Empowering Women of Color

D1309955

EMPOWERING THE POWERLESS: A SOCIAL WORK SERIES

EMPOWERING THE POWERLESS: A SOCIAL WORK SERIES

ALEX GITTERMAN

Series Editor

The Empowerment Tradition in American Social Work: A History

Barbara Levy Simon

Organizing for Power and Empowerment

Jacqueline B. Mondros and Scott M. Wilson

This series provides perspectives on empowerment strategy in social work, which seeks to help clients draw on personal, interpersonal, and political power to enable them to gain greater control over their environments and attain their aspirations.

Empowering

WOMEN OF COLOR

Lorraine M. Gutiérrez
and
Edith A. Lewis

COLUMBIA UNIVERSITY PRESS   NEW YORK

Columbia University Press
Publishers Since 1893
New York   Chichester, West Sussex

Library of Congress Cataloging-in-Publication Data

Empowering women of color /
[edited by] Lorraine M. Gutiérrez and Edith A. Lewis.
p.   cm. — (Empowering the powerless)
Includes bibliographical references and index.
ISBN 0–231–10116–3 (cloth : alk. paper)
ISBN 0–231–10117–1 (pbk.)
1. Social work with women—United States.
2. Minority women—Services for—United States.
3. Minority women—United States—Psychology.
4. Self-esteem in women—United States.
I. Gutiérrez, Lorraine M. (Lorraine Margot)
II. Lewis, Edith Anne. III. Series.
HV 1445.E45   1999
362.83—dc21   98–51518

Casebound editions of Columbia University Press books
are printed on permanent and durable acid-free paper.

Printed in the United States of America
Designed by Audrey Smith

c 10 9 8 7 6 5 4 3 2 1
p 10 9 8 7 6 5 4 3 2 1

Dedicated to
our daughters—Kamilah, Athena, and Julia
and mothers—Rebecca and Annie Laura

for all they have taught, and continue to teach, us.

CONTENTS

◆

EDITOR'S NOTE

◆

Many women of color have limited environmental resources and control over their lives. Historically, they have suffered from slavery, colonization, geographic dislocation, and numerous forms of domination and victimization. External oppressive forces and internalized reactions of hopelessness, despair, and alienation jeopardize their mental and physical health. In spite of these enormous barriers, many women of color valiantly persevere in their struggle to survive and succeed.

Empowering Women of Color is the third book in Columbia University Press's social work series Empowering the Powerless. In part 1, Professors Gutiérrez and Lewis provide us with a model to reduce vulnerabilities and risks for women of color and to strengthen and mobilize their resilience. They develop conceptual and practical means to engage and assess individual women of color and their families, groups, organizations, and communities. The emphasis is on helping women of color to gain personal, interpersonal, and political power.

Part 2 of the book contains the contributions of additional scholars. Each woman-of-color grouping is placed in a historical and social context. We learn about each group's unique roots, traditions, placement of women, family patterns, childbearing practices, and demographics. Each chapter concludes by applying an empowerment perspective to the specific population.

I present the series' third book, *Empowering Women of Color*, with excitement. The eloquent chapters prepared by Professors Gutiérrez and Lewis and the others contributing constitute a masterful contribution to the profession's literature.

Alex Gitterman
Series Editor

PREFACE

◆

The twenty-first century presents social work with particular challenges regarding its role and purpose. This is particularly true in the United States, where large economic transformations have created a society in which fewer and fewer individuals benefit directly from economic growth (Thurow, 1993; Smeeding, Danziger, and Rainwater, 1996; Hill-Collins, 1997; Bell, 1992). No longer are jobs secure, higher education accessible, or income supports adequate to help those displaced by these changes. Nevertheless, our society and others in the world have so subscribed to the tenets of the market economy that they appear to have abandoned concern for compassion, spirituality, and universality (West, 1998). Further, the social work profession and the communities it serves are increasingly scapegoated as causing these large system problems. Witness the major reductions in domestic public welfare spending, including the removal from the SSI program of many children formerly considered to be disabled, the cutbacks in health care for former veterans through the VA Hospital system, and the much studied changes in the former Aid to Families with Dependent Children (AFDC) program.

Among those hardest hit are women of color, who have, since this country began, joined their partners, fathers, and sons among those with the lowest life expectancies, the lowest incomes, the lowest rates of education compared to their gendered counterparts in the White population, and the poorest health (Lewis, 1988; Minkler, 1997; Ortiz, 1994; Gutiérrez and Lewis, 1994). Moreover, women of color experience discrimination based on race, ethnicity, class, sexual orientation, and gender. This intersection of "isms" has been posited as being far greater than that of any single social group membership (Hurtado, 1997; Hill-Collins, 1990; hooks, 1995; Lewis, 1988; Lewis and Kissman, 1989).

What is the role of social work within this context? How can we take an active role in confronting and immobilizing the forces that conspire to increase inequality while removing the tattered remnants of the social safety net? The empowerment tradition in social work provides one avenue for responding to these challenges in a proactive manner (Simon, 1994). By building simultaneously on social and individual transformation, it suggests ways in which social workers on many levels can work toward greater social justice.

In many ways, the empowerment model is built on the rich traditions of the settlement house movements of the late 1800s. Settlement houses emerged in the newly industrialized areas of the eastern United States and served primarily immigrant populations, first those from Eastern Europe and later poor people of color moving into manufacturing jobs in the North. The early settlement houses in both the United States and England were based on the social environment perspective, which also influenced the early mutual aid and support programs developed by and for populations of color in the United States (Jansson, 1997). Settlement houses viewed individual poverty as being a consequence of economic, social, and political as well as individual or familial forces (Macht and Quam, 1986; Jansson, 1997: Haslett, 1997). Settlement house workers lived in the communities where they worked and took an active role in political reform at the municipal, state, and federal levels. New Deal programs of the 1930s were established during a time when settlement house leaders such as Jane Addams, Alice Hamilton, and Rachelle Yarros were most active, both in terms of the literature they produced and the causes they espoused. These women and others influenced governmental agencies to respond to the social forces affecting individual poverty (Haslett, 1997).

Empowering practice with regard to women of color also owes much to the strong tradition of self-help and mutual support that existed among many populations of color prior to their arrival in the United States (Lewis, 1989; Gutiérrez and Lewis, 1992; Macht and Quam, 1986; Jansson, 1997). Populations of color in the United States brought with them practices that they adapted to offset some of the stresses and strengths of coping in their new environment (for examples, see chapters 10 and 11). Discriminatory practices within the wider society systematically excluded populations of color—a process that occurred in different ways for different populations, as illustrated in chapters 9 and 12, below—also fostered the emergence of parallel social welfare systems among populations of color, including the Hui and Ko (Takaki, 1993) among the Chinese and Japanese, and African-American systems of settlement houses in the northeastern and southern parts of the United States (Jansson, 1997; Burwell, 1995).

Like the social environment perspective, the empowerment framework for social work practice views individual or family problems as being at least partially shaped by economic, social, and political forces (McWhirter, 1994). And in the same way, this framework requires social workers to be agents of change and advocates in the political arena at the community and societal levels. What differentiates empowerment practice from the pursuits of the pioneering women of the settlement houses is its emphasis on helping consumers gain or regain power rather than on having social workers serve as intermediaries between consumers and social or political institutions.

Empowering social work practice requires that a number of activities occur simultaneously. Women of color develop a power analysis of the historical, social, and political influences shaping their past and present experiences—an exercise that, following Freire's liberatory education model (1970, 1994), we refer to as "critical consciousness." In evolving this analysis, women of color also develop new skills and become more confident in their capacity to change the individual, familial, group, community, and/or societal power imbalances in their lives. Among the new skills developed are those that build connections with others as a way of gaining power. This sequence occurs for both practitioner and consumer during the course of the intervention. Empowering social workers share practices of consciousness-raising, capacity building, and connection with consumers and colleagues to address the inequalities experienced by disenfranchised people and groups.

When working with women of color and others disproportionately affected by inequality, empowering social work practice provides a means to act in partnership to confront the assaults experienced by individuals, families, groups, and communities. Empowering social work practice, we posit, builds on rather than detracts from practitioners' knowledge of and skill with existing practice theories and methods. It does, however, require social workers to think strategically, in terms of the ability to access power and resources on all of the levels, about the impact on particular individuals, families, groups, or communities of using and combining theories and methods. Further, this partnership requires practitioners to take the time to focus on multiple factors influencing behavior, including spirituality, rather than simply assessing one level.

We acknowledge in this volume that our empowerment model is adapted from other, more widely recognized conceptual frameworks used in contemporary social work practice: ethnoconscious (Pinderhughes, 1983; Solomon,

1976; Davis, 1984; Comas-Diaz and Greene, 1994), feminist (Bricker-Jenkins and Hooyman, 1986; Van Den Bergh, 1995; Figueira-McDonough, Netting, and Nichols-Casebolt, 1998), woman-in-relationship (Solomon, 1982; Jordan, 1997; Comas-Diaz and Griffith, 1988), cognitive-behavioral (Greene, 1994b; Lewis, 1988), social group work (Lewis and Ford, 1990; Garvin and Seabury, 1997; *Social Work With Groups'* 1984 and 1990 special issues on ethnic minorities), life model (Germain and Gitterman, 1996), community building (Minkler, 1997; Checkoway, 1997), and multicultural organizational development (Chesler and Chesney, 1991; Cox, 1993; Gutiérrez and Nagda, 1996), among others. While we do not have space here to enumerate all the assumptions underlying all these frameworks, we do attempt to discuss the elements of certain models that have led to the development of our empowering practice perspective as these are identified within specific chapters in part 1. For example, we discuss the Stone School Model (Jordan, 1997) in chapters 3, 4, and 5 to help social workers understand the necessity for viewing women in their widest social contexts as a prerequisite to intervention. For those wishing to know more about the various models and their applications with women of color, we suggest beginning with the excellent volumes cited above.

Empowering Women of Color represents a paradigm shift. Unless our jobs specifically included community organizing or community development, we social workers have been taught to begin where the client is, as long as the "client" comes to our offices! Empowering social work practice requires us to join individuals, families, groups, and communities where they are: in their homes, at their workplaces, in their places of worship, and in their times of greatest distress (which seldom occur during the formerly standard nine-to-five workday). Both authors began their practice in the 1970s, a period when social work education routinely placed a greater emphasis on competence in generalist practice than is currently the case. While one of us has gone on to work more often with organizations and communities and the other to work more often with individuals, families, and groups, our real practice experiences with communities of color have found us engaging in a mixture of practice methods that require us to work across all these levels. A critical dimension of the practice model we learned was the importance of continually assessing ways in which multiple systems could be involved in the change process. It is from this mixture of practice methods that our perspectives on empowering practice with women of color have emerged.

It has been our experience that the paradigm shift we are proposing will not be readily accepted by all social workers or social work organizations. There are many ways to engage in social work practice, and this book presents one.

We consider it no more likely to be wholly adopted by all social work practitioners than, for example, structural family therapy has been. The choice of a practice method is often determined by a number of factors, including the socialized belief systems practitioners have about individuals, families, groups, and communities (as derived from life and educational experiences), the skill levels of these practitioners (including training and practice in varied methods and settings), and the resources or reinforcement for their choices in their practice environments (third-party payments, managed care). If these constraints do influence the choice of a practice model, as we suggest here, then it is likely that some practitioners will find useful the models and methods presented in this book.

This book is intended for the practitioners who will find some merit in our overall approach and for those who are working in a single practice method but wish to augment their traditional training with elements of what we term an empowering model of practice. The book is intended, secondarily, for those practitioners who already accept the ecological, symbolic interactionist, or eclectic systems, model. It is meant for those social workers who want to integrate their more macro-oriented skills with more micro-oriented skills. It is meant, moreover, for those social workers who are willing to question and hone their own practice assumptions and skills through the process of praxis: that is, critical reflection combined with action (Freire, 1970, 1994). The book is meant both for seasoned social workers who have worked in various fields of service over their career lifetimes and newer students of empowerment practice who may just be entering their first professional practicum experiences. We have attempted to include examples from each end of this spectrum but believe that most social work practitioners and other human service workers are somewhere in between these two extremes in their thinking and practice. If you find yourself resonating with one or more of these categories, then this book is for you.

The text is divided into two parts. In part 1, we identify the building blocks of empowerment practice and discuss how these building blocks relate to different social work traditions and levels of practice. Each chapter in part 1 begins with a vignette illustrating a method of applying the principles and strategies of empowering social work practice to women of color in real situations. Our rationale for using vignettes is both to pay homage to the rich narrative traditions from which we have both emerged and to illustrate the technique of storytelling or narrative voice used in both ethnoconscious and feminist practice (Minkler, 1997; Lamphere, 1992; Gutiérrez and Lewis, 1992). Most of the vignettes are composites, drawn either from our own practice experiences in several states across the United States or from those of our students, although some are the narratives of actual social workers. In each of the vignettes, we have attempted to be deliberate in our attention to the intersection of race, sexual orientation, ethnicity, class, and gender as these are reflected in the complex lives of women of color. The vignettes and voices included in chapter 1, "Empowerment: A Model For Practice," however, are ours, drawn from our own journeys to develop and integrate this practice model. We have included our personal voices to help readers understand that social work theory and practice are not color-blind, neutral, or independent of the historical, social, and political contexts of the practitioners.

Although the focus of this book is women of color, practitioners must investigate the extent to which the principles defined here are applicable to other groups, particularly White women and men of color. Throughout part 1 we attempt to address the variations and unique attributes of the many populations encompassed by the term "women of color." That term, however, tends to minimize the variations within and among African-American, Asian-American, Latina, and Native American populations. Moreover, our case illustrations and discussions of practice with women of color focus on women representing only two of the four overall populations we intended to include in this book. To do justice to an empowerment perspective, the actual lenses of women of color must be used to understand the rich traditions within their communities. Part 2 provides this additional perspective.

We have been fortunate enough to include in this section chapters by many guest contributors. These authors are scholars and activists who have lived and written about empowering social work practice for many years. Their rich insights into specific applications of empowerment theory demonstrate how the principles of empowerment practice have been historically integrated into communities of color. Their perspectives also provide additional examples of empowering practice that can be linked to the chapters in part 1 of the book.

Each of the chapters in part 2 furnishes basic demographic information about the population under discussion and then recognizes its—and its subpopulations'—contributions to empowerment practice. Chapter 9 addresses the way concepts of spirituality and environment affect social work practice with Native American women. In telling the story of Emily Salois, Lowery offers a concrete example of the utility of the small-group strategies in community work that are described in chapters 5 and 7.

Focusing on women from the African diaspora, chapter 10 suggests that the complexities of their historical, social, and political lives are masked with the term "African-American." It details how narrative voice can be used as a consciousness-raising strategy to tell the stories of women across the diaspora and provides illustrations of this technique in practice.

Gutiérrez and Suarez in chapter 11 use the examples of Yolanda and Ana to highlight demographic and social welfare program participation patterns among women described by the term "Latina." These composites of empowering social workers also demonstrate specific ways in which capacity may be built by Latinas within their communities of origin rather than in wider society organizations. In this way, mutual aid and self-help traditions are blended with the establishment of more formal institutions and organizations within home community.

Chapter 12, by Lie, and chapter 13, by Icard, Jones, and Wahab, might be read together and linked to the case of Emily Sato, described in chapter 8. Given the discrimination Asian-American women face in the workplace, cyclical anti-Asian backlash, and the wider society's sexual stereotypes of Asian women, Emily was indeed lucky to be welcomed by a youth center for gay, lesbian, bisexual, and transgendered youth.

Chapter 12 also discusses the demographic differences between Asian- and European-Americans. Lie's illustrations of the role of the press and the rise of associations and organizations to serve Asian women in the United States demonstrate the importance of connection in building supportive environments for these women. It also shows how members of one umbrella group with historical, social, and political differences might come together to increase their power in and outside of their communities through what is referred to as the Asian-American women's movement. Readers might compare the activities and structures of the organizations and associations identified by Lie to those available to Pamela, whose story is given in chapter 3.

In chapter 13, Icard, Jones, and Wahab demonstrate that sexual orientation is yet another complex layer of the lives of women of color, one that deserves specific attention lest social workers fall prey to the heterosexism so rampant in our society. Their use of data from focus groups highlights the specific concerns of lesbian and bisexual women of color in the Seattle, Washington, area. Data from these groups also illustrate the movement from individual empowerment to political advocacy, as in the case of Sherry Harris.

Another highlight of this chapter is the description of the Sistah-2-Sistah group and its implications for the critical consciousness and connection aspects of empowerment for lesbian, bisexual, and transgendered women of the African diaspora. In terms of sexual orientation, this homogeneous group may be compared to Unity, the group described in chapter 5, to examine the benefits and drawbacks of heterogeneous and homogeneous groups in empowerment practice. The Sistah-2-Sistah group further demonstrates the diversity that also exists within lesbian, bisexual, and transgendered populations.

Part 2 has two simple yet challenging goals. The first is to use the lenses of the populations in question to demonstrate the principles and strategies of empowering practice. The second, and probably more ambitious, goal is to challenge once again the direction of knowledge on populations of color by using their own historical, social, and political analyses rather than those of the wider society. By reversing the flow of information, colearners of empowerment practice receive insights into its roots within communities of color and the ways these roots have spread out to strengthen theory and practice in the wider society.

Overall, each chapter of this book is designed to assist practitioners with their own development of the knowledge, skills, and critical consciousness needed to engage in empowering practice with women of color. This journey will be different for each practitioner, moving in fits and starts, through times of great clarity and times of seemingly impenetrable blocks. We have been on this journey in our own work for over two decades and have had a number of transforming experiences along the way. We welcome you and invite you to join us on the journey.

It is difficult to find ways to acknowledge all those who have been a part of this birthing process. Over time, we have been involved in what might be thought of as a community-building project, and we are grateful to the many individuals, families, groups, communities, and organizations that have brought *Empowering Women of Color* to its fruition. While this is by no means an exhaustive list, we could not launch this project without specifically thanking the following people:

1. Alex Gitterman, editor of the Columbia University Press Empowerment Series and staunch supporter, who never lost faith in the project.

2. The other authors in the Empowerment Series (Simon, Gil, and Mondros and Wilson), whose work inspired us as we toiled to represent authentic social work practice in ways helpful to students. We must also thank our collective forebears, including Barbara Solomon, James Leigh, and Elaine Pinderhughes, whose work made it possible for all of us who participated in this series to expand the theoretical framework of empowerment.

3. Alexander Thorpe, our current editor at Columbia University Press. The words "The book is in publication" had never sounded as sweet as when he pronounced them. We are also especially grateful to Gioa Stephens, formerly

of Columbia University Press, for serving as our initial editor and helping to move us through the initial review and writing processes.

4. The University of Michigan Office of the Vice President for Research, for partial support of the production of this book through its Publication Subvention Grant Program.

5. The Hedgebrook Women's Writing Retreat in Langley, Washington, for providing a safe and quiet place for Lorraine to work on the book. The University of Ghana Department of Social Work Administration and Center for Social Policy Studies faculty, staff, and field instructors who furthered Edie's understanding of the parallel journeys of women of African descent in social work policy, practice, and research.

6. The readers of our early drafts: Linnea GlenMaye, Jacqueline Mattis, Gwat-Yong Lie, Alex Gitterman, and Christine Lowery, who gave us wise counsel and insightful critiques of the work. Along the way, numerous students in the School of Social Work at the University of Michigan also read portions of earlier drafted chapters and offered helpful feedback. Finally, we wish to acknowledge the anonymous reviewers chosen by Columbia University Press, who challenged us and made our visions clearer.

7. Tracy Washington, Kylo-Patrick Robert Hart, Emily Melnick, and Jennifer Toller, all former students who have gone on to prestigious careers of service to their communities and helped perform the hard labor of data collection, material acquisition, and secretarial support necessary to get this book to you.

8. Sarah St. Onge, our meticulous copyeditor, who worked diligently to ensure that our manuscript was consistent, clear, and accurate.

9. While this book is dedicated to our mothers and daughters, we must also acknowledge our partners and sons, who serve as further wonderful reminders of what really matters in life. Thank you, Bob, Jon, and Bakari.

10. And, finally, to our sisters—women of color throughout the United States—whose lives we have attempted to represent in the case studies used in this book. We thank those of you who are known to us (such as the participants in the Women of Color in the Academy Project at the Center for the Education of Women at the University of Michigan) and those for whom these stories may strike a resounding chord. Collectively, you have given us strength. Individually, many of you have given us support, friendship, and joy. spiritually, you have made it possible for us to write about our similarities and complexities through the life force that unites us all.

PART I

The Empowerment Approach
to Practice

ONE

◆

Empowerment: A Model for Practice

◆

It is 1984, and the presidential election is on. I have just entered a Ph.D. program in social work and psychology after six years of working as a social worker with multiethnic communities in Chicago, San Francisco, and New York. Ronald Reagan and Jesse Jackson are both running for president, and both are calling for the empowerment of individuals and communities. This juxtaposition intrigues me: empowerment was also something we spoke of when working to develop feminist multicultural programs in low-income communities. How could progressive social workers, Reagan, and Jackson be in such agreement? Or were we? Given the popularity of the word and its growing use in social work, it seemed that *empowerment* would be an important thing to understand.

—*Lorraine Gutiérrez*

◆

Empowerment has been a buzzword in the social work profession and society at large for the past three decades. It refers to a concept that reflects a variety of perspectives and practices. It has been used to describe both processes and outcomes, has been attached to individuals, families, communities, and societies, and has been misconstrued as something that can be conferred on another. This chapter focuses on two questions: First, what is empowerment, and what is its relevance to women of color? Next, can empowerment address the issues we face at the beginning of this new century?

The empowerment perspective is grounded in an understanding that separate groups exist within our societies, each possessing different levels of power and control over resources (Fay, 1987; Gould, 1987; Simon, 1994; Yeich and Levine, 1992). This perspective identifies ways in which individual problems can arise from the failure of society to meet the needs of all people. It holds that the potential for positive change exists within every individual, family, or group and that negative behaviors and symptoms emerge from attempts to cope with a hostile world (Pinderhughes, 1989). Although individuals can develop less personally destructive coping strategies, changes in the power structure of society are considered crucial to the ultimate prevention of individual problems (Albee, 1986; Rappaport, 1981; Solomon, 1982).

The concept of *social justice* is central to the empowerment perspective. Social justice refers to equity, equality, and fairness in the distribution of societal resources (Flynn, 1994). It includes a focus on the structures and outcomes of social processes and how they contribute to equality, places an explicit value on achieving social equity through democratic processes, and assumes that the social worker's role is to develop policy and practice that contribute to these goals (Flynn, 1994; Van Soest, 1994). Thus, although social workers may use empowerment methods with small systems such as individuals or families, the overall goal of empowerment practice is social justice and a reduction of social inequality.

In this chapter, we further develop our conceptualization of empowerment and how it can be translated into practice. We begin by defining elements of the construct of empowerment and then discuss empowerment as a practice theory and its relationships to other perspectives on social work. We explain how empowerment processes can occur on a grassroots level and also be a tool for social workers. In the second half of the chapter, we focus specifically on the empowerment practice method as an introduction to the specific techniques explicated in the remainder of the book. We focus specifically on how these methods can be especially relevant to the experience of women of color. This broad introduction to the empowerment perspective can be seen as relevant to other oppressed groups as well.

◆

The empowerment perspective rings true to my own experience and development. During my childhood on Chicago's South Side, no one asked African-American families what they needed; we were told what we needed. When as a girl of fifteen I told my high school counselor that I wanted to be a social worker, she told me, "You're a smart colored girl; learn to type," and then made it impossible for me to take the college preparatory classes offered by the school. I wondered why she thought she knew what was best for me. Later, at eighteen, when male adults in my community kept lecturing me about the "willfulness of women" who went to college rather than immediately marrying, I wondered why they thought they knew what was best for me. At twenty-two, when I had earned enough money and release time from my job to be able to return to college full time and the admissions officer said to me, "You're not college material," I wondered why he thought he knew more about my capacity than the instructors who had worked with me and encouraged me to complete my degree. When I received my undergraduate degree from that institution, *summa cum laude*, I went back to that admissions officer and showed him the credential.

Having been surrounded all of my life by children and adults who have thought through the options available to them and made informed decisions based on those options, I don't wonder whether people know what is really best for them. Instead, as a social worker, I wonder how options not open to them might be opened and how their confidence might be expanded through building their capacity to exercise those options.

—*Edith Lewis*

Elements of Empowerment

POWER

Understanding the multidimensional nature of power in social relationships is a critical element of empowerment. Empowerment theory is based on a dynamic perspective that assumes that power can be generated in the process of social interaction (Bricker-Jenkins and Hooyman, 1986; Pinderhughes, 1989; Solomon, 1976). Power gives one the ability to influence the course of one's life, to work with others to control aspects of public life, and to access mechanisms of public decision making (Leigh, 1985; Mathis and Richan, 1986; Pinderhughes, 1989; Weick, 1982). Power may also be used to block stigmatized groups' opportunities, exclude others and their concerns from decision making, and control others (Garvin, 1985; Leigh, 1985; Mathis and Richan, 1986; Pinderhughes, 1983; Weick, 1982). Understanding power and powerlessness and how they work are critical when using an empowerment perspective (see table 1.1).

Being a member of a disempowered group has personal as well as social costs. Powerlessness leads to a denial of valued identities, social roles, and social resources that limits self-determination and engenders a sense of dependency (Pinderhughes, 1989; Solomon, 1976). Indirect and direct power blocks

TABLE I.I Conceptualizations of Power

Positive	Negative
Ability to control one's own actions	Ability to control others
Capacity to affect public life	Capacity to exclude others from public life
Access to decision making	Ability to control political agenda

are the primary social mechanisms in this process. Negative valuation, or stigma, which indicates to members of oppressed groups that they are deficient in some way, represents one type of power block. Negative valuations become incorporated into the development of the individual and can interfere with their further development and/or the maintenance of adequate interpersonal, technical, and social skills. Negative valuations also engender inaccurate beliefs regarding status, opportunities, and resistance, encouraging individuals to accept the present social structure and preventing them from taking action to improve their lives (Freire, 1973; Gaventa, 1980). Consider the example cited above: if Dr. Edith Lewis had believed that she was intellectually incapable, rather than heeding her own voice and desires, she would have been less likely to make the enormous effort involved in stepping beyond the stereotyped roles that others had set out for her.

Direct power blocks, such as the provision of inadequate health services to the poor, also affect individuals in more concrete ways (Solomon, 1976). The apartheid system of discrimination in South Africa, for example, restricted the movement and access of the majority population of the country to political, educational, economic, and social resources until the mid-1990s. As a result, Black South African children had vastly diminished chances to improve their lives. While direct power blocks, too, can cause individuals to incorporate negative self-valuations, they are also more readily amenable to group consciousness-raising and direct-action strategies, as we will show later in this chapter.

PSYCHOLOGICAL TRANSFORMATIONS

Empowerment has been described as a process of development of change (Kieffer, 1984; Zimmerman, 1995). This process involves several intrapersonal and interpersonal changes, which can be described as consciousness, confidence, and connection. Together these changes in thinking can help individuals, families, groups, and communities overcome the effects of powerlessness (Fay, 1987; Freire, 1973; Gutiérrez, 1991; Pinderhughes, 1989; Solomon, 1976).

A crucial means for gaining power is the development of a *critical consciousness*: an understanding of how power relationships in the society shape one's perceptions and experiences, as well as an ability to identify how one can assume a role in social change (Gaventa, 1980; Gutiérrez, 1994; Kieffer, 1984; Swift and Levin, 1987). Consciousness has been identified as a "set of political beliefs and action orientations arising from the awareness of having ideas, feelings, and interests similar to others who share the same stratum characteristics" (Gurin, Miller, and Gurin, 1980, p. 30). Awareness of how group membership affects life circumstances is crucial to identifying powerlessness as a source of problems and understanding the need for social change (Gaventa, 1980; Gutiérrez, 1994; Simon, 1990).

Consciousness refers to beliefs about one's location and relationships. With regard to location, consciousness development provides an analysis of who the individual is vis-à-vis his or her own biological, emotional, psychological, and social placements within society. Although critical consciousness development is oriented toward social location, its focus is on how one has interpreted and internalized these external experiences.

Critical consciousness with regard to relationships extends to understanding the location of the self and social groups in society. It involves an interpretation of the distributive system in society, a perception of one's position in the social order, an overall evaluation of that order, and a sense of group solidarity (Kleugel and Smith, 1981). It includes *a collective orientation to social change*, feelings of *discontent with the distribution of power, relative deprivation, a rejection of the legitimacy of power disparities* between groups that includes blaming the system for outcomes, and an *identification with shared group values and interests* (Gurin, 1985; Gurin, Miller and Gurin, 1980).

Those in lower status groups, such as women, people of color, and the elderly, are often more critical of the stratification system overall. Conversely, members of more powerful groups in society are more approving of the social system and perceive greater opportunity; underestimate the disparities in income and resources between rich and poor, White and minority, or men and women; and overestimate the overall level of social mobility (Kleugel and Smith, 1981). Identifying people's perceptions of the legitimacy of social conditions is crucial to determining whether their beliefs will contribute to the endorsement of social change. Consciousness will only lead to social action if individuals believe that the system is unfair. Therefore, different components

of consciousness—discontent with the distribution of power, collective orientation, and the rejection of legitimacy—contribute differently to the
process of empowerment.

I grew up in southern California, in an area in which my father's family had lived
since the 1820s, when they came to Alta, California from Mexico to set up a black-
smith business near the San Gabriel Mission. Throughout my childhood I was
continually struck by the contradiction between the "Spanish myth" of California's heritage and the reality for those of us who were Mexican and Mexican
American. Although he was a fourth-generation Californian and his father had
helped to build the municipal pool, my father was not allowed to swim there
more than one day a week—the day the water was changed—because of segregation against African Americans, Asians, and Mexicans.

In studying California history in elementary school I was fortunate to have a
mother who corrected what my class was told about the early Spanish settlers in
our area. As presented in our history books, these "noble people" settled the area
and then somehow disappeared after the Mexican War in 1848. There was no discussion of the loss of land grants, the destruction of businesses, and the discrimination faced by those who remained in the area. As a child this version of "history" made me feel invisible and unimportant. The factual information I received
from my family about the history of California helped me to understand the
important role my family and other families had played in the development of
our community. These were the roots of my critical consciousness and my need
to reflect on and question what I was told.

—*Lorraine Gutiérrez*

To overcome the impact of powerlessness, one must have confidence in one's
abilities and actions. Efficacy theory provides a means of understanding how
individuals develop a sense of personal power when faced with conditions of
powerlessness and oppression (Bandura, 1982). Self-efficacy influences how
individuals judge their capability to perform specific tasks, judgments that go
on to affect subsequent motivation and behavior. Individuals avoid activities
that they feel exceed their capabilities. Feeling incapable of influencing the
social environment can contribute to feelings of futility, despondency, and
anxiety. Enhancing self-efficacy helps individuals to overcome these feelings
and approach their problems more effectively. In addition, efficacious persons
are more likely to attempt to modify the environment and to persist when
they encounter setbacks (Bandura, 1982).

Efficacy can be enhanced by four methods: personally mastering a new activity, seeing a similar person master the activity, being told one is capable of mastering the activity, and experiencing manageable levels of anxiety while attempting the new activity. Both individual capacity and supportive social environments are necessary for task mastery and for feelings of efficacy to develop. In contrast, feelings of futility are the result of low self-efficacy or a punitive, unresponsive, or negative environment. Assessment of the origin of feelings of futility guides how efforts should be focused: on changing the individual's response or on changing the social environment (Bandura, 1982).

Self-efficacy relates to beliefs about specific behaviors and domains. An individual who feels efficacious about many behaviors and domains will feel more generally competent than one who feels efficacious regarding only a few behaviors and domains (Bandura, 1984). Therefore, individuals in powerless positions have difficulty developing feelings of self-efficacy because of the negative effects of the social world. These feelings can be modified by providing activities in which they can feel efficacious and by working to change the social environment so it can be more supportive and rewarding (Bandura, 1982; Crosbie-Burnett and Lewis, 1993a).

Self-efficacy provides the basis for collective efficacy. Collective efficacy is the belief that group effort can achieve desired outcomes. High self-efficacy individuals who encounter an unresponsive environment are more apt to endorse collective efforts for change than are those who are low in self-efficacy (Bandura, 1982). Therefore, the experiences of self- and collective efficacy are linked and represent resources for gaining power.

Working with both homogeneous and carefully structured heterogeneous groups to achieve meaningful change has become a powerful tool in my practice. This perspective is rooted in my very first field placement as an undergraduate student, in a community-based group program for ex-offenders in Minneapolis back in 1971. The extraordinary people who served as my field instructors were incredible role models of empowering practitioners, although the term was not used in social work practice contexts at that time. I'm certain that their dedication to using a range of intervention modalities to address simultaneously the individual, family, and societal contexts of men and women newly released from prison has continued to stimulate my own thinking and practice today.

—*Edith Lewis*

CONNECTION

Connection serves two purposes: the development of social support networks and the creation of power through interaction. Involvement with others in similar situations provides individuals with a means for acquiring and providing mutual aid, with the opportunity to learn new skills through role modeling, with strategies for dealing with likely institutional reprisals, and with a potential power base for future action (Chesney and Chesler, 1988; Gitterman and Schulman, 1994; Gutiérrez and Ortega, 1991; Hirayama and Hirayama, 1985; Keefe, 1980; Pinderhughes, 1989; Reischl, Zimmerman, and Rappaport, 1986). The role of the group leader in helping to interpret experience and develop skills is crucial for the group interaction to contribute to empowerment (Gutiérrez and Ortega, 1991; Kieffer, 1984; Pretsby et al., 1990).

Groups play an important role in supporting the development of consciousness and confidence (Garvin, 1985; Gutiérrez and Ortega, 1991; Kieffer, 1984). Under most circumstances people do not perceive connections between personal and social problems. For example, although most women believe that discrimination against their sex exists, they deny that they personally have experienced it (Clayton and Crosby, 1987; Taylor and Dubé, 1986). Political involvement both assists the development of group identification and heightens an awareness of group-based inequity (Baca-Zinn, 1980; Padilla, 1985). Discussions with groups of similar backgrounds enable individuals to speak about common experiences, receive social support, and see the connections between personal and political life (Crosby and Hereck, 1987; Evans, 1980; Hurtado, 1982; Rosenberg, 1981; Lee, 1994). Ultimately, the experience influences individuals' behavior and their perceptions of reality. Group participation also provides an environment for engaging in risk-taking behavior (Zander, 1979). In homogeneous groups, members of oppressed populations can engage in verbal comparisons of social circumstances that involve both in- and out-group members. Through this exchange process, feelings of relative deprivation arise and are reinforced by other group members. A sense of group commonality and shared fate also grows from this process.

The empowerment perspective highlights the way in which change arising from intrapersonal transformations can occur. As individuals view themselves capable of acting in the world, they will use their self-knowledge and ability to work toward the transformation of larger systems (Freire, 1973; Gutiérrez, DeLois, and GlenMaye, 1995; Simon, 1994). This is one path toward achieving the goal of social justice.

Support and connection with others have made strategic contributions to my personal achievement and empowerment. To name and recognize all these people would mean another volume to this book! Individuals and groups have played strategic roles at significant times in my life. For example, a dedicated and courageous teacher in my junior high school worked with me individually on advanced work when I was placed in a less advanced "track" because my guidance counselor did not allow me to take more challenging courses. His belief in my abilities gave me the courage to enroll in advanced placement courses when I had the option. His support and willingness to take risks, to go the extra mile, are an example of the difference individual actions can make. Without people like him in my life—people like my mother, my social work supervisors, and caring colleagues—I could have easily lost the commitment and confidence necessary for the work I have done.

—*Lorraine Gutiérrez*

Methods for Empowerment Practice

Empowerment has been a theme in social work practice since the profession's inception. However, efforts to develop empowerment methods of practice are relatively recent (Simon, 1994). Empowerment practice can be focused at three levels: the personal, the interpersonal, and the political.

When empowerment occurs at the personal level, individuals develop feelings of personal power and self-efficacy. Powerlessness is so devastating that being able to experience oneself as powerful and capable provides a foundation for other levels of empowerment. Achieving personal empowerment involves recognizing and identifying the power one already has (Freire, 1973; Gutiérrez, 1990; Kieffer, 1984; Parsons, 1991).

With empowerment on the interpersonal level, people increase their ability to influence others, often through the development of specific skills, such as training in problem solving or assertiveness (Gutiérrez, Oh, and Gillmore, 1997; Hirayama and Hirayama, 1985) or learning how to influence the political process (Mathis and Richan, 1986). In some cases, developing skills to increase both interpersonal influence and political power occur simultaneously (Checkoway and Norsman, 1986; Garvin, 1985).

Political empowerment consists of social action and social change through a process of social support, coalition building, and praxis. It is based on both the personal and interpersonal levels of empowerment, with the additional goal of transferring power between groups in society. In political empowerment, individual change is considered to be as important a goal as social action (Fagan, 1979). This simultaneous focus on individual and political change distinguishes political empowerment from policy practice.

The three types of empowerment are unified by a central belief, namely, that social work's primary goal is to help individuals, families, groups, and communities develop the capacity to change their situations. The social worker's role is to help people change the situation and prevent its recurrence. The effects of powerlessness occur on many levels, so change must be directed toward both large and small systems; it is insufficient to focus only on developing a sense of personal power or providing skills or working toward social change. Practice at all three levels when combined comprises empowerment practice.

EMPOWERMENT PRACTICE AND WOMEN OF COLOR

Who and what do we mean by the term "women of color?" In our work we have argued vehemently and often that the use of umbrella terms such as "Latinos," " Asian Americans," "African Americans," or "lesbians" can create difficulties for effective social work because they may inadvertently imply that members of these groups are homogeneous, differing on few dimensions. Despite this objection, in this book we have chosen to use the term "women of color" to refer to African American, Asian American, Latina, and Native American women. Research and practice suggest that women who are members of these groups are likely to share experiences related to identity, culture, and inequality. Still, in the remainder of this book we will focus on deconstructing these identities to reveal their complexity and commonality (Comas-Diaz and Greene, 1994).

What do women of color share in common? Although the specific ethnic and racial groups encompassed by this umbrella term differ in many respects, together we share similarities in terms of our low social status and limited access to power. Women of color experience unequal access to power and resources in our society because of the effects of racism, sexism, and often classism. We are consequently hampered by average earnings lower than that of White women, by overrepresentation in low-status occupations, and by a low average level of education (Baca-Zinn and Dill, 1994a). Correspondingly, women of color are underrepresented in positions of power within our government, corporations, and nonprofit institutions (Comas-Diaz and Greene, 1994; Baca-Zinn and Dill, 1994a).

These statistics suggest ways in which our powerlessness as a group has very direct and concrete effects on our daily experiences. The poverty rate of women of color is two to three times that of White women: 36.5 percent of all Black women and 31.2 percent of all Latinas live below the poverty line, in contrast to 12.7 percent of all White women (U.S. Census, 1992). As a result, women of color are more likely than White women to suffer from conditions of poor or no housing, insufficient food and clothing, and inadequate access to health and mental health services and to be located within low-income and physically deteriorating communities (Kirk and Okazawa-Rey, 1998; Ortiz, 1994). We are disproportionately affected by the direct and indirect power blocks associated with low status and limited access to economic resources.

Women of color also share similarities in terms of strengths and coping strategies. Within our own communities we have developed values and behaviors that have allowed us to survive in the face of oppression. Economic necessity has led us to participate in the labor market at higher rates than European-American women. Although this has not always been voluntary, it has helped us to develop ties and a sense of self outside the family and has reduced our economic dependence on men. Women of color are also likely to have strong family ties and ties with other women in the community, to whom we can go for concrete and emotional support. These informal ties can be a source of strength. This history of coping and surviving within a hostile world has led many women of color to perceive themselves as strong and capable of dealing with adversity.

One important dimension in the lives of women of color is spirituality. Health and mental health fields in the United States have traditionally associated spirituality with religion, and religion was viewed as an unhealthy defense mechanism. Professionals were trained to work around rather than with the spiritual realities of their clients and to view spirituality as a crutch others leaned on. Practitioners even had to leave behind their own spiritual experiences, instruction, and realities. Be all that as it may, experiences of spirituality through meditation, fasting, writing, dance, music, prayer, the interpretation of spiritual signs, and service have been an important element in the survival of women of color in a hostile world (Boyd-Franklin, 1987; Adair and Howell, 1994; Mattis, 1995; Starhawk, 1992).

Social work and social workers need to recognize these ways in which women of color differ from White women and men of color. Social workers have most often recognized the impact of powerlessness on women of color from the perspective of institutional racism while overlooking the role of gender inequity in influencing the life chances of these women. We make an equally grave error when we group all women's experiences together without looking at ways in which women of color are impacted by racism and ethnocentrism (Comas-Diaz and Greene, 1994; Kirk and Okazawa-Rey, 1998; Baca-Zinn and Dill, 1994b). We have also overlooked the strengths and resources developed by women of color within their own communities. But in order to understand women of color in our society, a multidimensional perspective must be used that takes into account how multiple social identities have shaped the worldviews, life chances, and survival strategies of each individual woman (Comas-Diaz and Greene, 1994).

A multidimensional perspective dictates that multiple levels of practice and skills for working with individuals, groups, families, and communities are necessary for empowerment practice with women of color. Empowering women of color must focus specifically on how individual women have been affected by forces such as racism, ethnocentrism, and sexism and on ways in which social structures might be challenged. However, because women of color are at the bottom of our social hierarchy in terms of political power, social workers must also emphasize the interpersonal and political levels of empowerment. Gaining a sense of personal power must be viewed as only the first step toward the ultimate goal of changing oppressive structures (Bricker-Jenkins and Hooyman, 1986; Okazawa-Rey, 1998; Simon, 1994; Van Den Bergh and Cooper, 1986).

Empowerment practice with women of color was developed in reaction to the ethnocentric perspective of the profession, which positions, either explicitly or implicitly, the norms, values, and needs of the majority culture as the most desirable and places little value on the unique experiences of oppressed populations (Gallegos, 1982; Chau, 1990; Morales, 1981). In order to understand empowerment practice, we must understand its relationship to other social work practice models that have been used with women of color.

Ethnocentrism is present at the roots of the development of social work practice. In its most damaging forms, ethnocentrism has manifested itself in the provision of segregated services (Stehno, 1982), in the deportation of so-called aliens (Sanchez, 1993), and in Americanization programs that resulted in the loss of culture and community (Carpenter, 1980; Sanchez, 1993). For example, social service organizations have removed Native American children from their families and placed them in boarding schools or White foster families. This practice resulted in the breakup of families and communities and the loss of language and cultural heritage (Cross, 1986). For another example, during the Depression, southwestern social service agencies spearheaded efforts to "repatriate" people of Mexican descent in order to reduce public assistance costs. Over four hundred thousand people of Mexican descent, a large percentage of them American citizens, were sent to Mexico and separated from their homes, families, and sources of employment (Sanchez, 1993).

The impact of less direct forms of ethnocentrism has been just as insidious. The needs of ethnic groups have been ignored by service planners and providers (Lee, 1986). Some groups, such as Asian Americans, have been overlooked based on the premise that they "take care of their own" or may not respond well to the treatments offered at agencies (Land, 1988; Lee, 1986; Starret, Mindell, and Wright, 1983). Rather than looking at ways in which existing agency procedures, processes, or structures could be altered to respond better to the needs of ethnic minorities, the ethnocentric approach assumes that the problem in accessing and using services exists in the ethnic group and that it is their responsibility to change.

The ethnocentric approach reflects an *individual fallacy* assumption. This assumption, which evolved from the English Poor Law, views poverty and other difficulties as individual problems, often stemming from a lack of moral development (Simon, 1994; Jansson, 1997). The individual fallacy perspective supported the establishment of the Charity Organization Societies (cos) during the Progressive Era that monitored individual indigents in order to ensure that they did not receive too much assistance. The Charity Organization Societies viewed their mission as strengthening the existing social fabric by providing education for individuals so they could be more productive citizens (Macht and Quam, 1986).

In social work, the individual fallacy perspective took primacy in the 1920s, when many of the traditional casework techniques were developed; in the 1950s; and in the 1980s, which saw the erosion of many social welfare programs after the establishment of the Omnibus Reconciliation Act (Jansson, 1997). Social work has always been an interdisciplinary profession, and one of its contributing disciplines, psychology, also developed a set of theories that supported the individual fallacy argument. By the end of the nineteenth century in Europe, psychoanalytic theory, with its emphasis on the impact of unconscious forces on the individual, became increasingly popular. Borrowing heavily from the medical and physical sciences, psychoanalysis viewed individuals in terms of their mental health or illness. To return people to health, illnesses had to be diagnosed.

When viewed to the exclusion of other viewpoints, the individual fallacy perspective can be reductionistic and contribute to the development of programs and policies that blame individuals for their own misfortune. However, the psychodynamic and ego-psychological theories can provide useful lenses through which to view intra- and interpersonal processes. Transference and countertransference, which the early literature considered to be problematic therapeutic encounters, have more recently been recognized as factors to be addressed by practitioners in fieldwork (Greene, 1993).

In contrast to the individual fallacy perspective, the *social environment perspective* supports more fully the development of empowerment approaches to practice. The social environment perspective originated in the United States with the settlement house movement and the mutual aid and support movements of communities of color at the end of the nineteenth century. Its underlying assumptions were at odds in several ways with those of the COS. First, the settlement house movement viewed individual poverty as a consequence of the environment. Early settlement leaders sought to reform social systems and intervened at the community and governmental, as well as individual and group, levels. Second, settlement house workers viewed themselves as neighbors of those with whom they worked, as opposed to considering themselves to be morally superior to those receiving services. Living in the communities with which they worked, they worked as active change agents. Still, the degree to which women of color were welcome into social settlements has varied over time and in different regions (Iglehart and Becerra, 1995).

During the 1930s, the literature and activities of the settlement house movement leaders influenced governmental agencies to respond to social forces affecting individual poverty and were instrumental in the creation of the New Deal programs of that period. The Great Society programs of the 1960s, with their emphasis on urban community development programs, were another indication of this perspective's influence on social welfare policy.

Communities of color developed the *ethnic-sensitive approach* to social service organizations and programs during the late 1960s and 1970s (Chau, 1990; Devore and Schlesinger, 1987; Gallegos, 1982; Scott and Delgado, 1979). A response to ethnocentric approaches, ethnic-sensitive practice aims to create or re-create programs and organizations that are more responsive and responsible to the culture of populations of color. Training for cultural competence and the delivery of ethnic-sensitive services requires knowing one's own personal attributes and values, gaining knowledge about the culture of different groups, and developing skills for cross-cultural work (Chau, 1990; Gallegos, 1982) The emphasis is on learning to view the needs, values, and beliefs of different cultures as equally valid (Mizio, 1981).

The ethnic-sensitive approach to social services has led to changes in the training and thinking of service providers and the creation of new programs. However, the approach is insufficient to meet the challenges of the low status and power of women of color (Gutiérrez, 1990; Mizio, 1981; Morales, 1981; Solomon, 1976; Washington, 1982). If human service organizations are to be responsive to women of color, they must develop ways to contribute to their empowerment. Participating in the empowerment of women of color means going beyond sensitivity to questioning the structure and focus of existing practice and engaging in partnership with communities of color. Empowerment can be considered a form of *ethnoconscious practice* which integrates what we know about the significance of culture into the center of empowerment practice (Gutiérrez, 1992; Gutiérrez and Nagda, 1996).

TABLE 1.2 Elements of Ethnoconscious Practice

Values: professional, societal, culturally specific

Knowledge of self, of culture, of alternatives

Skills: ethnographic interviewing, culturally relevant assessment, empowerment methods

---

TABLE 1.3 Social Work Approaches to Women of Color

Perspective	Feelings	Goal of Polity, Program, or Practice
Ethnocentric	Repulsion, pity	To change individuals, families, or groups to reject their identities and adopt dominant values, beliefs, and behaviors.
Ethnic-sensitive	Tolerance, acceptance, and support	To have individuals, families and groups experience as sense of pride in their identities. To develop social work practice that takes into account the unique needs, values, and choices of diverse groups.
Ethnoconscious	Admiration, appreciation, nurturance, advocacy	To create social structures that are affirming of all people. To create social work methods that remove social barriers to the full development of all individuals, families, and groups.

Compiled by L. Gutiérrez, University of Michigan, based on work by D. Riddle and R. Simpson

EMPOWERMENT METHODS IN PRACTICE

Empowerment practice methods—*education, participation,* and *capacity building*—engender the psychological processes of change we have discussed. These methods, the building blocks of empowerment, apply to individuals, families, groups, communities, and organizations. In this section, we will discuss how these methods can be critical elements in a practice model. We begin with an example: a group- and community-based practice with women living in public housing in Ann Arbor, Michigan.

The *Network Utilization Project* (NUP) began as an effort to learn more from community members about ways in which low-income women have developed natural networks of support for survival. I had hoped that through working on this project I could learn how these women's strategies could be built into interventions for other women in similar circumstances. Through this process I learned more than I could ever imagine!

The NUP was initiated during a "power-over" period in the life of a community and human service agency. The agency, directed by individuals who did not live in or represent the community, had been receiving city and county funds as well as private donations with the hope that they would improve the lives of community residents. When I entered the community, residents had begun the process of developing their critical consciousness about the various micro-, meso-, and macro-level contexts of their social and political experiences so as to make the agency more relevant to their unique needs. I consider myself fortunate to have been able to work with the agency in its transition from a "power-over" through a "power-with" to a "power-within" organization.

—*Edith Lewis*

Education. Educational methods focus on improving participants' abilities to understand and act on their social environments. These methods emphasize techniques for increasing the individual's awareness of her own situation and developing skills to influence oppressive structures. They employ interactive processes and are grounded in the needs, capacities, and goals of the individual, family, or community involved in change. The role of the social worker is to serve as resource person, facilitator, or mentor rather than as teacher.

Consciousness-raising is one educational method that is a critical element of empowerment practice (Lee, 1994). It can take place in groups; through discussion, art, and writing; and via other educational channels. Social workers' awareness of a social issue in a personal problem raises the consciousness of the client and frames the structure of the program to reduce self-blame and, in some cases, to advocate for social change. Consciousness-raising helps individuals, families, or communities understand the societal nature of their problems.

Engaging in a power analysis of the situation, another important technique for empowerment practice, first involves analyzing how conditions of powerlessness contribute to the situation. Identifying sources of potential power represents a second step. One technique for engaging in a power analysis is dialogue between workers and clients aimed at exploring and identifying the social-structural origins of their current situations. Another technique focuses on analysis of clients' specific situations, either their own or from vignettes developed for the intervention (Pinderhughes, 1989; Wallerstein, 1992). Clients and workers often think creatively about sources of potential power such as forgotten skills, personal qualities that could increase social influence, members of past social support networks, and organizations in their communities.

Effective power analysis requires that the social worker fully comprehend the connection between the immediate practice situation and the distribution of power in society as a whole. This may require consciousness-raising exercises to look beyond the specific situation to problems shared by other women of color. Workers must not adopt their clients' feelings of powerlessness but learn to see the potential for power and influence in every situation.

Education also takes the form of the development of specific skills to address power deficits and develop resources to be more powerful (Mathis and Richan, 1986; Pernell, 1985; Shapiro, 1984). These skills could include formal training in computers or methods to avoid HIV infection and less formal training such as role playing, leadership practice, and interpersonal communication. The skill areas most often used when working with women of color include problem solving; skills for community or organizational change; life skills such as parenting, job seeking, or self-defense; and interpersonal skills such as assertiveness, social competency, or self-advocacy (Fagan, 1979; Garvin, 1985; Keefe, 1980; Schechter, Szymanski, and Cahill, 1985; Simmons and Parsons, 1983a, b; Solomon, 1976). Encouraging an interest in dance, the arts, sports, or crafts is another way to help clients develop self-expression and self-esteem.

◆

The NUP was designed as a small-group process that would involve women in moving from personal, through interpersonal, to community empowerment through a series of exercises and activities. Each level, or dimension, of the women's lives would be considered separately and sequentially. I would involve women in activities with increasing complexity and challenge.

In the first session of the group, I carefully explained the structure and the ideas behind it. First we would work on individual issues, then on family issues, and then on community issues. At this point, I was interrupted by a participant who stated, "But our individual problems are our community's problems; we need to talk about them together." She then described how her challenges in parenting and feelings of frustration were closely linked with the poor and often unsafe living conditions in public housing.

In this case, as in many, the consciousness-raising and educational processes were reciprocal. The participants in NUP didn't so much need education about community issues as skills that would allow them to apply their understanding of these issues to activities that would improve community and individual life. After this exchange, I changed the structure and processes of the program to reflect this dynamic more accurately.

—*Edith Lewis*

◆

Skills training often involves the use of rehearsal or role playing. For example, a mental health worker can prepare a client for a meeting with a social service bureaucracy through mock interviews. In these circumstances, skills in assertiveness and information regarding one's rights are particularly helpful.

Participation. Working collaboratively with participants requires the use of *participatory methods.* This helping relationship must be based on collaboration, trust, and the sharing of power. The worker acts as an enabler, organizer, consultant, or compatriot so as not to replicate the power relationship that the client may experience with other helpers or professionals (Schechter, Szymanski, and Cahill, 1985; Sherman and Wenocur, 1983; Solomon, 1976). The interaction between worker and client must be characterized by genuineness, mutual respect, open communication, and informality. The worker does not claim to hold the answers to the client's problems; instead, the client develops the insight, skills, and capacity to resolve the situation herself (Bock, 1980; Bricker-Jenkins and Hooyman, 1986; Fagan, 1979; Keefe, 1980; Pinderhughes, 1989; Schechter, Szymanski, and Cahill, 1985; Solomon, 1976).

Egalitarian interaction between worker and client can be described as *dialogue.* Dialogue connotes action and interaction, a two-way conversation between two mutually respectful people. The worker's revelation of self through self-disclosure, identification with the client, recognition of his or her own limits, and willingness to take risks is a component of dialogue.

Praxis is common to these activities: the wedding of reflection and action. For clients' active involvement in the change process to empower them, they must be encouraged to reflect on and analyze their experience. The knowledge gained can then be applied to future efforts (Bock, 1980; Burghardt, 1982; Freire, 1973; Keefe, 1980; Longres and McLeod, 1980; Rose and Black, 1985). This will in turn affect the shape of the intervention or activity.

The NUP project required me to be a shape shifter, able to work in several modalities simultaneously. At times this would mean doing individual work within the group by asking pertinent questions or shifting group discussion to a topic that would allow an individual's concern to surface.

NUP also relied on the social worker's ability to integrate several skills in order to provide the type of practice most appropriate at the time. It was built on several cognitive behavioral interventions as well as interventions from culturally competent and feminist practice. At times this meant learning the nuances of another language. At other times it meant developing a way to involve men of color into the practice in order to raise their consciousness about the experiences of their families, communities, or partners and to integrate their voices into the selected intervention.

—Edith Lewis

Participation can also play an important role in program or agency governance, ranging from collaboration in treatment planning to rule making and enforcement to representation on the board of directors. Many organizations committed to empowerment practice make efforts to bring empowering methods into their own administration (Gutiérrez, GlenMaye, and DeLois, 1995). In some organizations, this may mean a collective structure or the involvement of workers and program participants on all levels of the organization in the design, implementation, and evaluation of programs (Johnson, 1990). In this way, the governance of the organization becomes another mechanism for empowerment.

As I developed the NUP I knew it was based on the values of looking for strengths in some of the most discouraging places and believing that they existed. Throughout that work I was rarely disappointed, as the women engaged in levels of individual, family, and community change that I would not have predicted. By working on strengths and building capacity the NUP group was able to change the form and direction of support services and programming provided for families in public housing.

Holding on to this belief in individuals' capacities is the way I have been able to continue my current work on the conflicts involved in issues of race, ethnicity, gender, and sexual orientation in human service organizations. If I did not believe that human beings from different backgrounds could become bridges (without, as Moraga and Anzaldúa [1983] have noted, the bridge becoming one's back), I could not continue to do this work with my students, who are generally so different from me in terms of class and/or ethnicity.

—*Edith Lewis*

Capacity building. Capacity building requires methods that build from client strengths. Building from strengths means first identifying areas of positive functioning and using those areas to develop new skills (Mathis and Richan, 1986; Pinderhughes, 1989; Shapiro, 1984; Sherman and Wenocur, 1983; Solomon, 1976). Contributions from clients enhance self-esteem, further a sense of belonging, and break down isolation while increasing mutual assistance. For example, when working with a group of single parents on parenting their disabled children, one of the authors encouraged participants to share with the group their skills in such areas as baking or arts and crafts (Gutiérrez, 1991). This encouragement contributed to the parents' feelings of mastery, helped them to feel valued and important within the group, and provided a basis for future work.

Building from strengths often means recognizing and validating skills and capacities that may often go unnoticed and unrewarded. The worker must recognize that many women of color have been involved in a process of struggle against oppressive structures and that this has required considerable strength. By analyzing elements of the struggle, the social worker identifies client strengths, communicates these to the client, and then utilizes them as a basis for future work.

These methods—capacity building, participation, and education—have the potential to be interlocking and mutually reinforcing. Participating in programs within an organization can be educational and build on existing strengths. Unless social workers see participants and communities as competent, they will not treat them as equal partners. Moreover, a focus on education can guide the ways in which strengths are developed and participation is structured.

Doing empowerment work affects not only the service consumer but also the practitioner functioning as service provider. In fact, these labels no longer have the same meaning or importance for me as they did even ten years ago, when I believed them to be far superior to the then widely used terms of "client/patient" and "worker." I now strive to be a partner in the empowerment of individuals, families, groups, and communities in my professional work and am continually grateful for the ways I am transformed in my own capacity building, critical consciousness, and connection as those around me are engaged in their own transformations.

—Edith Lewis

Although this chapter presents empowerment theory and practice separately, these two faces of empowerment are closely interrelated. The methods of empowerment are techniques developed specifically to enhance feelings of confidence, consciousness, and connection. Empowerment as a perspective and method for practice calls for us to rethink our professional roles and identities. It suggests that we develop a working alliance with individuals, families, and communities to create and work toward a common vision. It acknowledges the commonality of our human experience while recognizing how social forces have shaped the standpoints of specific groups. Empowerment practice enables social workers to support collaboration and accept the lead of the client's perspective. In our subsequent chapters, we articulate further the standpoints of different subgroups of women of color and identify methods for work at different levels and phases of practice.

TWO

Empowerment Techniques: Engagement and Assessment

◆

Jacquie, a graduate student in social work, looked back on the day at her community mental health practicum placement. This was her second placement and infinitely more rewarding intellectually and interpersonally than her first. At this CMH, Jacquie was assigned to do the intake work with supervision and had encountered families and individuals from varied economic, racial, ethnic, and social backgrounds. Her supervision included training in bilingual and bicultural service provision, as well as specific attention to the potential for cultural nuances to influence assessment outcomes. Having just been terminated from a placement because she insisted that an elderly Lebanese man be allowed to have his imam pray with him and be involved in his discharge planning, Jacquie found her new agency to be a welcome change.

Today, Jacquie's intake roster included Kofi Baruch, a thirteen-year-old African-American male referred by his parents and school for behavioral difficulties at school; Rita Swanson, a twenty-five-year-old White woman from an inner-city neighborhood who had experienced severe childhood physical and sexual abuse that was interfering with her ability to sustain a romantic relationship; and the Joneses, a Puerto Rican family in which the aging mother, Rosario, was attempting to identify suitable arrangements for her forty-year-old, moderately retarded daughter, Monique, who remained at home. Each of these situations required Jacquie to choose different assessment instruments, identify additional pertinent questions for the social history, and moderate her behavior in order to engage most effectively the individuals entering the agency for the first time.

This was made more difficult today by the presence of a substitute receptionist at the desk who had been so rude to Kofi's family that they were in the process of leaving the agency when Jacquie came out to greet them. With much skill, she combined the lessons she'd learned as a poor child growing up on the island of St. Thomas in the Virgin Islands with those from her supervision and classroom experiences to encourage them to reenter the agency and participate in the intake process. All in all, Jacquie felt that this had been a great day!

Entering any new relationship can be difficult for people. This is no less true for service providers who are attempting to work from a culturally competent empowerment perspective. In addition to the basic interpersonal communication skills and knowledge, traditionally taught as forms of connection when performing engagement and assessment, working with women of color requires a knowledge of interpersonal skills and assessment techniques that raise all the parties' critical consciousness and confidence as well. Some of these interpersonal skills are gained from life experience, some from formal education, and some from the development of clinical expertise in practice situations. This chapter explores some of the varied tools, skills, and knowledge developed for an empowerment perspective on engagement and assessment, using Jacquie's experiences with the three intake cases from her agency as illustrations. As will be evident, this skill and knowledge base has implications for work with White women as well as women of color.

Negotiating the Initial Barriers in the Engagement Process

Much has been written about the general mistrust people of color have for professional helping services. Adebimpe (1982) identifies the historical roots of African Americans' mistrust of traditional forms of intervention in the reports of a higher prevalence of mental illness among free African Americans in the North versus those enslaved in the South during the period before the signing of the Emancipation Proclamation. Several scholars have produced studies identifying the increased probability for people of color to be misdiagnosed by psychologists, social workers, and psychiatrists (Greene, 1994a; Adebimpe, 1982; Mukherjee, 1983; McGoldrick, Pearce, and Giordano, 1982; Comas-Diaz and Greene, 1994), particularly when the diagnosis was schizophrenia. African-American and Latino/Latina individuals were more likely to be misdiagnosed as schizophrenic rather than as suffering from bipolar depression, a more likely diagnosis. Different toleration levels of chemical substances and treatment designs for substance abuse have also led to a lack of participation among populations of color in substance misuse treatment and prevention programs (Maultsby, 1979; Purnell, 1996; Henderson, 1994; Okazawa-Rey, 1998).

This mistrust has been exacerbated by the lack of attention to gender, ethnicity, race, economic status, and environment as variables influencing the engagement process for both service providers and service consumers (Lum, 1996). The tool used most extensively by clinical practitioners for the last forty-two years, the American Psychiatric Association's *Diagnostic and Statistical Manual of Mental Disorders*, has been criticized by many professionals—among them the Association of Black Psychologists—for its lack of attention to these factors (Kirk and Kutchins, 1992; Specht and Courtney, 1994; Comas-Diaz and Griffith, 1988; Lewis, 1993a). It is only in the new fourth edition, published in 1994, that ethnic, economic, and environmental factors influencing human behavior were given serious attention. Indeed, the *DSM-IV* includes an appendix entitled "Glossary of Culture-Bound Syndromes" that cites phenomena that may be experienced by some members of specific ethnic groups within their cultural contexts. Some examples are ghost sickness, reported by members of some American Indian nations, and *mal de ojo*—or evil eye—noted among some African, Indian, and Latin groups (American Psychiatric Association, 1994). As always, however, our knowledge of human beings in their social environments continues to grow. The new *DSM-IV* does not, for example, include the sleeping death increasingly documented among Hmong males who have immigrated from Vietnam to the United States (McInnis, Petracchi, and Morgenbesser, 1990).

This history of misdiagnoses and ethnocentrism, in addition to environmental factors such as traditional help-seeking behaviors appropriate to the ethnic community in question and the lack of affordable mental health coverage for individuals employed in the secondary labor market, have led fewer people of color to seek mental health assistance (Strand, 1997; Boes and van Wormer, 1997; Suarez, Lewis, and Clark, 1995; Comaz-Diaz and Greene, 1994). Many in the helping professions are concerned about this, and there has been a proliferation of literature on how to increase the numbers of people of color in the mental health field, as both service providers and consumers (Comas-Diaz and Greene, 1994; Comas-Diaz and Griffith, 1988). This chapter can only begin to scratch the surface of this wealth of material, and practitioners are encouraged to increase their knowledge base by reading as much of the new scholarship in this area as possible and attending all the professional meetings they can.

DEALING WITH THE DIFFICULT TOPIC OF DIFFERENCE IN THE INITIAL INTERACTIONS

We believe that the current state of racial and ethnic polarity in the United States has resulted in the institutionalization of ethnocentric models of assessment and diagnosis. We are supported in this belief by research that has pointed to the problems encountered by practitioners when they fail to discuss race or sexual orientation actively as potential issues with service consumers (McWhirter, 1994; Thompson and Jenal, 1994). Adopting an ostrich perspective because of our discomfort with issues of difference does not erase those differences. Indeed, it is our belief that they repeatedly emerge during the initial intake and intervention phases. To address these systematically— that is, to use critical consciousness-raising and education strategies to engage women of color in practice—is of utmost importance if these individuals are to complete the intervention process.

An example from Jacquie's experience might be useful here. On meeting with Rita, Jacquie might have ignored their different racial backgrounds at the outset. Instead, she chose to discuss directly the differences in their racial backgrounds and how these might affect their interaction. Here is a sample of what Jacquie did.

JACQUIE: Now that we've talked a bit about how we might work together on the experiences you've had, I'd also like to talk about other things that might affect our work together. I can start with some things that sometimes happen when two people of different backgrounds enter therapy, but I want you to add to this list if you think there are other things that might be important for the two of us to get on the table right away. Is that okay with you?

RITA: Okay, uh, I think so. What kinds of things are you talking about?

JACQUIE: Things that might make us feel uncomfortable sometimes. For example, people of different races often have been taught things about each other that sometimes make it difficult for them to focus on their work together rather than thinking about what the other person is really thinking. I'd like to say right up front that I noticed that I'm Black and you're White [Jacquie smiles]. But I'm more than Black, and you're more than

White. I'm from an island and consider myself an Afro-Caribbean woman who grew up poor. I know you've grown up poor as well, and so even in our differences there are some similarities. Plus, we both use expressions when we speak that come from our backgrounds. That we do it is a similarity, but that we might not understand each other's expressions is a difference. I want to make a contract with you, if you're willing, to have you stop me when I am saying something that doesn't make sense to you and to keep asking me about it until it does make sense or until you want me to drop it because it doesn't fit in your case. I also want you to feel free to do the same with me.

RITA: You mean like when I said that people thought I was "pwt" and you didn't know what that meant?

JACQUIE: Yep, exactly! What you helped me do was to keep asking questions until we both understood that what you meant was that you were more than where you were born or how much money you made. You were a woman who was special because of how you lived and loved other people, not someone who didn't care, take care, work hard, or have "family values" because you happened to be poor and White. Then you told me that I'd gotten it right. That's what I'd like to have us keep trying, okay?

RITA: That really makes a lot of sense to me! But I think I'll get nervous sometimes because I don't want to hurt your feelings.

JACQUIE: We need to trust enough so that we can try this out with each other. I have an idea. How about we make an agreement to stop at the beginning and ending of each of our sessions to check in with each other on whether we have really tried to accomplish this?

RITA: Okay, I think I have one. Can we talk about why there are no White people in the pictures on your walls?

What Jacquie did well in this last dialogue was to establish that she and Rita had a potential problem that could interfere with their ability to work together effectively (connection). She named the problem as racial difference and talked about the strengths of both their differences and similarities (critical consciousness). In addition, she gave examples of how she and Rita might use a back-translation technique (Jackson, Tucker, and Bowman, 1982) to unravel their potential misunderstandings and voice their realities (Boes and van Wormer, 1997) in the therapeutic sessions. She checked for Rita's willingness actually to raise these differences and reinforced any effort on Rita's part to redefine their interactions (confidence and skill building). This example illustrates all three of the principles of using an empowerment perspective in the engagement process.

Had Jacquie not addressed the issue of racial difference early in her interactions with Rita, it might have been raised at a later and more emotionally charged time in their interaction. That situation would likely have been confrontational, as the party who had held onto her concerns about the issue of difference could use it as a bombshell to attack the other (McWhirter, 1994). Instead, each person here had room to speak her own truths about the situation, one of the tenets of feminist practice (Bricker-Jenkins, Hooyman, and Gottlieb, 1991).

HOW TO AVOID ONE OF THE CLASSIC BLUNDERS IN THE ENGAGEMENT PROCESS

All too often, our attempts at enacting an empowerment perspective in our work are undermined before we actually meet the people with whom we are working. Jacquie encountered this in her initial meeting with the Baruch family. Today, one of the more striking public service announcements on the prevalence of HIV disease is that adults are not only having sex with a new partner, they are having sex with every partner that person has ever had sex with. To a certain extent this is also true of all our initial encounters with people, particularly women and men of color, whose daily encounters with negative experiences—so-called everyday racism—often color the new experiences in their lives. Jacquie had been having a marvelous day at work, but the Baruch family had not. The parents were sincerely concerned about their son's ability to continue to excel in the public school system. They had been overcharged for car repairs earlier in the day but knew that they had to have the transportation, in part to avoid the high prices charged at the grocery store in their neighborhood. In their anxiety about Kofi, they had arrived early for their appointment with Jacquie, who was running five minutes behind because she had not been contacted by the substitute receptionist and told of the Baruch's arrival. As the family waited, the receptionist filed her nails, refused to respond to their question about when Jacquie might be available to see them, and laughed at their son's haircut. Understandably, the Baruch family had just had enough!

Before Jacquie could start her work with the Baruch family, she first had to undo the damage they had experienced at the hands of many others in the course of the day. Jacquie viewed her initial task as establishing connection between herself and the Baruchs. She introduced herself to the family, apologized for her delay, asked if they would like a beverage, and asked them to accompany her to her office. Noting that the receptionist only began to appear to be working when she entered the reception area, Jacquie asked the Baruchs whether they had been told she was seeing another person. When informed that the receptionist had been rude to them, Jacquie went on to acknowledge the frustration the Baruchs must have experienced, to apologize again, and to state that it was the agency's policy to provide top-quality service to everyone who sought it; at the same time, she encouraged the Baruchs to file a formal complaint about their treatment in the reception area if they chose. These efforts to establish connection allowed the Baruchs to relax and refocus on the reasons they had come to the agency in the first place.

In summary, engagement is a process that brings into perspective not only the interaction of the empowered social worker and the service consumer but everyone else in both parties' environments. It is a delicate negotiating process that can offset the historical distrust women of color feel for mental health service provision. An empowering social work practitioner can use the tools of critical consciousness, confidence, and connection to forge a therapeutic alliance among all parties.

Issues in Assessment

In today's harried world of multiple competing responsibilities, social workers find themselves juggling large caseloads, taking on administrative responsibilities, and trying to maintain their traditional commitments to working jointly on individual and societal problems (Gutiérrez, Lewis, and Nagda, 1995; Soderfeldt, Soderfeldt, and Warg, 1995). With these sometimes conflicting roles, it is all too easy to skimp on the tedious work required to arrive at an adequate assessment of a consumer's concerns. Our agencies and disciplines further support such skimping by providing us with shortcut methods of assessment that do not always consider individuals in their social environments. We noted in the preface that taking the time to focus sincerely on the multiple factors influencing behavior is essential to empowered practice with women of color. This section identifies some ways to accomplished this. Integrating the empowerment themes of critical consciousness, confidence, and connection with those of culturally competent practice (viewing the individual as part of larger social networks; recognizing the historical, political, and social factors influencing behavior; embracing class, ethnic, racial, gender, sexual orientation, and ability differences in terms of their utility for the service consumer) can lead to a mutually agreed-upon course of action.

USE OF STANDARDIZED INSTRUMENTS

Ongoing research has both helped and hindered practitioners by developing scales and assessment instruments that purport to provide accurate diagnoses of presenting problems. In the aggregate, these scales have been tested on large numbers of individuals and, through factor or cluster analyses, have given practitioners general constructs to guide diagnosis. There are, however, problems with relying solely on these instruments for diagnosis, as we noted above. If the actual items in an instrument have little or altered meaning for the respondents, then the constructs they measure will also have little or altered validity in the assessment process. Empowering social workers must be very careful in their use of instruments that have not been normed for the populations they meet in their practice settings. For example, Jacquie wished to gain additional knowledge of Monique Jones's adaptive and cognitive skills, even though she had access to the WISC-R scores from the school Monique had left when she was twenty-two. Rather than assume that she understood what an earlier diagnosis of moderate mental retardation meant in Monique's case, Jacquie gathered further information from both Monique and her mother about Monique's adaptive behavior in the house. She found that Monique had been taking responsibility for the family shopping, had helped with household tasks, and was fully capable of managing all her daily hygiene chores. When Mrs. Jones had broken her arm ten years before, Monique had also learned to write checks and pay the household bills, with some supervision. A simple reliance on the earlier diagnosis would not have been sufficient in this case, as most individuals diagnosed with moderate mental retardation are not able to perform all the tasks at which Monique was quite competent. Jacquie appropriately reinforced both Monique and Mrs. Jones for their successful efforts to increase Monique's skill level at home after she left the public school setting (an integration of the concept of confidence during the assessment phase).

That there is a danger in relying solely on standardized instruments during the assessment process does not mean that these instruments must be altogether ignored in this phase, however. By the third session with the Baruch family, Jacquie recognized that Mrs. Baruch's continuing complaints of stomach pain might be connected to depression. Her agency routinely used the CES-D and/or the Hudson Generalized Contentment Scale for diagnostic purposes. Neither of these scales focused on the somatic complaints so often documented in depressed women of color (Maultsby, 1982; Adebimpe, 1982; Lewis, 1993; Comas-Diaz and Greene, 1994). To explore further her concerns about Mrs. Baruch's depression, Jacquie asked her to complete the African-American Women's Stress scale (Watts-Jones, 1990), a hundred-item scale addressing a wide variety of physiological as well as psychological elements of depression that has been tested with African-American populations and found to be as useful as the CES-D. The results revealed that Mrs. Baruch was experiencing a number of stressors in her life that would have to be addressed before she could effectively work with her son and the school system.

Most standardized instruments do not simultaneously address individuals and their social environments, a prerequisite of effective empowerment practice. For this reason, social workers must have at their disposal a number of nonstandardized tools that can further this assessment process. A variety of these tools have been developed during the last two decades (Lum, 1982; Cheetham, 1982; Lewis and Ford, 1990; McGoldrick and Gerson, 1982; Hartman and Laird, 1978). They allow practitioners to identify the number of people who are actively involved in the service consumer's network, the extent to which these individuals are active in decision-making processes or exert other types of influence on the service consumer, and the quality and quantity of their economic, social, or emotional support (Lewis and Ford, 1990; Henly, 1994; Lewis, 1988). For example, Jacquie used the Network Utilization Project (NUP) Assessment packet (Lewis and Ford, 1990), which asks consumers to diagram their entire social network of family, friends, romantic partners, church or other religious supports, and professional supports. The packet also includes an instrument that identifies the quantity of support available from these various networks. The final portion of the assessment packet is a systematic analysis of each of the target problems brought to the treatment process, a task analysis of those steps needed to address the first of the target problems, identification of network members who might be asked to provide support to the consumer, and an appraisal of the pros and cons of having a particular person involved in the intervention process. Monique Jones's NUP assessment is reproduced in table 2.1.

Monique's network analysis revealed a relationship with her church, an extended family of support including her paternal grandparents and an aunt, three good friends, and a boyfriend, Paulo, with whom she had been "keeping company" for over ten years. She also identified Jacquie as a significant part of her formal network, along with Mr. Johnson, who managed the sheltered workshop in her community, and Johnnie, the pharmacist from whom she purchased her mother's hypertension medication.

Monique, Mrs. Jones, and Jacquie identified the most pressing concern facing Monique as the need to find an alternative placement in the event of her parents' deaths. Table 2.2 presents the second part of the NUP analysis, construction of a task analysis for an appropriate placement.

After determining what tasks needed to be accomplished for Monique to move, Jacquie, Monique, and Mrs. Jones then identified who in the natural

TABLE 2.1 Monique Jones's NUP Assessment

Family	Friends	Partners	Church	Others
Mama/Papa	Cece	Paulo	Iglesia Bautista	Jacquie
Abuelo Carlos	Jean		Mrs. Bell	Johnnie
Abuela Carla	Patrice		Fr. Tucker	Mr. Johnson
Tiá Lupe				

TABLE 2.2 Strategic Determination of Monique's Relocation Goal (Preliminary)

Task	Who's Responsible	Date of Completion
Identify an appropriate place to live based on Monique's current abilities and prognosis for the future		
Determine the costs		
Who will move Monique?		
How will costs be met?		
Explain move to grandparents		
Care for parents		
A job for Monique		
Transportation to and from job		
Carry out the move		

helping network could either assist or deter Monique from meeting her goal of moving from her parents' home to a more independent living situation (Lewis and Suarez, 1995). Each member of the network was reviewed in light of the pros and cons of his or her involvement in helping Monique meet her objective of making the move within one year (for more information on the construction of goals, objectives, and task analyses, see Cormier and Cormier, 1998). Table 2.3 reproduces the pros/cons list for Tiá Lupe.

It is clear from the pros and cons list for Tiá Lupe that the positive aspects of her being involved in Monique's move outweigh the potential negative aspect, though eventually Jacquie will need to find out how problematic it will be for Tiá Lupe to behave in a manner that may not adhere to the principle of *respeto* (respect) that governs the Joneses' extended family system. At this juncture, however, it appears that Tiá Lupe should be retained as a support person in Monique's move.

After doing the pros/cons analysis for each person on Monique's original network chart, those involved in the assessment process then returned to the original task analysis to fill in the blanks of who would be contacted to assist with the move (see table 2.4).

Note that not everyone originally included in Monique's social network chart was included in the final tasks. The grandparents were determined to be so opposed to the potential move that they could not be enlisted in the process. Monique's friend Jean was also not involved because she wanted Monique to live with her but her home would not provide the type of super-

TABLE 2.3 Tiá Lupe's Pros and Cons List

Pros	Cons
Tiá Lupe loves Monique	Tiá Lupe might support Monique's parents' opposition to Monique's move away from home. This could cause a conflict in the family.
Tiá Lupe has access to a friend who owns a moving company.	
Monique has talked with Tiá Lupe on several occasions about her desire to move.	
Tiá Lupe loves her brother and knows that this move is something the Jones family wants.	

vision Monique herself decided that she needed. Looking at the entire Iglesia Bautista as a support entity was impossible. Instead, the strategic planning assessment allowed Monique and Mrs. Jones to identify those individuals in the church who could be counted on to provide the care for the Joneses that Monique had been providing before. As much as Monique cared for her friend Paulo, it was determined through his pros/cons list that his involvement in planning the move would not be as helpful as his actual presence during the move. (The NUP assessment process helps women make reasonable appraisals of network members who may not be helpful to them in a particular series of tasks. Not including certain people does not mean they are excluded forever from the network, merely that they are not included in a particular task [Lewis and Ford, 1990].)

In this case, using a range of assessment tools helped Jacquie in her work with the Jones family. She used an analysis that supported the recognition of Monique's participation in a broad social network including family, friends, partners, religious organizations, and professional helpers (the connection element of empowerment). At the same time, she collected formal assessment data using the results of the WISC-R and several adaptive rating scales with

TABLE 2.4 Strategic Determination of Monique's Relocation Goal (Preliminary)

Task	Who's Responsible	Date of Completion
Identify an appropriate place to live based on Monique's current abilities and prognosis for the future	Monique, Mom, Dad, Jacquie and Mr. Johnson	March 1, 1999
Determine the costs	Jacquie, Mom, and Dad	March 1, 1999
Who will move Monique?	Tiá Lupe, Monique, and Mom	April 30, 1999
How will costs be met?	Jacquie, Mom, and Dad	March 24, 1999
Explain move to grandparents	Monique, Tiá Lupe, Dad	May 1, 1999
Care for parents	Jacquie, Mom, Dad, Fr. Tucker, Mrs. Bell	March 1, 1999
A job for Monique	Monique, Mr. Johnson	June 30, 1999
Transportation to and from job	Monique, Jacquie	June 30, 1999
Carry out the move	Tiá Lupe, Monique, Paulo, Cece, Patrice	October 30, 1999

Monique and Mrs. Jones. In doing so, she used critical consciousness construction knowledge to determine who in the network would actually be able to assist Monique in meeting her goal, without eliminating those individuals who might hinder the process from the network. In supporting Monique's decision to move to a more independent living situation and adequately assessing her capacity to do so, Jacquie reinforced Monique's confidence that she would indeed be able to meet her goal (Renz-Beaulaurier, 1998). Having had prior experiences with social workers who had told her more about her limitations than abilities, Monique found this reinforcement was to be significant.

Women-in-Relationship Models

This chapter has demonstrated some of the issues in assessment and engagement with regard to working with women, particularly women of color. As we stated at the outset, in this chapter we adopted the view that an empowerment perspective on assessment requires that social workers look first at the woman of color in her social environment. This is a basic tenet of both feminist and culturally competent practice as well (Lewis and Kissman, 1989; Bricker-Jenkins and Hooyman, 1986; Devore and Schlesinger, 1987). In recent years, this perspective has led to the creation of several models of practice in psychology, public health, family therapy, and social work, including the ecological framework, culturally competent practice, ethnic-sensitive practice, ethnoconscious practice, feminist practice, and the Stone School woman-in-relationship perspective (Comas-Diaz, 1981; Lum, 1982; Chau, 1990; Longres, 1990; Lewis and Kissman, 1989; Jordan, 1997; Turner, 1997).

This chapter introduces the Stone School woman-in-relationship model, and elements of it will be cited throughout the text. This model is a conceptual framework congruent with empowerment practice because it includes attention to the issues of different gender constructions as well as those used in the other frameworks: race; ethnicity; economic, social, and political history; age; and ability. Recognizing the extent to which the women of color we encounter in practice are both women and people of color is essential to appropriate engagement and assessment. Jacquie's experiences as outlined in this chapter demonstrate the use of skills, values, and cultural competence to inform the assessment and diagnostic phases of the intervention process.

Equally important, incorporating an empowerment perspective during the assessment and engagement phases of the intervention process gives all the participants clues about the appropriate level of intervention. In the case of Jacquie and Rita's interaction, this systematic empowerment strategy led to future modeling and role playing of new skills as both parties progressed through the intervention. With the Baruchs, Jacquie assisted in the facilitation of two forms of intervention: Having identified the problem with the receptionist, Jacquie provided the family with the range of grievance options available to them both in and outside of the agency. As she learned more about the range of concerns the Baruchs had about their son, she was also able to refer them to the team of parents, teachers, and administrators in their son's school who were responsible for improved relations among all school members. The Baruchs began to take turns linking their participation in the Black Parents Support Group with that of the School Improvement Team and reported findings and requests from each group to the other. As a result, critical consciousness was built across both entities (Okazawa-Rey, 1998; Manning, 1998). This model of sharing information across issue groups in the school was reported to the district office, and the Baruchs later became consultants to other schools that wanted to replicate the program. Lastly, Jacquie's use of the NUP model with the Jones family led to systematic skill development with those of Monique's family, friends, neighbors, and teachers who were strategically placed to help her reach her stated goals. Without this strategic analysis, much energy and time could have been wasted and emotional distress increased by working ineffectively with individuals or institutions unable or unlikely to facilitate the changes Monique sought to make in her life.

The following chapters address ways in which the specific incorporation of an empowerment model can be used at the individual, family, group, and community levels to address target problems facing women of color in their social, historical, and political environments. At each of these levels, issues of engagement and assessment must be addressed via use of standardized and nonstandardized instruments and strategic problem solving so that the intervention is congruent with the needs and desires determined by service providers and consumers at that level of service. While each chapter primarily addresses one level of intervention, it is important to note that multiple levels of intervention may be enacted simultaneously in real-life situations, as issues at all levels interact with and affect issues at all other levels.

THREE

Empowerment Techniques: Practice with Individuals

◆

"So hum." Pamela said her mantra as she sat for a few moments in the early morning preparing herself for the day. "So hum—That I Am" she breathed in and out again and thought about how using this affirmation had really affected her life. Her work with Aisha, the social worker she had been meeting with during the last six months, and the widows' support group had helped her to view herself as an integral part of not only her own family and community but her society and world. Her daily meditation time of twenty minutes had also reconnected her with her spirituality in ways she had abandoned in the two years since leaving the church she had joined in the United States after marrying her husband, Anthony, some thirty years before. In the two years since Anthony's death, she had become more aware of being isolated in a racially mixed urban community as a widow whose three children had reached adulthood, as a Japanese immigrant, and as an individual experiencing the onset of a painful chronic illness: fibromyalgia.

Pamela's journey to this morning had not been easy. She remembered the period immediately following Anthony's death as excruciatingly painful. She felt isolated and believed that no one cared for her. While she thought she was coping well with her losses, her children became concerned about the depths of her depression, evident in her increasing lack of daily hygiene and indifference to caring for her home and pets. Moreover, she began having severe sleep disturbances and grew unable to hold coherent conversations with family, friends, or neighbors.

As her isolation and problematic behavior increased, those who cared about Pamela became very concerned. One evening, approximately six months after Anthony's death, Pamela's children and a neighbor came to visit her and explained their concerns. Pamela's first reaction was anger, followed closely by denial of the situation. The neighbor, Maude, a member of the widows' support group, gently talked about her own experiences with her husband's death and the types of support they had offered for her. She also discussed her experiences with breast cancer in a community where being open about illness was frowned on and most women kept silent about their needs until it was almost too late. Maude invited Pamela to come to the group meetings, but she declined, stating that she did not need help with her problems because she didn't have any.

Pamela discounted that evening's conversation for three more months, although periodically Maude would come to visit her and invite her to the group meetings. One evening when Maude stopped by, she found Pamela in tears, having suffered a painful episode related to the fibromyalgia. Maude had done some reading on the disease as part of her participation in the support group and helped Pamela connect words to her anguish. The next day, she brought another woman to Pamela's house, a member of the support group who had been diagnosed with fibromyalgia. Pamela believed that she had finally met someone who understood what she was facing on a daily basis and agreed to come to one meeting of the group.

While she still sometimes felt afraid and overwhelmed by the number of challenges in her life, Pamela had begun to reacquaint herself with the skills that would help her offset the pain, worry, and negativity that were limiting her. Aisha and the members of the widows' recovery group she had been involved with during the past nine months had helped her to practice daily acts of "remembering" the "so hum."

◆

The Contexts of Individual Work with Women of Color

This chapter focuses on some of the methods used to work effectively with women of color, integrating some of the more widely used intervention strategies with an analysis of how they might be incorporated into individual practice. But working with an individual woman of color does not necessarily mean working only with that woman without her significant others or using a single strategy with no other methods of intervention (e.g., community work and group work) (Jordan, 1997; Hodges, Burwell, and Ortega, 1998). As we have already noted, working with women of color requires the ability to view them as parts of families and communities of color with both unique and overlapping social, political, and historical experiences. Using an empowerment framework to view women of color requires an acknowledgement of all those past factors and the ways in which they interweave and manifest themselves in people's lives. From an empowerment perspective, individually focused intervention is a point of entry from which the individual can connect with her or his influencing social systems. We will use Pamela's case to illustrate these methods.

Working with Different Systems

INTRAPERSONAL

From an empowerment perspective intrapersonal work with women of color—that is, work on the internal emotional, psychological, and spiritual health of the individual—requires a focus on capacity building through the regular practice of skills that will allow them to view themselves as agents of change both within themselves and in their world (McWhirter, 1994; Glen-Maye, 1998). It also focuses on using the existent strengths of these women as tools in the skill-building process. Pamela and Aisha began their work by engaging in what might be thought of as simple case management. Together, they determined the level of knowledge Pamela had acquired about managing her personal finances and her health. Then they used that information to develop a contract for working together on securing more information about her physical health and adaptive living skills. While assessing the level of an individual's knowledge might seem like an interpersonal activity, an intrapersonal standpoint involves interpreting the knowledge acquired. For example, Pamela's initial reaction to the news of her fibromyalgia was denial, which allowed her to disconnect the symptoms she was experiencing from a physical illness. Aisha's recognition of Pamela's thinking about the illness helped her to understand Pamela's reactance to the situation (Rooney, 1992). Rather than blaming Pamela for being resistant, she could see that Pamela's intrapersonal constructions of reality were a natural response to confusing news about a malady she did not quite understand. With Aisha's help, Pamela then gained a greater understanding about how she viewed her world and the impact of that worldview on her decisions.

At all times, the interactions among intrapersonal, interpersonal, and community levels are at the forefront of the empowering practitioner's mind. Additional information about possible connections among these levels and others (such as societal or international) is continually elicited in the empowering practice relationship. Thus intrapersonal work is not divorced from any other system in which intervention may take place to benefit the service consumer (Baines, 1997).

Individual practice with women of color can be viewed from a woman-in-relationship perspective (Jordan, 1997). From a symbolic interactionist or ecological perspective, often used in feminist practice, this means that even intrapsychic conflicts can be viewed in the context of their interpersonal stimuli (McWhirter, 1994; Lipchik, 1991). In Pamela's case, for example, the feelings of worry and accompanying negativity had their basis in Anthony's death and Pamela's perception of her subsequent status as a widow in her community. While it would have been possible to focus an individual intervention on her inner feelings of self-esteem, a woman-in-relationship focus more profitably explored with her how her feelings were reinforced by interactions with others and by wider issues such as the ageism, racism, and sexism in our society. The following dialogue is indicative of one of the later individual sessions between Pamela and Aisha on the topic of Pamela's self-worth.

PAMELA: Aisha, it's happened again! Another notice from the social security office with another denial for ssi. What is this! How many times do I have to explain to these people that I am disabled? How many more doctor bills do I have to run up getting more assessments? Here's Anthony dead, and I am back to being a new immigrant all over again. Will I never be worthy enough to be taken seriously and considered a real citizen of this country?!

AISHA: Okay, Pamela, I hear you! This is your second denial from the ssi office, and you have the right to be angry about it. Let's take a step back and survey this situation in its entirety, though, so that you understand it as a systemic rather than a personal problem. That way you can use the anger productively to assert your rights until you get them. Let me ask you a question. How many women in your widows' group have had difficulty getting benefits they were entitled to?

PAMELA: Well, Kyoung did, . . . so did Pearl, and Etta, now that you mention it.

AISHA: Were Pearl and Etta immigrants?

PAMELA: Well, no . . .

AISHA: Are there any other commonalities between you and the other people you know who were denied ssi?

PAMELA: Hmmm, I get it. Certainly there are many. We are all poor, we are all women, and we all live in this neighborhood.

AISHA: Okay, while we both know that these denials are not restricted to poor women living in the neighborhood, we also know that there may be a higher percentage of poor people applying for benefits who may not be able to get them, in spite of the fact that they deserve them.

PAMELA: Well, richer women, even if they're widows, have lawyers and accountants to help them, and we don't.

AISHA: So what are you saying about this situation?

PAMELA: Well, perhaps if our widows' group had some help from a professional, or at least some information, we might be able to get that Social Security office to at least listen to us.

AISHA: So, do you still think that this is a personal problem related primarily to your immigrant status?

PAMELA: No, but it's a problem related to some of my other statuses. I guess my first reaction was to view it from the memories of my first days here in this country when all of the hurt was really related to my inability to speak English in ways people understood and their nastiness to me.

AISHA: Without a doubt! We all have things that trigger our past experiences. The important thing is to take a deep breath, step back, and examine the triggering situation and how accurate our thoughts about what it means are. The support of others is often helpful in doing this, but you can also do it alone. If we can grasp the real reasons things are happening in our lives, and not just respond to the triggers from our pasts, we can take action to change them. Look at what you have just done by thinking of organizing your women's group to seek justice in receiving benefits! This will have a positive outcome not just for you but for your friends in the group and, when the word gets out about how powerful you are, for the whole community as well.

PAMELA: That's right! Bring on the Social Security Administration!!!

In the preceding example, Aisha used a modification of Albert Ellis's (1962) Rational-Emotive Therapy (RET) to engage Pamela in an analysis of her ssi denial. With the goal of determining whether Pamela's thoughts about her immigrant status were accurate, Aisha used a form of Ellis's concept of disputation to elicit Pamela's perspectives on that accuracy. The analysis included the replacement of the inaccurate thoughts with more accurate ones that would address the situation productively (McWhirter, 1994). Beyond that disputation process, however, Aisha helped Pamela to link her individual concerns with a larger social action that would potentially benefit at least several members of her peer group.

Three things in the preceding example provide additional examples of empowering intrapersonal practice. First, Aisha heard what Pamela had to say and did not try to disabuse her of the reality she brought into the session. It is completely possible, given the increase in legislation aimed at restricting immigrants' rights to supportive social services, that women like Pamela would be excluded from access to those services, and that possibility must be assessed by the interpersonal practitioner (Lewis, 1995; Baines, 1997; Boes and van Wormer, 1997; Okazawa-Rey, 1998). In other words, before placing blame on service consumers for what may appear to be faulty thinking based on personal experience, the empowering practitioner should make certain that there is actually no historical, social, or political reality in the thinking.

Second, Aisha's role was to walk with rather than direct Pamela through the process, a method of capacity building. RET is often criticized for its directive and negating processes (McWhirter, 1994) and can be quite disempowering to those who are not interested in a constant argument about their perceptions. What Aisha did was to take a standard intervention technique and modify it for use with the real person she was meeting at her office. As a result of her modification, Pamela was able to build on the existing strengths in her life (e.g., the widows' group) and tie them to some meaningful goals in her own life.

Third, Aisha and Pamela's interaction provided a mechanism for building a collective response to the oppression and discrimination faced by women in the widows' group. With the exploration of the interactions between racism and classism for public assistance recipients, seeds were laid for a joint response to their common experiences by the widows' group members. Eventually the widows began to write and send letters to the local newspapers' editorial offices about the double whammy of being a poor widow of color in the city. Many of these letters were printed, and one of the city's newspapers did a Sunday feature on the widows' group and their individual and collective challenges and triumphs. Critical consciousness, in this case, led to a connection to others with like experiences and the crafting of productive rather than paralyzing responses to the discriminatory experiences (Wallack, 1997; LaBonte, 1997; Cohen, 1997).

INTERPERSONAL

The relationship between service provider and service consumer is as complex as any other interpersonal relationship and must be examined in the context of building an alliance for work, as the previous chapter discussed. Essentially this means that empowered practitioners must engage in a series of questions about their historical, political, and social realities—as well as those involved in their professional status—and how these interface with the therapeutic alliances they must try to establish with those seeking assistance. This does not mean that the practitioner is trapped in her own self-analysis of the alliance to the detriment of the service consumer. Rather, empowering practitioners are open to receiving as well as providing information about the critical consciousness experience (Coll, Cook-Nobles, and Surrey, 1997; Castex, 1993; Cohen, 1990).

It is important to illustrate here how empowering practitioners may use transformed understandings of the issues of transference and countertransference in empowering practice (Miller et al., 1997; Scharff and Scharff, 1991).

One of the tenets of this book is that knowledge is socially constructed, supported, or punished by those in a position to influence our thinking and behavior. Socially constructed knowledge, unlike that in the physical sciences, is fluid: what we hold to be truth is based on an aggregation of people's experiences. This aggregation, however, only captures a portion of these experiences, and social science knowledge and methodology are only able to capture snippets of people's realities.

The same holds true for interpersonal practice techniques, which are likewise historically and socially constructed. Whether a service provider chooses a particular one or not depends on the other information she receives about the appropriateness of a particular method and on her ability to use it effectively. While this is to be expected, sometimes service consumers teach us about the uses of interventions we might not have thought about.

Pamela's work with Aisha on her concerns about practice with women of color offers one such example. Aisha had been involved in interpersonal and group practice for almost ten years and had dedicated most of her life to working with people of color. In the inner city of the urban area where she lived, however, that meant working almost exclusively with African-American and Latino/Latina populations. Pamela's arrival at the agency Aisha worked in was quite unusual, and Aisha felt at a disadvantage when deciding how best to approach working with her. Aisha, herself an African-American woman, had been raised to be suspicious of Asians and Asian-Americans but knew that these suspicions were based on someone else's social construction of reality, one that Aisha had never had to test. Pamela, in the first session, sensed some unease on Aisha's part and raised it with her.

PAMELA: Okay, now I think I can talk to you, but you seem to be having difficulty talking with me.

AISHA (hesitantly): I don't know what you mean . . .

PAMELA: I was raised to hear what people said with both their mouths and their bodies, and your body says that you may be uncomfortable with me. I know I am an immigrant. Does that bother you?

AISHA (on the defensive): No, of course not. I have worked with Haitians and Nicaraguans in this agency before.

PAMELA (quietly, but glancing occasionally at Aisha's face): Ever worked with someone from Japan before?

AISHA: Actually, no, but I am willing and competent to work with you.

PAMELA: Then let's work, but let's be honest about our backgrounds with one another. I have lived with my husband's family for the last thirty years, and one of the things they taught me both in the South and the North was that when Black people look you straight in the eyes for a long period of time, you cannot trust that they are giving you the truth. My family in Japan was the same. Looking directly in the eyes was a sign of contempt not respect. I look at you, and you're looking at me straight in the eyes, but I don't feel that your soul is here in the room. Am I right?

AISHA (still somewhat evasive, but surprised): And where did your husband's people come from?

PAMELA: From Mississippi, originally, although many of them live in this city now. My husband was a Black man. But I just asked you about the use of your eyes. Was I right?

AISHA (now looking somewhat sheepishly at the floor but smiling): Okay, you caught me. But I like the way you did it. You still allowed me my dignity even while I was sticking my foot in my mouth. You're right, Pamela, I don't have a lot of experience dealing with people from Japan or with any other Asians, for that matter. The relationships between our groups have been very strained lately, and I guess I've been responding to this discomfort.

PAMELA (softly but firmly): And it has shown. Of course, you need to know that the tensions haven't been focused on Japanese and African-American conflict for several decades now. The tensions have, however, been very clear between African-American and other Asian populations, such as the

Koreans. I'm only saying this because my daughter helped me to become sensitive to our being viewed as one group in this society, even though there are so many different Asian groups represented in America. I always think of myself as a Japanese-American, not as an Asian-American, and I want you to think of me in that way, too. To do so, you will need to know something about who I am, though.

AISHA: I hadn't thought of the differences in this way before. You're right, I have been thinking of you as "Asian." Will you tell me why you don't think of yourself that way?

PAMELA (clasping her hands together): Ah, so we begin to talk about group identity, yes?

AISHA (laughing): Okay, so is this not a topic I should be familiar with . . . ?

This interaction could have been quite painful for both Aisha and Pamela, but instead it became a capacity-building exercise for them both. This occurred for several reasons. First, the psychological distance the service provider sometimes places between her professional self and the service consumer's real self may not provide enough information about the practitioner's true self to let the engagement process continue. The professional self, which may not incorporate enough salient aspects of the practitioner's true self, may in turn trigger the past experiences of the service consumer (Greene, 1994c; Morrow, 1996; Cohen, 1997). In the preceding dialogue, Aisha benefited because when Pamela was triggered by Aisha's use of eye contact, Pamela called attention to it in the session. Even then, Aisha's evasive first response could have been Pamela's last opportunity to heighten Aisha's critical consciousness. Aisha could have responded that the problem was Pamela's alone, even though it was clear that the issue affected both of their true selves equally. The simple but incorrect thing for Aisha to have done would have been to label Pamela as having the problem or being resistant (Rooney, 1992). Instead, she acknowledged, with Pamela's help, that an intricate web of transference and countertransference issues was affecting the interaction of their true selves. In other words, both Pamela and Aisha were being triggered by past experiences, and, in this case, Pamela's information was much more accurate than Aisha's. Aisha's willingness to engage in dialogue with Pamela about their mutual reactions to an issue not directly related to the concerns that brought Pamela into the social work context in the first place expanded the knowledge base for both parties.

Second, Pamela was able to build on her own understanding of the ways in which U.S. citizens often erroneously think about Asians to help Aisha understand that the beliefs she had historically operated under were not uncommon (see chapter 12). In fact, Pamela modeled that she, too, had been able to expand her own skill building by being educated by her daughter. Pamela's statement set the tone for Aisha to understand that we all can draw lessons from unlikely sources.

Third, Aisha was able to recognize that she had been exposed to some stereotypes about Asians and Asian-Americans through her own past experiences as well. Too often, women of color in professional practice believe that only White Americans can discriminate. That belief rejects the personal and referent group power each ethnic group has to exclude other groups—the very experience that Pamela faced as a Japanese widow in an ethnically diverse but primarily African-American neighborhood. Aisha's recognition of her own capacity for discrimination further solidified a foundation for the exploration of discrimination and prejudice in Pamela's life, as well as the search for useful strategies to offset these experiences in the wider society. In fact, Aisha's experience of the interaction led her to share the experience and the new skills she had acquired with other social workers in her own case supervision group.

Finally, Pamela and Aisha were engaged in truthful discussion, during which each could use humor and tenderness to continue to bridge their individual misconceptions. This truthful discussion allowed them to discuss other cultural cues Pamela was experiencing in her interactions with family, friends, and neighbors and to decode them as she had done with Aisha.

In this example, transference and countertransference experiences were considered a part of everyday interpersonal interaction. An empowering framework views such constructs as normative rather than as interactions to be avoided or minimized (Jordan, 1997; O'Hanlon, 1990; Suarez, Lewis, and Clark, 1995). Further, the framework recognizes that both service consumers and service providers undergo such experiences and that this must acknowledged by both equally, rather than the professional power broker attaching the label of transference to the so-called patient alone or the disgruntled client leveling the charge of countertransference (perhaps explained as "that therapist has a problem with folks like me") at the practitioner.

FAMILIAL

While later chapters of this book are devoted to family and group practice, empowering individual practice must also link the woman of color to her significant and proximal others, as defined by her (Hodges, Burwell, and Ortega,

1998; Dill, 1994; Aswad and Gray, 1996). In Pamela's case, this family is international in scope, incorporating the experiences of two ethnic groups of color in two very different societies. For thirty years, Pamela had worshiped at an African Methodist Episcopal Church that Anthony's family had attended for two generations. This signified a dramatic departure from the spiritual practices she had been raised with in her own family of origin. She had left the church after Anthony's death, because of the ways married women in the church treated her (widows were erroneously considered to be interested in other women's husbands, although Pamela suspected that the stand-offishness of other church members was also related to her ethnicity). Her referent group, then, was the membership of the church.

After joining the widows' group and developing a new referent group, Pamela was exposed to the practice of meditation, which group members had adopted as a healing technique (Sermabeikian, 1994; Smith, 1995). The process of meditation was congruent with Pamela's earlier spiritual learning but at odds with the practices of the church that her children and the rest of Anthony's family still belonged to. One day, Pamela entered the widows' group in tears.

THELMA: Pamela, what's wrong?

PAMELA: I am so angry with Anthony's sister Deborah!!!

AISHA: What happened?

PAMELA: Well, we had a celebration for my son last night, and Deborah came with her family, along with my mother-in-law. Before they arrived, I had centered myself by doing my evening meditation, and I'd been burning incense in my house. Deborah smelled it when she came in and asked what I was burning. I told her that I had begun to meditate again, and she started yelling at me. She told me that I was "going to hell in a handbasket" for dealing in the devil's work! Then she told everyone who came in the door—including my mother-in-law—that I was involved in witchcraft!!! Deborah has decided that my case needs to be taken in front of the church council and minister and that I need to be reconciled with the church!

MAUDE: Ooohh, this sounds like it was a big mess!

PAMELA: You're telling me! I don't think I can bear to show my face in front of the family again.

THELMA: How did your children respond?

PAMELA: Both of them tried to change the subject. I know that Caroline supports what I do, but I'm not sure about my son, Anthony III. I think he thinks this has something to do with cults, and I didn't expose him to the religious practices I had grown up with when he was a child because I didn't want to confuse him or make him uncomfortable with what he was learning in Sunday school.

AISHA: It sounds like what you did was to love your children and try to give them a firm spiritual foundation where you were living but that did not deny who you were. Is that accurate, Pamela?

PAMELA: Of course it is!

THELMA: So how do you feel about your meditation practice now?

PAMELA: I will not be made ashamed of my place as a part of the universe, supported by a universal spirit who loves all creatures. Meditation, as we have been reading about it and practicing it, is really about showing compassion for all creatures and not placing our individual selves above others or presenting ourselves in ways that will hurt others. It seems to me that this is the Golden Rule as I have learned it at the AME church, isn't it?

MAUDE: Pamela, you know that I was also a member of that church but left for the same reason you did when Bobby died. You know that some people are frightened of things they don't understand and that their first reaction to that fear is to run in the opposite direction. My friends in the choir reacted that same way your family did to the news that I was starting to meditate. I told them that I was going to continue the practice, and some of them even stopped talking with me. What's so funny is that later my best friend from the choir came to see me when she was feeling low. I started talking with her about the meaning of "so hum" and how she could begin to listen to what God was telling her through being silent and waiting with an open heart. She began to do some reading on her own and then asked me to do a presentation on meditation at the women's auxiliary retreat. Now there's a group of ten women who meet weekly to meditate together before the auxiliary meeting. Does Deborah even know about this? I know that the pastor does!!!

PAMELA: I've never heard of it, and I'm sure Deborah hasn't either. I feel so relieved now.

THELMA: I think that Maude is making a point for all of us, though. People's first reaction to something they don't understand is to make like a jackrabbit and run away from it. If we withdraw at the first sign of their fear, we may miss out on something special that was meant for us. We have to learn to love our families in their being themselves and know that they will find their paths as we have found ours.

AISHA: No one could have said it better, Thelma. You are becoming the distinguished teacher among us.

PAMELA: Maude's comment also makes me think that I can develop a plan to demonstrate the gains I receive from meditating, even when people make fun of me, and talk about them with my family. I certainly feel more present as a whole being when I am with them than I used to when I was always worried about what they were thinking of me. In fact, I have an even better idea. Maude, would you go with me to ask the meditating women in the church to do a workshop for the entire church at the next women's day program?

MAUDE: I'd be delighted!!

AISHA: Could we use the next few minutes of the group to work with Pamela and Maude on their plan?

EVERYONE: Why not?

The previous dialogue combines work with families, communities, and referent groups in a group setting. As is immediately evident, learning took place for all members of the group. Maude's explanation of people's reactions to new information is presented as normative rather than as something to be overcome. This explanation mirrors that of Rooney's (1992) discussion of reactance as an everyday by-product of human congress.

A second lesson from the previous dialogue is provided by the actions of Aisha, the service provider or group facilitator in this case. She recognized the level of capacity in the group and allowed for the connection of group members to further Pamela's growth. Aisha could have given the explanation Maude furnished about the familial response to Pamela's expanded spiritual outlook or made the suggestion to Maude and Pamela about approaching the church to expand the knowledge base of its members (thus effecting environmental change), but she knew enough to allow the group to come up with its own answers. In doing this, she provided yet another excellent example for empowering social work practitioners.

Summary

This chapter has examined a number of ways in which individual practice is transformed when an empowerment perspective is employed by social workers. The range of intervention methods is as fluid as the practitioner, who should constantly be expanding her or his knowledge base to be most effective with service consumers. Empowering interpersonal practitioners should also recognize that they are not restricted to the standard two-person relationship but can incorporate family, friends, groups, and communities as intervention mechanisms for individual growth and vice versa. Women of color are considered in relationship with others, and those others—whether present in the interaction or not—are seen as contributors to the gains and losses of the relationship between service consumer and provider.

In an empowering interpersonal practice setting, issues such as resistance/reactance, transference, and countertransference can be viewed as avenues for growth rather than as evils to be avoided. Empowering practitioners understand the relationship between the development of social work practice methods and their temporal creations. That is, the development of key concepts in social work practice are intricately related to historical, social, and political forces present at their inception. An empowering practitioner listens to the service consumer and herself and places the presenting concern in context. When this is accomplished, the most appropriate practice method can be chosen.

This chapter has also illustrated ways in which a spiritual framework can be viewed positively in a practice setting. Releasing the fear that can result from turning one's back on one's spirituality or recognizing the importance of spirituality for some service consumers—whether or not the service provider herself has a spiritual base—may enhance the consumer's capacity and foster the intervention alliance.

Consistently employing the strategies discussed in this chapter is not always easy, particularly when empowering practitioners are attempting to work in disempowering agencies (a topic to be discussed in the chapter on organizations). Thus this chapter provides some guidelines for empowering individual practice with an understanding that new information on how best to participate in the development of critical consciousness, capacity building, and connection will emanate from daily attempts to incorporate some of these suggestions and find new answers that can be shared with other providers and consumers.

FOUR

Empowerment Techniques: Practice with Families

◆

Catalina works in a multiservice community mental health agency. She has been trained as a family practitioner and works with all the members of a family group who are identified as family by those initiating the intervention and are willing to participate in the intervention. Catalina's agency is unique in its geographical area because of its acceptance of this definition of "family." As a result, it sometimes faces great funding obstacles because county and state reimbursement formulas treat individual and family work equally, although the latter is more time- and resource-consuming for the agency. Nevertheless, the agency always has a long waiting list for family practice.

Because of her willingness to work with extended family systems, Catalina's work often involves a myriad of intervention styles, as different parts of the family constellation are involved in various parts of any familial conflict. Catalina is currently working with the Ade family. This includes two biological parents, one adolescent female (Rita), aged 17, two sets of actively involved grandparents, and a set of godparents who were married at the time of Rita's birth. All family members except Rita were born in Nigeria; however, they have lived in the United States for at least twenty-five years. The godparents have been separated for nine years. Catalina has determined, through use of a modified genogram, that the most pressing present conflict is, on the one hand, among the mother, the adolescent, and the godmother and, on the other hand, between the father and the godfather. The controversy stems from the adolescent daughter's desire to choose her own dating partners and her male parental figures' desire to have her escorts screened by male family members prior to her receiving permission to date them. The consequences of this familial controversy have included the escalation of tension between the parents and godparents, which has been dichotomized by gender, and the father's desire to have his parents involved in the decision-making process, which has not happened before. Familial interactions in the intervention setting have become heated, and Catalina is faced with various options for working with the family. How will she make an appropriate choice?

An Empowerment Model for Family Practice

The example of the Ade family allows us to explore some parameters for family practice with women of color. Some of these choices are based on the conceptual frameworks guiding family practice as drawn from the field of family social science, some are based in the social/political and historical contexts of the Ade family, some stem from Catalina's own strengths and biases or cultural competence with respect to working with extended family systems, and some are based on subjective/objective orientations with regard to ethnically diverse families. These all combine to form intervention strategies, and the purpose of this chapter is to illustrate how various combinations of the parameters may lead to quite different intervention styles (Hartman and Laird, 1978; Congress, 1997; McWhirter, 1994; Congress and Lynn, 1997). Empowerment practice with families requires an understanding of the potentially different outcomes of combining conceptual/ideological practice methods with particular social/historical/political realities. It interweaves multiple rather than singular critical consciousness, confidence-through-skill-building, and connective perspectives into negotiated agreements by family members. Empowerment practice with families also includes an analysis of the interactions of families with their environments and addresses change strategies for those interactions. Table 4.1 summarizes the components of the empowering approach to family practice.

The chapter focuses primarily on the use of the Stone School woman-in-relationship, interactionist model we introduced in the previous chapters as one illustration of empowering family practice, examining its relationship to other traditional models of family intervention and exploring some of the implications of this approach for family practice and research. Again, it is important to note that empowering family practice requires knowledge of and

---

TABLE 4.1   Elements of Empowering Family Practice

---

1. Understanding the assumptions underlying most "objective" family practice conceptual models.

2. Recognizing the ways "subjective" orientations inform these models.

3. Strategically crafting intervention strategies specific to the family based on both a knowledge of their social/historical and political realities and objective and subjective practice orientations.

4. Taking multiple critical consciousness, confidence-through-skill-building, and connecting perspectives from each family member and then sharing the information from these multiple explorations with all family members.

5. With a focus on the family, incorporating elements of community, group, and individual practice, with an emphasis on critical consciousness, confidence through skill building, and connection with others.

---

the ability to transform current conceptual frameworks guiding family practice to support change within and among families.

CONTEMPORARY CONCEPTUAL FRAMEWORKS
GUIDING OUR UNDERSTANDING OF FAMILIES

Family scholars have relied on numerous theoretical frameworks to identify, understand, and categorize families. These fall under four major groups: structural-functionalist, interactionist, psychodynamic, and developmental/life-span (Boss et al., 1993). Social work scholars have also developed conceptual frameworks to guide our understanding of family functioning, perhaps the most widely used of which is the eclectic systems approach of Germain (1973). Table 4.2 summarizes some of the contributions and limitations of each of these conceptual frameworks.

The structure-functionalist model views the family as the unit of analysis, as opposed to individuals within families. This approach concentrates on the various structures family units may assume and the corresponding functions of these structures. With a premise that family units exist and are arranged for carrying out maintenance tasks necessary to the unit, this approach has been widely utilized in cross-cultural studies and has its origins in anthropological research. The approach is criticized chiefly for its inability to account for changes outside the family structure that affect overall family functioning. For example, Hunter (Hunter and Ensminger, 1992b; Hunter, 1993, 1997) illus-

TABLE 4.2 Contemporary Theories of Families

Theory Type	Contributions	Limitations
Structural-functionalist	Focus on various structures of family units and their corresponding functions	Inability to account for changes outside of family structure that affect overall family functioning
Developmental (life-span)	Identifies family stages tied to the existence of children, with specific tasks required of each stage	Lack of consideration of overlapping stages, recognition of the element of family crises, and capacity to account for changes in families without children
Psychodynamic	Extrapolates from individual psychodynamic theory; views families as organized to meet demands of environment based on historical and biological determinants of members	Family members must gain "institutional memory" of precipitating factors affecting current family functioning
Eclectic systems approach	Social work-centered; expands from systems theory; explores complex relational systems within families and between families and their environments, using an "ecological metaphor" of person-in-environment	Family members' differential perspectives of race/ethnicity, class, gender, and sexual orientation both within the family system and between it and the wider society
Interactionist	Notion that humans acquire symbols, to which they ascribe value, and these are determinants of behavior	Necessity for a varied array of symbols under stood by both family members and practitioner

trates how a failure to acknowledge structural economic changes within society between 1900 and 1936 directly affected southern African-American women's decisions to work outside the home when young children were present. This strategic decision making influenced by external, macro systems might determine various forms of family structures and functioning.

Developmental theory has been viewed by many scholars as a preferable approach for the study of families (see, e.g., Allen, 1978; Troll, Bengston, and McFarland, 1979). Goldberg and Deutsch (1977) view the approach as incorporating elements of both structural-functionalism and interactionism (to be discussed later). According to the developmental (or life-span) model, all families have tasks that arise at specific times in the life cycle. These tasks must be accomplished for the family to move successfully to other stages and tasks. Familial stages incorporated in the model are systematic, tied to the existence of children in the family, and begin with the identification of the family unit's emergence in marriage, continuing with subsequent stages: childbearing, the preschool family, the launching family (the nuclear family from which children are leaving), middle-aged parents, and, finally, aged parents. Goldberg and Deutsch criticize the approach for not accounting for differences in families without children or with varying numbers of children, ignoring the element of crises confronting families and the potential for developmental stage modifications as a result of crises, and for not considering the overlapping stages in the approach. One illustration of this last criticism would be a nuclear family, such as the Baruchs in the last chapter, who were launching Kofi's adult siblings while simultaneously settling in with a new baby.

Psychodynamic family theoretical frameworks have been a part of social work practice for decades. Most recently, the work of Margaret Spencer (1983), among others, has distinguished itself for extrapolating from individual psychodynamic work to apply its tenets to family interaction. From a psychodynamic framework, families function to meet the demands of their environments, and these demands are based on both biological and historical determinants from members' backgrounds. It is useful to think about families in terms of "institutional memory" from this perspective. Family members have institutional memories about the family that influence their interactional patterns with one another. In the Ade family, for example, the institutional memory is illustrated by the conflict about who should choose the young men Rita dates. The goal in therapy from this framework is to find the underlying "institutional memory" currently affecting the interactional patterns in the family and to focus energy on understanding it. In the Ade case, the institutional memory is interpreted by the women in the family as a necessity in Nigeria but of limited utility in the United States. Of course, identifying the institutional memory assumes that the family members are aware of the precipitating institutional memory currently affecting their behaviors, which is not always the case. The men in the Ade family, for example, may not be aware that the origins of their institutional memory regarding women and dating is a hundred-year-old incident in which a woman from the extended family disappeared while walking outside the compound with a man unknown to the family.

The great strength of the eclectic systems approach to understanding a social work–centered conceptual framework is its connection of individuals, families, and their social environments. It accounts for differential perspectives both within and across families on the basis of social group memberships such as race, ethnicity, gender, class, and sexual orientation. Further, this conceptual framework acknowledges that interactions within families are complex and require a great deal of disaggregation to disclose how family members are interacting. The eclectic systems approach focuses on these complex relationships. In the case of the Ade family, the eclectic approach would normalize the extended family system, including so-called fictive kin, such as Rita's godparents.

The weaknesses of the eclectic systems conceptual framework, however, are the limits it places on the agency of family members in defining their systems and giving meaning to the role these systems place in their lives. Instead, the practitioner defines the systems influencing the family system and determines the social group memberships. For example, while social work educators have long recognized the importance of family membership and/or ethnic/racial and gender socialization in the lives of women of color in social work programs, it is only in the last four years that the discipline has developed expanded approaches to the discussion of sexual orientation as a factor in the lives of these women (see chapter 13, below).

Interactionist theory is based on the work of early psychologists and sociologists who believed that concepts had no meaning unless they could be applied either directly or indirectly and so insisted on pragmatic applications for any developing concepts. Among the assumptions underlying interactionist theory are the following: human beings acquire a complex set of symbols through their interaction with others; these symbols are given value by the human beings; the interaction of the symbols and the value ascribed to them is an important determinant of human behavior; humans respond to and act on their symbolic environments, creating new symbols and selecting or interpreting the symbols to which they will respond (Crosbie-Burnett and Lewis, 1993; Boss et al., 1993).

Interactionist perspectives are criticized for their loosely organized frameworks; however, their loose structures are also the source of their attraction for those working with the multidimensional relationships within and outside families (Crosbie-Burnett and Lewis, 1993; Bandura, 1986). The limitations of incorporating a symbolic interactionist perspective also include the necessity for a varied array of symbols that are determined not by practitioners but by service consumers. This is understandable, however, given that this perspective is a response to structural-functionalist, developmental, and psychodynamic frameworks that impose their own definitions of reality on families. It also expands eclectic systems approaches in that it explores the meaning family members give to their social group memberships and actions. For example, families may define their own structures and interactional patterns in ways different from the definition imposed by the researcher or theorist, with corresponding values placed on the presence or absence of these symbols. In the cases of the Ades, their bond with Catalina is such that they view her as one of their close relations.

Each of these frameworks makes specific assumptions about the nature of families and optimal family-life interactional patterns. Some practitioners unwittingly base their practice methods on particular patterns without being aware of these underlying assumptions or indeed of the theories themselves. As a result, these practitioners may choose methods either not in keeping with the realities and needs of the families they work with or in conflict with each other in terms of potential outcomes. While social work practitioners working from an empowerment perspective are likely to have an eclectic approach to practice, it is important for them also to be aware of the conflicts inherent in the assumptions of selected approaches and to try to minimize these potential conflicts whenever possible. One way of doing this is to focus not only on the objective conceptual frameworks guiding their practice but also on the subjective conceptual frameworks from which they operate (Reed et al., 1997).

Subjective Versus Objective Frameworks: How Families of Color Have Been Viewed in Family Practice

In 1978 Allen provided a quite useful—and still accurate—mechanism for understanding how objective conceptual frameworks based on empirical findings and replication are also influenced by subjective and usually unrecognized assumptions about the nature of familial interactions. According to Allen, these subjective orientations have strongly affected both research and practice with people of color. The first subjective orientation, cultural deviance, has permeated mental health practice with people of color in general, as outlined in our introductory chapters. In a cultural deviance perspective, individuals (or, in this case, families) are considered functional to the extent that they meet some predetermined, externally constructed norm of structure and/or function. Family research on families of color has been widely criticized for operating precisely from this culturally deviant perspective, where the predetermined normative behavior is identified as that of a mythical European-American middle class.

The second perspective, called cultural equivalence, has often been described as a response to the predominance of culturally deviant models, particularly in research and practice with people of color. In cultural equivalence, families are viewed according to the extent that they are similar to or different from the predetermined normative family, but these differences are not connoted as deviant, merely as different. There is an assumption that those similar in characteristics to the family are best able to design effective interventions for it. In terms of empowerment practice, however, this assumption ignores the ability of social work practitioners to develop culturally competent skills and knowledge.

The last of the subjective orientations discussed by Allen is that of cultural variance. Families are recognized for their diversity on the basis of characteristics other than ethnicity, and for the potential of families of color to share

TABLE 4.3 Subjective Frameworks Guiding Family Theories

Type of Framework	Focus	Impact
Culturally deviant	Examination of the extent to which families meet a predetermined norm	Predetermined normative behavior is considered based on mythical European-American middle-class ideal family type
Culturally equivalent	Predetermined norm still standard of measurement for families, but those who do not meet the norm are merely considered "different"	Limits those able to work with "different" families to practitioners who have the same characteristics
Culturally variant	Recognizes similarities and diversity within as well as across families	Uses culturally competent perspective as a tool to enhance empowerment practice

SOURCE: Allen, 1978

characteristics with those of European-American backgrounds. Thus an African-American family may share economic, educational, geographic, and gender constructions with a German-American family in the same residential area while simultaneously sharing historical and political experiences of deprivation with African-American families far removed from their geographic, economic, or educational locations. The culturally variant perspective encourages social workers to identify through culturally competent assessment how families construct their social, historical, and political environments in conjunction with the wider society (Schacter, 1996). Further, this perspective accepts that practitioners, through their own development of critical consciousness, can work effectively with families of ethnic backgrounds different from their own (Castex, 1993). In the case presented at the beginning of this chapter, Catalina's ethnic background is that of a Chicana, but the basis of her culturally competent work with the Nigerian-American Ade family stems from her ongoing interactions with the Ades, her colleagues, and new literature to maintain her critical consciousness with the family (McWhirter, 1994; Reed et al., 1997). For example, the importance of the extended family of biological and fictive (non-blood-related) kin had to be considered in the Ade case, as did the influences of first-generation immigrant status for the grandparent generation (as opposed to second-generation status for the parents and godparents and third-generation status for Rita). Further, Catalina's attention to political events shaping the social lives of Nigerians living in the United States and Nigeria helped her develop interventions perhaps as much as did understanding the types of help-seeking behaviors of the extended Ade family itself (Paulino and Burgos-Servido, 1997).

Table 4.4 illustrates how workers may be influenced by the subjective orientations they use to make judgments about families in practice. It is imperative for empowering practitioners to analyze critically the subjective orientations underlying their work in order to avoid the negative consequences of misapplying labels to family interactions.

How can practitioners recognize their uses of objective and subjective frameworks? The process of self-reflection and critical analysis that forms the foundation of empowerment practice is of great importance in meeting this challenge, as outlined in chapter 1. While uncommon in practice settings, it is nonetheless useful for practitioners to stop for a few minutes before and after family therapy sessions to reflect on their own use of specific practice techniques and the underlying assumptions to be made about the families when these are used (Reed et al., 1997; Gutiérrez, Ortega, and Suarez, 1990; Scharff and Scharff, 1991). What have these choices meant for the ways in which indi-

TABLE 4.4 Applying Subjective Orientations to the Ade Family

Subjective Orientation	Interaction in Ade Family	Potential Subjective Meaning and Action for Practitioner
Culturally deviant	Several individuals involved in decision as to the conditions under which Rita is to date	Family is "enmeshed" and "triangulated." Rita needs to individuate. Practitioner needs to focus on Rita as an individual member of her family, regarding only biological parents' wishes, as she is still a minor
Culturally equivalent	Extended family includes many members	Family is "different," and strategies used in conventional family work have no meaning for Ade family
Culturally variant	Extended family includes parents, godparents, and grandparents, as well as Rita, whose dating is the central familial concern at present	Family is "different," Practitioner is working with multiple interactional patterns (i.e., parents, godparents, grandparents), each of which must be explored in terms of its relationship to Rita and the others; the meaning incorporated by members in each of these relationships must also be explored

vidual family members view themselves and/or each other? Have the choices been limited to the practitioner's "comfort zone"? What specific skills and knowledge of the historical, social, and political realities of family members and their communities is the proposed intervention based on? What assumptions have been made by family members about the interactions of race, ethnicity, class, gender, and sexual orientation in their particular family formations (Frankenberg, 1993; Baca-Zinn and Dill, 1994b)? Practitioners such as Catalina who engage in this process of critical self-reflection and action are expanding our knowledge base concerning the most effective methods to use in family therapy under specific circumstances.

Using an Empowerment Strategy for Understanding Women of Color in Families

Once more, this chapter uses the Stone School model (Jordan, 1997) to understand women in their social environments. The empowering practitioner's acknowledgment of the woman-in-relationship aspects of the lives of women of color is especially useful for empowerment work with women in their families. This model emphasizes the recognition of women in relationship with others and the interactions between women's individual decision making and family or community consequences. This women-in-relationship model has been applied to women of color's relationships by Comas-Diaz and Greene (1994), Pinderhughes (1989), Attneave (1982), and Lewis (1988).

Certain elements of the Stone School model are most useful in understanding empowerment work with women of color in families, and this was particularly true in the case of the Ade family. The woman-in-relationship variable includes, in this instance, multiple women: Rita, her mother, two grandmothers, and a godmother. Each of these individuals has different perspectives on her roles and statuses within the extended family, based in part on these statuses and roles in conjunction with their communities of origin (which differ) and the wider societies of both Nigeria and the United States. Rita, as a third-generation family member, for example, lives within an extended family system whose normative expectations for her as an adolescent are often in conflict with those experienced by her classmates in high school. The public school system that she has attended for four years has held "advisory group" sessions each morning emphasizing individual responsibility and rights for adolescents in preparation for their adulthood in an individual-oriented society. Rita's godmother, in contrast, recognizes the extent to which her divorce has placed her squarely between two worlds: that of her homeland (often re-created in ethnically homogeneous communities in the United States) and that of the United States, where divorce is more prevalent (Crosbie-Burnett and Lewis, 1993). In negotiating contracts with other family members, the godmother's status can be reinforced as a legitimate adaptation to live in the United States by Catalina, who must also be aware that the godmother's role in determining Rita's life course may be automatically diminished by those family members who consider it inappropriate to use the U.S. court system as a remedy for settling family problems. Rita's mother, in joining with Rita's godmother, may appear to refute the norms and values of the extended family system and may be viewed as encouraging Rita to become more Americanized than is actually the case. Finally, the grandmothers (and particularly the paternal grandmother), who are recognized in their own home societies as the conduits for tradition in the care and nurturance of children, have the potential to be viewed by Rita as not to be involved in decision-making processes that affect her life. All these women may develop confidence in their perspectives on the situation through skill practice and continuous assessment of the relative benefits and consequences of taking actions in light of their membership in the family, the community, and the wider society (Turner, 1997). In other words, empowerment practice with the Ade family first requires the practitioner to engage family members in a critical analysis of their location within their countries of origin and the U.S. society and the implications of these locations for their involvement with one another. This approach focuses on knowledge building for family members, allowing them to share their knowledge of their location(s) with one another so that meta-communication can take place.

The woman-in-relationship perspective also includes the men in family situations and recognizes through culturally competent assessment practices their roles and statuses (Bergmann and Surrey, 1997). In families where lineage is traced through males and decision-making power invested in them, social workers must be particularly careful to involve them in consciousness-raising activities, as it serves little purpose to help the women develop a critical consciousness if those with whom they interact are not growing along with them. The benefits and consequences of Rita's increased decision-making power for individual family members and the family unit can be explored in a joint session. Family members may also be encouraged to join multiple-family groups, an intervention gaining increasing popularity in family therapy, which will be discussed later in this chapter.

An empowerment approach to combining skill building and critical consciousness in the Ade case means moving all family members through the cultural deviant perspective. When conflict occurs within families, it is quite easy to define difference as deviance. When people don't think alike, particularly in families from or with ties to societies that think of them as monolithic units, at least one family member will usually make firm attempts to change the thinking of the "deviant" member(s). That family member, however, seldom thinks of reconstructing his or her own thinking patterns. Explicit attention to the potential for meanings of cultural deviance to occur among family members allows them to recognize the differences in the meaning of their relational systems and the challenges and opportunities of choosing options among these systems to enhance family growth.

In the Ade case, Catalina must also remember the importance of her presence as an intervenor in the family system (Jordan, 1997). As a woman of color, she must make clear to all of the Ades how her gender, ethnic, and class constructions lead her to develop ideas about interventions in conjunction with the multiple ideas of the family. This delicate strategy is necessary to interject continuously in family sessions, so that family members are aware that all involved in the intervention (including Catalina) are using their multiple lenses to construct a reality with which all of them can live. Figure 4.1 presents an excerpt from Catalina's journal that discusses negotiating these multiple lenses with regard to her work with the Ade family.

Week 5: We are still in the trust-building stage in this intervention. I am aware that Rita, Mrs. Ade, and Mrs. Akintunde view me as an ally, but this is sometimes to the detriment of building an alliance with Mr. Ade. I must be more careful about actively seeking out his opinion and perception of reality as we discuss issues. Use of the modified back-translation technique with all members of the family would probably be helpful here, as would having them mirror what they hear from each other. This is an extraordinary family, and the strengths they have developed to thrive in this foreign environment need to be highlighted for all of them so we can build on them.

In some ways, our experiences are very similar, but I am increasingly aware that we are very different in these interactions as well. I'd like to side with Rita, but I know that Rita's independence may cost her familial support at a later point. The family is in transition, and I represent a part of that transition or what could possibly happen to Rita if she continues to flout familial norms by wanting sole responsibility for her decisions. Mr. Akintunde, in particular, eyes me with great suspicion, I believe. I need to check in more about the role of the court-mandated counselor in his divorce from Mrs. Akintunde.

I know I am a role model for Rita, but I think some strategic analysis about the costs and gains of total independence versus interdependence are warranted here. There can be some lonely days when one chooses to be out there completely on one's own, and Rita's perceptions of my worldview need to be addressed.

FIGURE 4.1 Notes from Catalina's Journal

Many terrains identified by scholars using a woman-in-relationship model must be traversed in the Ade family case. Multiple perspectives on family structure are evident here. While Rita has been socialized to the wider society's norm of the biological nuclear family as decision-makers, clearly her parents, godparents, and grandparents have competing ideologies. Some negotiation between family members must occur, taking into account the different historical, political, and social contributors leading to the establishment of these different ideologies by actors in the family. Multiple perspectives are also evident in child-rearing practices and establishment of partnerships, and these must be negotiated as well.

One of the increasingly popular ways of assisting families in establishing a critical consciousness, developing the confidence to enable them to assume their power in negotiating conflicts, and reinforcing their connections to one another and others facing life situations similar to theirs is participation in the multiple-family group. Multiple-family groups incorporate all the members of several families simultaneously and allow for multiple perspectives to be shared by more than one family member. A multiple-family group that might be helpful for the Ade family would include other extended families with teenaged members, members who had experienced separation or divorce, and those in which some conflict between negotiating cultural expectations was evident. In such a group, the versions of reality experienced by all the Ade family members would be reinforced. This construction of a multiple-family group would also stress the importance of the culturally variant model, in which similarities and differences among families are recognized and the similarities capitalized on to strengthen individual family outcomes (Bergmann and Surrey, 1997). The multiple-family group further allows for the establishment of political agency among the families, which can lead to change in the wider society in the future. For example, an ideal outcome of a multiple-family group for the Ades would be the formation of an adult subgroup that might meet with the district school board to address the consequences of "advisory groups" in the public schools (Congress, 1997).

Multiple-family groups are used in different ways in family practice and serve different purposes. We advocate here for a multiple-family group procedure that maximizes the interactions and connections between and among family group members rather than focusing on multiple rounds of leader-imposed questions to which members respond. A emphasis on "what did you mean?" or the use of a back-translation method is imperative for maximum use of the empowering multiple-family group. Figure 4.2 illustrates ways in which multiple-family groups can function.

Monday evening, 7:00–10:00 P.M., Catalina and Barbara, facilitating

Present: The Rodriguez, Ade, Oni, and Montserrat families—twenty-five people!!!

Summary: We used an "inner-outer circle" or "fishbowl" technique this evening, with several "trigger" questions for participants to share information about differential aspects of women's lives in the city. Everyone present participated fully, although it was difficult at first to keep the norms of noninterruption by those in the outer circle. It helped to let all participants know that there would be reaction times to what was learned.

We began with the teens and asked them what it was like to be young women of color in their schools. They were surprised at the degree of similarity in their stories about how other students treated them, how they sometimes felt ostracized by their teachers for their names, and how they just wanted to fit in. It was clear as we processed afterward that many of the parents had not heard some of the horrors experienced by their children at school before.

The second inner circle was for the mothers/godmother/grandmothers present, beginning with the question: "What is it like for you these days as a _____ woman in this city?" The teens were surprised to hear the extent to which their mothers felt dislocated and missed the certainty of life in their homelands—even Mrs. Ade, who has been here for twenty-five years, and Rita's godmother, who was a successful businesswoman in the city. The mothers, however, were thrilled to know that other women shared their experiences and that they weren't alone in their feelings.

At this point, it was important to bring the men into the circle and use a similar question to that posed to the mothers. It was clear that having the other two groups precede them had been helpful in modeling the openness we were seeking from all participants. At the end of the fishbowl, as the men turned their chairs outward to hear the responses of the mothers and teens, there were indications that, while the reasons for coming to the United States and the histories of the families were different, there were similarities in all the families' experiences with public agencies.

This led to a second set of fishbowls, each begun with the question: "What one thing would you have your family help you with to make your situation better?" This led to a series of requests by teens to parents, parents to teens, and families to one another. Homework was assigned to each family to try to fulfill one request made by another family member before the next week. At the next session, we will begin with a report of whether attempts were made to meet these requests and what the outcomes were.

FIGURE 4.2 Cofacilitator's Notes from the Ade Family and Others in a Multiple-Family Group Session

Summary

As indicated in table 4.5, there are multiple intervention activities involved in empowering practice with families. Some of these are joint activities between the practitioner and family members, some are solely the responsibility of the family, and some require care solely on the part of the social worker providing service. This interplay among theoretical perspectives, assumptions, and actions is indicative of the complexities of empowering family practice, all which must be negotiated, often simultaneously, to maximize the benefits for the consumers of service. An ancient African proverb states "It takes an entire village to raise a child." From the perspective of incorporating empowerment principles into family practice, the service provider becomes a part of the village and joins the family with other village members (both those of close proximity and those who may be able to provide more institutional assistance, such as public schools) to raise the family members of all ages.

TABLE 4.5 Potential Empowering Processes in Family Practice

Target Unit	Activity
Catalina and Ades	Modified genogram; woman-in-relationship model employment; consciousness-raising for men and women in family; examination of impact of power shifts within family; management of the ways in which a culturally variant interactionist perspective informs family functioning
Ade family	Multiple-family groups; subgroup for school change; reconciling multiple perspectives on child rearing and member interactions; employment of a culturally variant perspective
Catalina	Self-reflection of impact of her gender construction on working with Ade family; clarity on her role in and rules for working with Ades; employment of a culturally variant perspective

FIVE

Empowerment Techniques: Practice with Groups

Unity, a group of ten women, has been meeting for five weeks with two cofacilitators trained in empowerment practice, named Liz and Anna. The group members include two Native-American women, one Korean woman, one Singaporean woman, four African-American women, and two women who grew up in the southeastern United States and have identified themselves as "hillbillies." The group evolved from Liz and Anna's work with them individually in a community mental health setting in a large midwestern city. All the women went to the CMH because of concerns about their relationships with their partners, whom they consider to be abusive. Jiwan, the Korean woman, and Imani, one of the African-American women, are involved in lesbian relationships, and Imani and her partner have two children. Liz, who traces her background to the early German settlers, also has a lesbian partner and has been in this committed relationship for ten years. Anna, the African-American cofacilitator, and all the other women are involved in heterosexual relationships, five of which have resulted in marriage. Alice, one of the women from the Southeast, has come to the sixth group session having just entered a women's shelter as a result of a battering incident during the previous weekend. She is concerned about how she will continue her life and still raise her three children having made the decision to leave her partner. The group has decided to employ an empowering problem-solving strategy to assist Alice in making decisions about her next steps. What can they do to be effective and collective empowering agents? How do Liz and Anna fit into this process as leaders and cofacilitators of change? How are cohesion and group process issues modified to effect group and individual outcomes?

Race, ethnicity, and gender have occasionally received attention in studies of group work as "extra" rather than "integral" variables. It is often argued that anyone adequately trained in group work will be able to work effectively with all people, regardless of race or gender. Multicultural empowering group practitioners, however, instead of ignoring gender, race, and ethnicity as variables, are sensitive to issues of bicultural and even multicultural socialization. In incorporating a multicultural perspective, these practitioners include a recognition of differences within racial, class, ethnic, sexual orientation, and ability groupings of women as critical elements of their gender construction (see chapter 13, below; see also GlenMaye, 1998). An explicit acknowledgment of the racial, ethnic, or other stereotypes group members in a heterogeneous group may apply to one another is a theme for initial group meetings as well.

An empowering perspective on group work also involves linking group techniques to women's social, historical, and political environments to effect change, both for facilitators and members. These group work strategies include the ability to identify "invisible group members," that is, those extended family, significant other, and friend networks that influence group members' behavior and actions in the group (Hodges, Burwell, and Ortega, 1998; Turner, 1997). The potential power discrepancy inherent in professional leader–lay member group construction is another integral part of the group's initial discussion (Lewis and Ford, 1990; Pinderhughes, 1983). Thus culturally competent practice in group work interventions addresses issues of power, consciousness-raising, self-identification, bicultural (or multicultural) socialization, and oppression, all of which affect group process and outcomes, as indicated in table 5.1.

Sadly, many group leaders and members fail to consider the factors of ethnicity, race, gender, sexual orientation, class, and ability or how they influence groups. Given the predictable realities of life in the United States in the next century, however, these complexities, as well as their interactions, must be examined and incorporated into interventions if groups are to attract and retain women of color and contribute to their empowerment experiences. This chapter focuses on group work strategies and examples pertinent to work with women of color across these potential interactions.

Designing a Group

Specific attention to group design issues both in the pregroup screening process and later in actual group sessions is important. One design issue

TABLE 5.1 Incorporating Empowerment Strategies in Group Work

Strategy	Issues Addressed
Addressing stereotypes of members and leaders explicitly	Eliminating unconscious use of racial, ethnic, sexual orientation, class, ability, or gender stereotypes in group process
Attention to coleadership/facilitation as modeling and skill-building strategies	Coleadership composition; coleadership styles; power
Recognition of historical, political, and social worlds of group members as sources of capacity building and connection	Oppression; current state of conscious ness; gender construction based on bicultural and multicultural socialization
Evaluation	Repeated measurement; measures of capacity building and connection taken within and outside the group; measurements of cofacilitators' leadership; use of multiple measures

relates to the content and meaning of symbols used by group facilitators and members (see the discussion of symbols in chapter 4, above). Gaining a clear mutual understanding of the content and meaning of symbols used by group participants is useful in the prescreening process, as all members may not view the same concepts identically. This often stems from racial, ethnic, class, and sexual orientation differences, as well as the different symbolic meanings of terms (Tatum, 1997; Cohen, 1997; see also chapter 4, above). When these discrepancies go unaddressed, irreparable damage to the possibilities for group cohesion may occur. For example, irreparable damage could result from conduct as blatant as a group facilitator asking a Puerto Rican group member if she would prepare tacos for the last group meeting (tacos are not even a staple dish in Puerto Rico). It could occur in gestalt groups that hold the basic assumption that one must live in the "here and now," which negates the realities of those who view their lives as intricately linked to the past and future, as is the case for many American Indian and Asian-American ethnic groups (Attneave, 1982; Lum, 1996; see also chapter 9, below). Persons from ethnic groups where the survival of the community is valued over the individual may find difficult participation in assertiveness training groups, which traditionally value the individual at the expense of the community (McWhirter, 1994). Reticence on the subject of negative family themes could be misconstrued as a lack of self-disclosure in a group, whereas the actual problem may be a strong sense of filial piety, common among some Asian-American or Middle Eastern groups, that cannot be superseded by a group norm (Chu and Sue, 1984; Ho, 1987; Aswad and Bilge, 1996)). Clearly, it is critical for empowering group facilitators to be conscious of the potential traps to group design.

HOMOGENEOUS AND HETEROGENEOUS GROUPS

Heterogeneous groups may only be functional for women of color to the extent that leaders and members are willing explicitly and repeatedly to identify (1) the sources of diversity within the group, (2) the different approaches that can be used to resolve target problems, (3) the different resources brought to the group setting by both leaders and members and, in particular, (4) the potential for bicultural or multicultural socialization of group members, as outlined in table 5.2. The bilingual abilities and elaborate patterns of decoding and encoding among ethnic groups of color have been documented (Falicov, 1982; hooks, 1994; Tatum, 1997). Unless specifically tracked, these are often missed in the ethnically homogeneous group.

Attention to the woman of color's view of her gender and of others is of utmost importance in the prescreening and early group sessions, especially if the group is composed entirely of women. The historical exclusion of women of color in women's movements in the United States makes work in mixed-ethnic or mixed-race groups that include European Americans difficult (Giddings, 1984; hooks, 1994). In groups in which the authors have participated, women of ethnic backgrounds different from ours have often remarked that they felt more comfortable in their attempts at self-disclosure within a mixed-ethnic group that included no European-American women than they did in those in which European-American women were present.

TABLE 5.2 Considerations for Heterogeneous and Homogeneous Groups

---

- Identification of sources of diversity within the group

- Ability to incorporate different approaches to resolving target problems that are congruent with the social, historical, and political realities of group members

- Recognition of the different types of resources brought by members and cofacilitators

- Use of bicultural or multicultural socialization as a strength within and outside of the group

---

One of the best illustrations of diversity arising within supposedly homogeneous groups is given by Ho (1987). He suggests that there are still many segments of the Asian population who harbor ill feelings against other Asians because of past conflicts. This may be especially true of individuals not born in the United States. Without careful planning, placement of Hong Kong–, Taiwan-, and U.S.-born Chinese in the same task-oriented group can result in a composition as problematic as that of any other heterogeneous group, in spite of the fact that from a U.S. standpoint all of these people are Chinese.

Initial sessions must assess the extent to which women of color may be interested in using a group approach to address their problems. Organizations in and around Detroit, Michigan, have often attempted to integrate Middle Eastern women into existing group programs. Many of these women report that group participation seriously jeopardizes their families' perceptions of their filial loyalty, which requires that all personal information be kept within the extended family (Aswad and Bilge, 1996). The extent to which group designers can modify their designs to include a group composed of women from extended families with this kind of ethos may influence whether a group approach can be effectively used in these situations (Khoury, 1995).

Perhaps one of the greatest potential errors in designing or implementing heterogeneous groups with women of color is the creation of an artificial support community outside the extensive network of familial and community supports generally available to the woman of color (McAdoo, 1982; Lewis, 1989; Lewis and Ford, 1990; Jordan, 1997). It is important to remember that there is a rich history of mutual support and aid networks in many communities of color. These have evolved as a result of discriminatory practices that restricted access to resources in the wider society. The process of bicultural socialization assists women of color in becoming aware of these mutual support and aid networks (Gutiérrez and Lewis, 1994). Women of color will then often turn to these networks instead of formal mental health services, even when the networks are not consistently or appropriately helpful (Manning, 1998). Proponents of culturally competent practice have noted that effective work with populations of color requires the creative incorporation of both these natural helping networks and formal mutual aid organizations into the intervention (Atteneave, 1982; Lewis, 1989; Lum, 1996; Lewis and Suarez, 1995). This can be done by using a modified genogram to map out the significant and proximal others involved in the potential participant's network and then discussing with the member the extent to which an individualized plan can incorporate these individuals (see chapter 2, above, on assessment and engagement). In one use of this method, extended family members came to the group meeting to ask for specific support for the family member participating in the group (Lewis and Ford, 1990).

On Group Cohesion

Guadelupe Gibson (1983) tells the story of a practitioner in a community mental health setting who was incensed at the cancellation of an appointment by a woman who reported that her *muñeca* was broken. The practitioner, who spoke some Spanish, understood *muñeca* to mean "doll." A second meaning for the word, however, and the one meant by the woman, was "wrist."

Few group practitioners are given opportunities in their training to think critically about the potential for differences stemming from race, ethnicity, class, or gender/sexuality construction. Development of a critical conscious-ness of this is essential even for practitioners, however, and this can be accom-plished through reading, thinking, and discussing the interaction of race/class/gender/sexual orientation/ethnicity with others (Reed et al., 1997; McWhirter, 1994). Group leaders and members without an understanding of the way the culturally deviant perspective (see chapter 4, above) colors their daily interactions with others will often accept racial stereotypes without ques-tioning them (Coll, Cook-Nobles, and Surrey, 1997). Liz's first days of employment within the CMH system help to illustrate this issue.

◆

When Liz began working within the CMH, her professional training in feminist practice had limited her clinical experiences to women from European-American backgrounds in neighborhoods similar to the one where she herself had grown up. While facilitating her first groups in the setting, she formed a group of women of African descent. During the second session, Liz suggested that every-one discuss their personal experiences with gang membership. Three of the six women did not return for the third session. Two weeks later, in a case confer-ence, Anna informed Liz that the three group members had lodged a formal com-plaint of racism against her. It seems that these women, while of Caribbean and African-American backgrounds, had grown up in upper-income nuclear families and neighborhoods and had had no prior experience with gangs. Liz's training had confused issues of race and class, which left her open to the charge of racism.

She remedied the situation by meeting with the three women, offering her apologies, getting extensive information on their backgrounds, asking Anna to be a cofacilitator with her, and asking the three women to rejoin the group. She then apologized to all the members present and talked about how her lack of knowledge had led to a potentially fatal error.

If the isms (e.g., racism, classism, sexism, heterosexism, ableism) are not discussed in the group setting, cohesion, one of the desirable characteristics of groups, may not be possible. Garvin and Reed (1995) posit that people grow into stereotypic role sets that are played out in group situations. It is necessary to uncover these role sets in the group so that it can move to a higher level of cooperation, honesty, and mutual support. This move toward mutual support and cooperation may be problematic for women of color and lesbians, who have been socialized to wear a mask when interacting with European-Americans or heterosexuals (Greene, 1994b; Giovanni, 1994; DeLois, 1998). Putting aside this mask for purposes of group cohesion and interaction is a risky business, as it may result in having to give up coping strategies for interacting with members of the wider society that have proven effective as survival tools (i.e., a lack of eye contact). Instead, it has been our experience that women, and particularly women of color, will adapt or drop the mask according to whether its use surfaces as an effective survival strategy in group sessions (Turner, 1997). The safety of the mask may no longer be perceived as necessary when its utility in some situations is validated and the need for members' stereotypic role behaviors are eliminated (Comas-Diaz and Greene, 1994).

Jiwan and Imani, the two lesbian women in Liz and Anna's group, sat together during the first group meeting. No mention of it was made. As the second group convened, however, these same two women moved to occupy adjacent seats. Jean, one of the women from the Southeast, said aloud to Anna, "Why is it that the lesbians always sit together?" Liz overheard the remark and responded, "Probably for the same reasons that all the heterosexual women have sat together." Somewhat perplexed, Jean then looked around the room at how others had chosen to arrange themselves and found that group members had indeed organized themselves in this fashion. She responded, "I never thought of it that way before!" Liz and Anna then began the group with a discussion of choices and their multiple interpretations, using the seating experience as an illustration. As all members of the group began to understand their collective lack of comfort in this new situation, they also began to gain additional information about choices others made that they had previously misunderstood. Seating options in later group sessions began to vary from the pattern exhibited during the first two weeks.

◆

Liz was able to take her early experiences of confusing race and class and turn them into an increased sensitivity to her own and others' potential for this confusion (Ewalt, 1994). Her skills had increased such that she could identify the isms operating in the situation, raise them for others, and then link them to overall issues of group process and content.

Differences in styles of communication are often evident in groups, but some styles have been erroneously considered deviant rather than different when they occur in the context of the group. Unfortunately, they do not disappear and are often misrepresented by members and leaders. Placing members with different interactional styles in the same group requires special monitoring during group sessions, and when differences occur, the group leader must make sure to address them as style differences (Tatum, 1997; Lewis, 1993). Sensitivity to the potential lack of understanding based on the content of communication must also be addressed explicitly in groups; for example, nonverbal communication does not equal nonparticipation. Incorporating creative methods to encourage shared participation is a critical task for group leaders. Among these may be the use of stress management techniques, rounds that provide the opportunity for more quiet individuals to express themselves in the group setting, the use of dance and art as forms of expression, and role-playing techniques (see table 5.3). Explicit ground rules designed, modified, and agreed on by group members and then revisited throughout group sessions are also helpful. After the second session of Liz and Anna's group, for example, a new ground rule was added: "We will not assume that we understand the meaning of another member's actions without first checking out that meaning with her."

TABLE 5.3 Strategies for Enhancing Group Cohesion

- Establishing and modifying ground rules for the group
- Maintaining flexibility in cofacilitation styles
- Clarifying meaning of symbols and behaviors
- Recognizing attributes ascribed to sole leaders, particularly when they are women of color, and addressing these in terms of impact on the group

Aries (1977) suggests concentrating on ways to ease sex-role pressures within groups, a recommendation that can be extended to the interactions of race/gender/class/sexual orientation/ethnicity in groups that include women of color. Noting in the initial group that members enter with different perspectives about their world that will influence the group process paves the way for group members to clarify those things that are a part of their own realities and how they may differ from the realities of other group members (another way of building critical consciousness among members). Taking care to "unpack" these interactions by clarifying meanings and perspectives in group sessions is particularly helpful (Bergmann and Surrey, 1997). In planning sessions, practitioners may purposely provide space for explicit discussions of these interactions. In the case of surfacing heterosexism, for example, the group leader or facilitator may wish to draw attention to the restriction of discussions to heterosexual lifestyles and traditions and the impact of this on lesbians and bisexual women in the group or on even gay/lesbian/bisexual invisible extended family members whose lives intertwine with group members. This capacity-building exercise may be done during debriefing activities at the end of the group session or during the session itself by stopping the general discussion to do a "fishbowl" with subsets of the group to identify verbal and nonverbal behaviors, their true meanings, and their impact on group cohesion. Some flexibility in session design is necessary to incorporate this idea, and practitioners should view these activities as group-building or connection activities rather than as diversions.

Group Process Issues: Consequences of Leadership Styles and Evaluation of Member Participation

LEADERSHIP

Leader competence is viewed as one of the cornerstones of group effectiveness; however, a lack of attention by leaders to their own stereotyping behavior can cause serious consequences for group members. In describing the importance of group leaders' development of a critical consciousness, Gutiérrez, Ortega, and Suarez (1990) have remarked:

> The group worker is visible to all members, and is likely to receive both verbal and nonverbal feedback about how members are reacting to the group

and its worker(s). In all forms of practice, knowledge of oneself is important—of one's skills and limitations, and how one's background and conflicts can influence judgments. . . . Self-knowledge must include our own
gender socialization, the various cultures in our background, and resulting
social values and expectations that one has about human behavior. We
must learn to recognize areas of privilege and disadvantage in our lives and
how they have shaped us.   *(p. 184)*

Leaders are sometimes trained to serve as conduits for the group experiences
in such a way that the leader's perception of reality is expected to be the
group's view of reality. Formal gestalt training is an example of this. This
approach fosters a belief system for leaders that focuses on their own creation
and interpretation of the experience rather than the members'.

Another context in which the sociocultural information that influences
group members may differ from that of the group leader is in cognitive-behavioral therapies, especially Rational-Emotive Therapy (RET) and cognitive
restructuring. Women of color have developed patterns of communication
and behavior that are based on their interactions with both their communities of origin and the wider society (Lewis, 1993a). As noted earlier, the consequences of giving up or modifying these patterns may bring considerable
harm to the individual in her daily interactions outside the group. Cognitions
that have proven to be effective perceptions of the self, the community of origin, and the wider society by women of color and have ensured the survival
of these populations may not be lightly dismissed as "negative" or "inappropriate." When challenging cognitions in intervention groups, leaders must
acknowledge the role that the cognition has played in strengthening the individual as well as how it has been detrimental to the person's overall functioning. Thus, when encountering a statement such as "I feel I'm in danger every
time a White person from the South comes into the room," an unpacking
process must take place that identifies under what conditions that cognition
is held or disavowed, in what ways it has been helpful to the group member,
and, most importantly, how it is put into operation by that person. Comas-
Diaz (1981; Comas-Diaz and Greene, 1994) has incorporated this consideration in using the cognitive-behavioral approach with depressed Puerto Rican
women, placing an emphasis on the "reassessment" of key cognitions rather
than their combative restructuring or elimination.

Experiences of women group leaders (Reed et al., 1997) and African-American group leaders (Davis, 1984; Davis, Galinsky, and Schopler, 1995) can be
confounded when the leader is a woman of color in a racially or ethnically het-

erogeneous group (Lewis, 1993; Pinderhughes, 1983). The bicultural influences shaping the lives of women of color (both as women and as individuals of color, at least) bring one perspective to the group process. These influences may be in direct conflict with those of the other group members. The woman of color as leader may face one or two competing sets of perceptions in the group, unless these are clearly identified in the early stages of group process. She may be viewed as less (or more) competent than a European-American woman in the same role because of her dual lower-caste statuses as woman and person of color (Ogbu, 1981). In some cases, the woman of color as leader is perceived as having more power in the group, as being a "superwoman" or matriarch (Davis, Cheng, and Strube, 1996; Comas-Diaz and Greene, 1994). Directly addressing this potential for misunderstanding can be an effective strategy in an initial group meeting. We have done this in our work with groups when introducing ourselves, adding that we value the contributions our life experiences as women of color bring to our formal training and expect to make those contributions explicit when applicable. At the same time, we note that we are engaging in a process that is transforming not only group members but ourselves as well (Cohen, 1990; Castex, 1993; Gutiérrez, Lewis, and Nagda, 1995). As such, all group members are experts on their own experiences and the way these experiences can be utilized by others.

What are the advantages and disadvantages of a single person serving as the group leader in empowering group work with women of color? When power is invested in one sole leader in an empowerment group, the leader may be empowered, but other group members may not experience their own agency and thus may be denied the chance to gain confidence through action (Cole, 1993; Gutiérrez, Parsons, and Cox, 1998). Sole leadership also results in hierarchy and domination within the group, with group members engaged in gaining cohesion with the leader rather than with each other. Another consequence of sole leadership, even in professionally facilitated clinical practice groups, is that there is only one available source of data on group process and outcomes within and across sessions.

To avoid these potential dangers, we suggest two remedies. The first is coleadership when both leaders have had some training. It is not necessary for both leaders to have identical training backgrounds but instead for there to be balance that incorporates each leader's strengths. For example, the Women's Initiative for Self-Employment Project (WISE) in Ann Arbor, Michigan, holds group sessions for low-income women attempting to start their own businesses. The groups are co-led by women who have earned professional degrees in business, social work, and/or psychology and women who have been through the training program and begun businesses of their own. In this case, both individuals can alternate responsibility for carrying out the session and then compare their perceptions of session activities. The resultant data is richer than would be data collected by either facilitator alone.

The second method of cofacilitation is alternating leadership among group members. This is a method used in many self-help groups and natural helping networks (Lewis and Suarez, 1995). The method models different styles of cofacilitation that can be critiqued and refined by participation. Another benefit of this method is that leadership is distributed in the group in ways that allow the group to continue after its relationship with professional leadership personnel has been terminated. Rather than the professional serving as a model, other group members provide the modeling of facilitation skills. Hence members use their connection with one another to build confidence in their abilities (Lewis and Ford, 1990).

Summary

This chapter has focused on issues of group design, composition, cohesion, process, and leadership. We have attempted to offer concrete examples of strategies that may be used to enhance overall group outcomes in working with women of color in groups and discussed the development of critical consciousness as it affects individual members and coleaders of the group, as well as their families and communities. Confidence is achieved through capacity building and modeling both in and outside of the group, as in the case of the informational campaign on domestic violence and the individual members' experiences with changing familial patterns of violence against women. A sense of connection can be forged through strategies such as the establishment of ground rules. Key to all these strategies, however, is the explicit recognition and interaction of difference and similarity in group settings, whether groups are considered homogeneous or heterogeneous.

SIX

Bringing an Empowerment Perspective
into Organizational Practice

♦

Ines Marcano works at a large community coalition focused on AIDS prevention, education, and early intervention. She was attracted to this job after her brother had died of AIDS a few years back and she became aware of the great risk of HIV infection for people in the Puerto Rican community. She was hired by the coalition right after receiving her bachelor's degree in social work (BSW) and feels fortunate to work in an organization that has infused multiculturalism and empowerment into its programs and practices.

Ines's main role is that of outreach and training in the Latino community. Her job involves identifying existing organizations in the Latino community that can provide AIDS/HIV prevention education. The groups she works with include block associations, Head Start centers, PTAS, and merchant groups. She has learned that in her community an effective strategy has been to work with parents—particularly mothers—to educate their children to reduce the risk of HIV infection. She knows that in this way she can reach women at risk who may feel uncomfortable talking about their own sexuality.

When Ines talks with other friends who graduated from her BSW program she sees the degree to which her organization is empowering of workers and clients. Within the coalition each unit operates as its own self-governing team to identify its own mission, priorities, and services. The workers in each unit in collaboration with community members make up the self-governing team. Each team has the power to hire, supervise, and fire its own staff. Staff is encouraged to use their ideas and knowledge to create and test new programs. Although Ines sometimes is frus-

trated by the demand to participate and work on the governance of her organization, she also recognizes the benefits gained for herself and her community

◆

Empowerment practice does not exist in a vacuum. If we are to contribute to
the empowerment of women of color, the organizations and institutions in
which we work must be supportive of this practice (Gutiérrez, GlenMaye, and
DeLois, 1995). We have noted earlier in this volume that most attempts at
infusing practice with an empowerment perspective have focused on work
with small systems. Seldom do organizations recognize the need for the
empowerment of workers at all levels. Indeed, those attempts to infuse an
empowerment perspective to date have focused on the use of strategies such
as Total Quality Management (Latting, 1994) or training directed at selected
employees. We consider attempts that target stakeholders, staff, or clients only
to be incomplete strategies and propose in this chapter a more comprehensive
perspective on organizational empowerment.

We begin with a discussion and description of organizational empowerment and its structures and processes. We then present a model for organizational change focused on the goal of creating multicultural and empowerment-based organizations. This change process can begin at any point in the
organization but will eventually require the support of administration. Our
discussion of organizational change is based on the work on multicultural
educational and organizational development.

Some may consider laughable, indeed oxymoronic, the project of thinking
about empowerment at the organizational or educational level. Most human
service organizations are hierarchical in nature, and the literature has presented
much about the changes organizations experience as their clientele, staff, and
funding increase over years (Cox, 1992; Jackson and Holvino, 1988; Dodd,
1994). Those wishing to create empowering organizations must look beyond
the status quo to models that show some promise of providing increased consciousness, confidence, and connection to the world interacting with the organization. The strategies employed, as noted in earlier chapters, include education of all members of the organization, their participation in activities that lead
to actual change, and an expanded definition by those who are chosen to serve
in leadership positions of who can best manage the organizational mission.

One last caveat concerning organizational empowerment is that it is a work
in progress. Those of us in social service organizations who have experienced
the benefits of client empowerment have most likely had that experience for
only a short time. Most of us who have worked in large organizations have
probably never had the experience of empowerment at all. Even as you read

it, therefore, this chapter is being rewritten and critiqued by countless others struggling to do this work.

Understanding Organizational Empowerment

Organizational empowerment can be looked at from two perspectives: that of the empowered organization and that of the empowering organization. The empowered organization has the resources and power to meet its goals. An empowering organization maximizes the power of its workers and constituents to participate fully in the governance of the organization (Crowfoot, 1972; Gerschick, Israel, and Checkoway, 1990; Zimmerman, in press). In this chapter, our focus is on the empowering organization, with the understanding that through the processes of worker empowerment the organization can enhance its own effectiveness.

Research on organizational empowerment suggests that the ways in which social service organizations are structured will affect individual and community empowerment. The ability of individual workers to share their power with clients and engage in the range of interventions required for empowerment practice can depend on the support they receive for this type of work and their own feelings of personal power (Gutiérrez, GlenMaye, and DeLois, 1995). Social service organizations that contribute to the disempowerment of workers may undermine their ability to empower clients and communities: in response to feelings of powerlessness, many social service workers may become ineffective, hostile toward clients, apathetic, or burned out (Mathis and Richan, 1986; Pinderhughes, 1983; Sherman and Wenocur, 1983). Organizations that empower workers to make independent decisions about their work through participatory management, communication and support from administrators, and opportunities for skill development can be more capable of empowering clients (Bredeson, 1989; Gerschick, Israel, and Checkoway, 1990; Zimmerman, in press).

The implementation of empowerment-based programs, such as those described throughout this book, will require particular administrative practices. For example, empowerment practice is consciously consumer oriented and driven and involves clients or consumers in the planning, governing, or implementing of programs. Thus the successful implementation of empowerment-based programs will require the use of participatory management techniques and the creation of an organizational culture based on working in partnership with others.

Empowerment in organizations follows the framework we have been using throughout this book. The structure of empowering organizations is characterized by a flattened hierarchy, teamwork, and the participation of workers and consumers in issues that affect their lives. Attention is paid to staff development, and responsible leaders provide the means to make organizational vision a reality. Table 6.1 identifies some of the administrative supports found to be crucial for engaging in empowerment practice (Gutiérrez, GlenMaye, and DeLois, 1995).

Although these organizational factors are described as parallel, the critical dimension is that of leadership. Effective leadership can be the linchpin that makes the other organizational elements possible. Within an empowering organization, leadership is not the responsibility of a few individuals but is shared throughout the organization and into the community. All individuals draw on their strengths and build new skills to provide organizational leadership.

When Ines first came to the organization, she was asked to sit on a committee to develop a new client grievance procedure for the entire organization. When she first heard about this assignment, she worried that she didn't know enough about possible policies and procedures or the laws governing them. She became even more worried when she went to her first meeting and found out that no one else knew much more than she did.

Recognizing that lack of information was an issue for the committee, the group began by identifying a strategy for learning more about grievance procedures. This included activities such as talking with attorneys specializing in administrative law, getting sample procedures from the United Way, and interviewing staff and clients about the procedures they would want. These strategies led to the creation of policies that were legally sound but also grounded in the expectations of the people who would use them.

TABLE 6.1 Supports for Empowerment Practice

Staff Development	Collaborative Approach	Leadership
training	teamwork	vision
entrepreneurial support	peer support	influence
rewards	safety to take risks	
flexibility	shared philosophy	

This form of leadership is also dependent on an administration and governing board who are invested in the philosophy and practice of empowerment. Administrators and board members who are able to share power and encourage the growth of staff are critical. Administrative staff who are able to advocate for the organization with external systems that can support the empowerment-based programs within the agency are also very important. These administrative supports will develop an organizational culture that is supportive of the empowerment of board, staff, volunteers, and consumers.

Resources to develop and support staff are also a critical element of the empowering organization. Viewing staff on all levels as human resources for the organization and community means that providing opportunities for further education and training will be a priority. Access to conferences, training workshops, and other educational opportunities is integral to the empowerment atmosphere of the organization. Staff can also be supported through flex time and other policies that encourage flexibility and self-care. Similarly, providing opportunities for staff to develop programs and professional skills that match their own personal interests is an important part of the empowerment of staff within an agency. These supports for staff utilize the empowerment methods of building on strengths and providing opportunities for skill development.

One responsibility of each work team at the coalition is to participate in developing its budget for the upcoming year. Through this process the team can determine the direction of its programs and what kinds of resources can go into supporting staff. In the past, the work team has budgeted funds to support the participation of each staff member to attend one conference or workshop a year of his or her choice. Other years, the work team has pooled its training funds so members can bring a consultant to work with them on particular issues such as time-management skills.

One critical aspect of supporting and developing staff should not go unmentioned: providing promotions and salary increases. The opportunities for adequate salaries and room for advancement within human services are often limited. Funding resources will often prescribe how much salary an organization can pay its staff. Managers who focus on developing diversified funding sources will have more latitude in their opportunities for providing raises and promotions for staff. Workers who join or organize a union in their workplace will also have a mechanism for negotiating for livable wages.

An empowering organization will only function effectively if work-group relationships are healthy. In order to share power and information, staff must feel free to take risks in confronting each other, venting frustrations, and developing new programs and ideas. Intragroup conflict should be identified and worked on constructively. Although a shared philosophy for programs and services can be a basis for group cohesion, it cannot eliminate all the conflicts that can occur in a diverse workplace. As mentioned in previous chapters on groups and communities, however, when conflict is framed as healthy and inevitable, it can lead to creativity and further growth.

———————————————————◆———————————————————

Every year the coalition holds an all-day retreat to review the previous year and identify program goals for the coming year. Staff and community representatives work together on particular issues in small groups.

At one retreat, an intense debate arises over the involvement of churches in the coalition's outreach programs. One of the largest and most powerful ministers in the African-American community has denounced the coalition for "supporting immorality." Reactions to this issue vary: some advocate using pickets on Sunday mornings to confront the minister about his homophobia; others suggest that allies on the interfaith council speak with him; a third group proposes that they downplay the more controversial aspects of HIV infection. After some discussion of these three major perspectives, a small group representing different reactions is empowered to develop a strategy to work through the issue and bring it to the rest of the group. The group recommends setting up a meeting with the minister, staff, and two board members who are ministers to see how they can work together on the common goal of health care for African Americans.

———————————————————◆———————————————————

From this brief discussion, the linkages between organizational and other forms of empowerment become clear. Table 6.2 outlines how the structures and processes we have covered can lead to the development of consciousness, confidence, and connection among workers. What distinguishes organizational empowerment is "parallel process": the notion that the treatment of workers within human service organizations should parallel that expected for clients (Gutiérrez, GlenMaye, and DeLois, 1995). Through organizational empowerment, the empowerment of workers as people can be enhanced.

This form of human services management involves an element of risk and presents challenges in implementation. Workers must attend actively to the needs of their program and those of their clients. One responsibility of working in an organization with a participatory management style requires a different kind of demand for work. These two relationships must be negotiated carefully. The following example illustrates the type of conflicts that can develop.

♦

Each month the community education unit takes time for a half-day retreat. During that time members review their work for the month, review the budget, and make plans for the coming month. Workers are active participants in the process and are expected to make reports on their activities and to use the time for group consultation.

This month, Ines has a problem. A local Head Start center would like her to give a workshop the morning the monthly retreat will be held. The center director has told her that it is the scheduled time for their parents' council meeting and so the best time to reach the parents. Her supervisor had told her that the retreat is a priority and she will be expected to attend and participate actively. Ines must now decide which obligation is more significant.

♦

Although, as we have argued, the needs of workers and their organizations cannot be separated from those of their clients, the client-driven nature of the empowerment perspective suggests that such conflict should be analyzed from the perspective of client services. Ines and her supervisor and coworkers would be wise to discuss how she might meet the needs of the Head Start center

---

TABLE 6.2 Organizational Processes for Empowering Workers

Consciousness

       1. Education of members about the nature and structure of the organization

       2. Demystification of organizational processes

       3. Dialogue regarding organizational mission

Confidence

       1. Skill building to increase leadership capacity

       2. Identification of areas of power and control

       3. Increased opportunities for professional growth and development

Connection

       1. Development of teams to make program decisions

       2. Use of coordinated top-down and bottom-up approaches

       3. Ongoing evaluation of the change process

---

while honoring her obligations to the work team. Through brainstorming together they could identify strategies for meeting both sets of obligations.

Strategies for Organizational Change

In the first section we described the empowering organization and how it is managed. Few social workers work in such organizations, however. How can the rest of us work to transform existing organizations into more effective instruments of empowerment for their workers and clients? In this section of the chapter, we will present a strategy for changing organizations so they can be truly empowering for women of color as workers and clients.

USING EMPOWERMENT METHODS FOR ORGANIZATIONAL CHANGE

Lydia Vasquez works in the permanency planning program of a large child welfare agency employing more than three hundred people; her job is to help develop permanent solutions for children in the foster-care system. Three years ago Lydia was hired as a Spanish-speaking caseworker who would focus her efforts on the large Mexican-American population served by the agency. She and one other African-American worker, Veronica, are the only people of color in professional roles at the agency. Over the past year they have started having lunch once a week to talk about some of the issues they have faced as social workers of color at the agency.

   Some of the issues they raise would be faced by any worker: large caseloads, lack of resources for clients, sadness over the abuse and neglect they see in the families. But other issues are more specific to their status: calls by other workers for help when they are working with families of color, community demands to provide outreach and education, and concerns over the lack of culturally relevant services provided by their agency and others. In their lunches together, Veronica and Lydia have begun to talk about ways in which they and their clients can receive better support from the agency.

   The issues identified by Veronica and Lydia are not unique. Many social workers of color are concerned with the need to provide more effective culturally competent programs and services. As token members of a specific group, they often experience feelings of marginalization with regard to their own community and the organization in which they work (Comas-Diaz and Greene, 1994). These experiences can be disempowering and contribute to feelings of burnout and despair. What can social workers do to transform the organization in which they work?

Organizational change work requires the involvement of individuals on all levels of the organization. Direct service workers can play a critical role in identifying the specific unmet needs in a community (Germain and Gitterman, 1980; Kettner, Daley, and Nichols, 1985; Netting, 1993). They are in the unique position of interacting with the community and being able to translate their needs and potentials into program issues. Administrative staff play a critical role in helping to translate these needs and potentials into actual changes in policy, practice, and procedure. Only when both groups work together can changes take place.

The empowerment processes of consciousness, confidence, and connection can be used as means for organizational change. Workers can gain consciousness and knowledge through dialogue with community members and each other about unmet needs. For example, in their lunches together, Lydia and Veronica identified common issues in serving clients of color. By expanding the dialogue to others, individual workers can begin to connect with a larger community that shares their concerns. When Lydia and Veronica attended a training workshop on culturally competent practice in child welfare, they met many other workers in their region who shared their concerns. Such processes of consciousness and connection can lead to the development of confidence to make ideas more concrete and seek organizational change.

When deciding to be agents of organizational change, Lydia and Veronica followed a planned change method that can be used to change large systems (Netting, 1993; Kettner, Daley, and Nichols, 1985). They had been introduced to this method through a required macro practice course in their master's of social work (MSW) program. This method presents a way for involving direct service workers, administrators, and the communities they serve to work together to create effective and responsive programs, projects, and policies.

IDENTIFYING AND ANALYZING THE CHANGE OPPORTUNITY

Organizational change requires careful planning and strategy. In their meetings together, Lydia and Veronica began to identify and then analyze the change

---

TABLE 6.3 Steps in the Planned Change Process

---

1. Identifying the change opportunity

2. Analyzing the change opportunity

3. Identifying strategies for change

4. Selecting change strategies

5. Implementing the change strategy

6. Evaluating the change strategy

---

opportunity. After much discussion, they identified the goal of creating more culturally competent services for client families of the agency. But before they could come up with more specific objectives, they knew they needed to draw on more perspectives. They divided up the list of workers in their unit, planning to talk to each of them about culturally competent services. After a series of individual coffee-break meetings with their coworkers, they were able to identify which workers were supportive and which were not. They were encouraged by their discovery of a broad range of support within their unit.

They now felt they needed to gain some organizational sanction and support for their efforts. In order to do this, they needed the support of the larger administration. They used a "force-field analysis" to identify potential sources of support and resistance in the organization. In a force-field analysis, the change agents identify all possible actors who would have an interest or formal relationship to the change process. These actors are then classified according to their degree of support, resistance, or neutrality with regard to the change. The names are then listed on a sheet of paper so that a change strategy can be mapped out. Based on their analysis, Veronica and Lydia were able to move to the next step: bringing their ideas to a staff meeting.

◆

Within the organization there is a bimonthly social work staff meeting in which policies and procedures are discussed. This meeting is facilitated by the clinical director of the agency. The meetings are very formal and often consist of the director discussing procedural issues such as statistical forms.

Before the next meeting, Lydia and Veronica decide to go to their individual supervisors and discuss their concerns regarding culturally competent services for clients. They would like the need for culturally competent services to be discussed at the next staff meeting. In preparation for these meetings, they have pulled together existing agency statistics to demonstrate that over 50 percent of their clients are either African American or Latino. They also provided materials from the child welfare conference on culturally competent practice with Latinos and African Americans. They have asked a former professor from their MSW program, who is the field liaison to the agency, to call the supervisors early that week and ask about the provision of culturally competent services.

Lydia and Veronica receive a positive response from their supervisors. They agree that the concept of culturally competent services is important but are unsure if the agency has the resources to provide them. However, they see no problem with discussing the topic in the staff meeting. Lydia and Veronica then prepare for the meeting.

IDENTIFYING AND SELECTING STRATEGIES FOR CHANGE

To prepare for the meeting, Lydia and Veronica have lunch with the workers in their unit who are most sympathetic to the idea of culturally competent services. They decide that their objective for the meeting will be to raise the issue so as to gain support and resources from the clinical director. Their ultimate goal will be training for the entire staff and a commitment that any new staff have knowledge and skills for work with families of color.

As a strategy, Veronica and Lydia ask if any of the other workers would like to speak at the meeting and present a case in which cultural factors were important. They know that if many workers are involved in presenting the material the administrators will see that there is a broad base of support. They also believe that if a European-American worker speaks for the need of culturally competent services, their concern may be less likely to be identified as a special issue. One of the workers, who has been with the unit for many years, agrees to present a case in which her efforts to find an adoptive family for an African-American child were unsuccessful until she met with a minister in the African-American community. The minister set up a meeting for her with interested members of his congregation, and she was able to find a family that was able to adopt the child. However, this process also led her to question some of the agency's procedures for home studies and preadoption services. For example, the fees they charged for adoption services were prohibitive for some of the families in the community.

This brief example identifies some of the methods and skills that might be used by social workers who would like to initiate a change process in their organization. As demonstrated by this discussion, it is critical that the process involve multiple perspectives and participation of all who will be affected by the change (Kettner, Daley, and Nichols, 1985). This example also demonstrates the degree to which processes of organizational change are ongoing: once a change has been initiated it can require a considerable level of commitment to deal with the consequences of change work.

Organizational change for empowerment can involve external consultants who can provide processes and procedures for planned change. Consultants will often enter an agency only after groundwork has occurred within the organization that provides impetus for committing time and money for the change. Effective work by consultants will require the involvement of a wide range of organization members; it will build on and reinforce work that has already taken place within the organization.

Pearl and Jean have run a successful consulting firm for the last decade. One is an African-American, and the other a European-American. Both women are in their mid-forties and live in the northeastern part of the United States. While they have specialized in helping large corporations identify their "workplace diversity" concerns about gender and race, they have been disturbed that there has been little in the way of follow-through by their clients once the contract is over. Pearl and Jean support long-term change, but they have found that, without building a base within the organization, this cannot occur.

They have been negotiating a contract with the child welfare agency where Veronica and Lydia work. The executive director of the agency describes the organizational goal as improving the practice skills of the staff through a series of workshops on culturally competent practice. Although they would like to hire more qualified workers of color, they feel they cannot because of limited resources for recruitment.

Jean and Pearl are interested in working with this organization, but they must first evaluate the commitment to change.

Before getting involved in organizational change work, the level of commitment within the organization and the expectations for change must first be evaluated. Transforming an organization's culture and structure will require the participation of individuals at all levels. The interests of board members, administrators, line workers, and support staff must be evaluated. This can most easily be done by interviewing individuals representing these groups to identify their vision of what a change process could and should accomplish. Before entering an organization to make change occur, there must be a moderate level of agreement among individuals in the organization regarding their vision for change.

After entering an organization officially, this process of gauging consensus should be continued by using an assessment tool (see figure 6.1) to begin to identify each staff member's strengths, challenges, and commitment to the organizational change process (Jackson and Holvino, 1988).

Once information was received from the majority of individuals, Jean and Pearl were able to develop an initial map of those individuals who might be interested in or critical to the development of a core group. This core group, in a small agency, may be thought of as an organizational empowerment team that will provide the major leadership for a change process. Such a team would carry out the tasks outlined in table 6.4.

The members of the group must first identify the ways in which each contributes to the organizational mission (or the one that will be developed). If necessary, the very structure of the organization must be modified to accommodate the in-depth work of this facilitating team so that members do not feel their participation is an add-on rather than an integral part of their job descriptions for the period of their most intensive work.

◆

Veronica and Lydia were excited to see that their initial attempt to make change had resulted in a broader approach to training and organizational change. When Jean and Pearl first began working with the organization, they attended a clinical staff meeting where all members filled out the assessment tool and then discussed goals for the organization. A week later, a memo was circulated among the staff asking for participation in a Cultural Competence Committee that would work on long-term change. This group would be composed of representatives of the board, administration, line staff, and support staff and would report to the board and executive director. Lydia and Veronica recognized that this meant a change in the agency's governance structure.

◆

Multiple tasks are assigned to the leadership group. First, it is expected to engage in activities that will help model consciousness building, connection,

TABLE 6.4 Tasks of an Organizational Empowerment Leadership Team

- Define initial organizational goals, objectives, and strategies for change
- Monitor long-term agency change strategies and report these to others in and outside of the organization
- Design and implement agency innovations based on agency needs

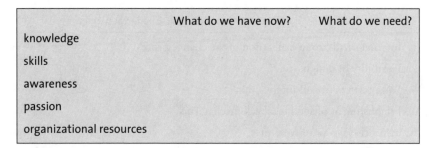

	What do we have now?	What do we need?
knowledge		
skills		
awareness		
passion		
organizational resources		

FIGURE 6.1 A Sample Organizational Assessment

and confidence for other members of the workforce. The first sessions must be spent unpacking the knapsack of isms encountered by those in the group and the organization at large (McIntosh, 1995). The second task is to complete the agency or organizational assessment process, identifying goals and objectives, as well as task analyses to meet these. To complete this process, members of the team work with board members and individuals in each unit in order to tap into their perspectives.

IMPLEMENTING, MONITORING, AND
EVALUATING CHANGE STRATEGIES

A third task of the leadership team is to monitor what is being done to meet the goals, objectives, and task analyses over time. As they monitor, leadership team members can communicate innovations being tried in parts of the organization to the rest of the organization and to other stakeholders. A last task of the organizational leadership team is to design and model innovations based on agency needs stemming from their own increased awareness of the organization's diversity.

The leadership team can engage in a number of intervention strategies for organizational change. These strategies focus on mechanisms for involving a broad representation of staff and institutionalizing change. Table 6.5 outlines some characteristics of the strategies involved in this process, which are discussed more fully below.

Internal small-group facilitation of the change process. In a method congruent with other levels of empowerment, we propose that the small group is a useful vehicle for influencing change in a larger organization. While at some later point

---

TABLE 6.5 Empowering Organizational Change Strategies

---

1. Internal small-group facilitation of the change process

2. Flexibility of design

3. Long-term nature of intervention

4. Establishment of solid feedback mechanisms

5. Institutional reward structures

6. Specific organizational change goals

7. Skill building and connection activities linked to overall organizational vision, mission, and development

---

in the organizational change process multiple small groups throughout the organization may be useful, we propose that a group representing all levels of the organizational structure and all forms of diversity be constructed to spearhead the organizational change. The warnings about heterogeneous groups given in chapter 5 should be heeded, and only those individuals interested in being involved in a long-term interpersonal, intrapersonal, and organizational change effort should be included in the group. Cofacilitation of this group will eventually be undertaken by group members, although some outside facilitators/trainers may be identified to take the group through its initial sessions.

◆

Jean and Pearl, after compiling the list of core empowerment team members, invited them individually to a meeting (an important aspect of group composition, as explored in chapter 9). The team began meeting on a weekly basis at first. Initially, Jean and Pearl shared cofacilitation responsibilities. By the end of the third meeting, however, Jean and Pearl began to alternate their cofacilitation with one of the team members. Within two months of contact, the team members took responsibility for cofacilitation, based on a review of their own strengths, and Jean and Pearl began to serve as consultants, providing information, access to training/consciousness-raising, and other skill development resources. Part of the progression of the team's activities is explained in the excerpts from Jean and Pearl's notes on the intervention, reproduced in figure 6.2.

◆

In this example, the organizational empowerment leadership team is a leadership model in which power is shared in a lateral rather than hierarchical manner. The team represents all the functions within the agency and is diverse in terms of sexual orientation, gender, class, professional status, ethnicity, and

By week 8, the team had developed its initial list of organizational goals, objectives, and change strategies. Each team member took responsibility for meeting with a group of agency staff monthly to share information developed within the empowerment team, to solicit staff perspectives about proposed changes, and to refine further and assist in the implementation of agency innovations based on agency needs.

At the end of the fourth month, the team held an all-agency meeting and presented the second revision of goals, objectives, and strategies for the organizational change. The ten team members were prepared with charts identifying who was responsible in the organization for the change; where overlaps in responsibilities had occurred, with rationales for the separate assignments of these responsibilities; and a time frame for initial changes to occur. Each staff member was included on the charts, and all were able to determine where they fit into the total picture of the organizational change. The staff completed an evaluation of the overall proposed structure that was later reviewed by the core team.

FIGURE 6.2 Notes on the Organizational Change Intervention

racial social group memberships; all, however, are of similar ages, and all have children. The team is representative of the organizational community and develops skill-building activities in keeping with the needs and mission of the organization. All members of the organization are able to see their role in the change process.

Flexibility of design. Human service organizations are constantly changing and are influenced by their own social, political, and historical contexts. Empowering organizational change must reflect this organizational fluidity. Designing a program with a canned set of options does not allow for the development of long-lasting rather than person-specific changes, as is evident in the following example.

Lydia has been an integral part of the empowerment core team for two months. She had taken responsibility for sharing information with the agency social workers and bringing information about design problems back to the core team. Two days following the last meeting of the agency social workers, Lydia was struck by a car during a home visit. She was forced to take a medical leave of absence from the agency. The other social workers met together, asking for a representative of the core empowerment team to join them. At that time, they nominated Steve, another committed member of the social work staff, to replace Lydia on the core team.

Had all members of the organization not been aware of the plans for the long-term change effort or prepared alternative strategies for the organizational design, Lydia's leave of absence could have derailed the entire intervention. Too often, person-specific designs invest too much power in one individual (often the agency director) and only nominally address the shared-power model. Flexibility of design addresses both the internal and the external changes that normally occur in agencies and educational institutions in their social-historical-political contexts.

Long-term nature of intervention. Everyone knows that Rome was not built in a day. The same holds true for organizational change. When Pearl and Jean were initially contacted by the organization about facilitating workshops on diversity, they requested a meeting with the staff development representative and the agency director, instead. During this time, they explored what these personnel expected from the workshops. After learning that they expected the workshops to transform the organization's ability to respond to communities of color, Jean and Pearl explained clearly that workshops could have only a limited impact on organizational change. At the same initial meeting, they began laying the groundwork for a consciousness-raising and skill-building program with key staff in the agency that would enable this staff to communicate with others in the agency about the proposed intervention.

Establishment of solid feedback mechanisms. Participating in organizational change requires that the process be communicated to all members. One of the reasons for developing a leadership team with representatives from all units is to provide feedback systems regarding the process. An important responsibility of team members is to communicate their activities to coworkers. This communication should be a two-way process: team members should also bring back ideas and reactions to members of the leadership team.

---◆---

Steve is a member of the leadership team who works in the family preservation unit. His involvement in intensive wraparound services for families in crisis has convinced him that understanding cultural resources is imperative. He is one of two MSW social workers on the unit; much of the footwork in his team is carried out by case aides recruited from the community.

At a unit meeting, Steve reports on plans for recruiting and hiring more workers who understand communities of color. He is surprised that the case aides—the majority of whom are African American and Latino women from the community—have become silent and seem displeased by the discussion. When he asks for questions and reactions, there is more silence, and then a case aide, Delia, says, "Why bother recruiting people from the outside; why not give us what we need to do our jobs better?" A number of the case aides nod and murmur their support. They then spend the next twenty minutes discussing the need to recognize the expertise that exists in the agency and to support the further education of paraprofessional staff. Steve brings the ideas from this discussion back to the leadership group. This results in a recommendation that the agency support the education of current staff through release time and limited funding.

Institutional reward structures. The process we are discussing is time and labor intensive. Although change can be its own reward, organizations must develop means to support and recognize the change process. Rewarding work toward change is one means to maintain motivation and vision. Rewards can be simple and informal, such as taking the time during each meeting to review the progress made and thanking individuals and groups for the work they have done. Rewards can also be more formal, such as modifying staff performance reviews to include acknowledgment of staff activities in the project and its implementation.

The organizational leadership team developed a number of ways to reward the agency's work on diversity. Pearl and Jean modeled a process that included a review of accomplishments at the end of each meeting. This process was replicated by the leadership team and all subsequent task groups. At the end of the sixth month, a section of the agency's quarterly newsletter was devoted to the progress of the leadership team. This report highlighted the work done by the team as a whole, by the task groups, and by individual units and included photos from training sessions and community meetings. The newsletter, which is distributed to all staff, board members, funders, and public officials, was another means of recognizing staff participation.

Specific organizational change goals. Lofty or vague goals can be strategic weapons in the suppression of a change process. In the same way that we encouraged specific activities to be agreed on in individual and family practice, we recommend the same in organizational change work. Different orders of intentions can be useful to guide the change process: a mission statement can be generated to identify the overall vision of what is to be achieved; a goal can define a general desired end; an objective can indicate the specific outcome that needs to be achieved (Kettner, Daley, and Nichols, 1985; Netting, 1993).

Continually identifying operational definitions for agency change goals and refining them with stakeholders is as essential in organizational practice as it is in individual, family, or group practice. Given the flexibility of design, these goals may change. Consultants can serve as recorders who map out changes in the overall mission, goals, and objectives of the organization/ agency/institution over time so that those who are new to the group can understand what has happened in the past, what is currently perceived, and what may happen in the future. Each working group should develop its own mission, goals, and objectives, which can then be integrated into a larger plan for the organization. Table 6.6 provides one example of the relationship between mission, goals, and objectives for the permanency planning unit.

Skill building and connection activities. Skill building is linked to overall organizational vision, mission, and development. This is how we began this chapter and also how we end it. Continual attention and linkage of skill-building work to the real and changing mission of the organization are critical. It is unethical to state as part of an organization's mission that all constituents will have equal access to the organization's decision-making process if this is not true. Furthering connections between staff and service consumers for the sole purpose of an organizational intervention is not empowering practice; new structures and processes must be created as a part of this work. This process of change is never ending, as all organizations are continually evolving.

TABLE 6.6 Relationship of Mission, Goals, and Objectives	
Mission	To provide permanent and culturally congruent living situations for children who have been abused or neglected
Goal	To hire and develop staff who are culturally competent
Objectives	Each social work staff member will engage in a self-assessment to identify his or her level of competence for working with Latino and African-American families
	Each social work staff member will develop a plan for improving cultural competence
	Each social work staff member will be reviewed annually on progress on their cultural competence plan
	Administrative staff will develop resources for funding participation of staff in appropriate conferences and workshops
	Administrative staff will identify individuals and groups in the community that can consult with staff on specific cases

The process and vision of empowerment with organizations that we have presented here calls for a radical change in the management of human service agencies. The goal is the development of organizations that are primarily accountable to the communities they serve. This requires the full participation of all stakeholders in the governance of the organizations. Without the support of this type of empowering organizational process, empowerment practice will not lead to fundamental change (Gutiérrez, 1992; Gutiérrez and Nagda, 1996). With this support, empowerment can be carried out to its fullest potential.

◆

Since Lydia and Veronica began the process of changing their organization to become more culturally competent, the child welfare agency has undergone a number of changes: consultants have worked with the organization, its board, and community to initiate a change process; all staff have received intensive training in cultural competence; personnel policies have been changed to reflect the multicultural priorities; paraprofessionals have been provided with resources to receive further education; and self-governing work teams have been initiated on the unit level.

This change has not occurred easily. Some individuals chose to leave the agency when they did not like the direction it was taking. Many found it painful when community members and clients began to communicate directly with them about the ways they viewed the organization. The Department of Social Services, which provides a large percentage of agency funding, has questioned some of the changes in organizational structure.

However, this change has also benefited the community it serves. The permanency planning unit now works closely with community-based organizations and informal groups in communities of color. The staff is much more ethnically diverse. Improved communication among staff has resulted in more efficient and effective work with all cases. And the organization has spearheaded efforts in the city to improve child welfare through improving overall economic and social conditions. By broadening its focus, it is now working for the empowerment of individuals, families, groups, and the community as a whole.

◆

SEVEN

Empowerment Techniques: Practice with Communities

◆

Ada Deer, the first American Indian woman to receive an MSW degree, has had a long and distinguished career working with Native American communities to increase their levels of self-determination and empowerment. A member of the Menominee nation in southeastern Wisconsin, Ada was aware from childhood of the implications of interpersonal and societal power imbalances as they affected the Menominee people. From 1634, when the French first landed in the Menominee homelands, through Chief Oshkosh's reign in 1827, interactions with other European settlers were relatively harmonious. By 1836, however, the U.S. government through the Wisconsin Territory was attempting to make the Menominee move west of the Mississippi, and Chief Oshkosh negotiated the Treaty of Cedars, selling part of the land but allowing the Menominee to stay on land near the Fox River. By 1854 the Menominee's interactions with the federal government had resulted in the establishment of their first reservation, with homes, schools, churches, and a sawmill. By 1870, however, smallpox, discrimination, and war had reduced the nation to fewer than fourteen hundred members (Kalbacken, 1994).

In the 1950 the U.S. termination laws resulted in the loss of the Menominee's sovereignty, including its access to medical care, management of its own lands, and educational facilities. In 1953 hundreds of Menominee marched the two hundred miles from the reservation to the state capital to regain their rights; however, the termination laws were not repealed until the 1970s. Ada Deer was a part of this tribal action to return the land to the people, and her voice and conviction were honored by her people. In 1973 she was chosen the leader of the Menominee Restoration Project.

Ada Deer's accomplishments in concert with her tribal members have resulted in the reestablishment of a nine-member tribal council, four reservation schools, a clinic, a lumber mill, and a casino. When the federal government wished to store nuclear waste on the reservation lands in 1986, the tribal leaders, including Ada Deer, protested, and the project was scrapped (Kalbacken, 1994).

Concern for her community of origin also led Ada Deer into the struggle for agency for other tribal nations, populations of color, and societal change. She is responsible for advocating for and modeling scholarship about Native American peoples, leading to the establishment of an American Indian Studies Program on the University of Wisconsin–Madison campus. There, she also served as mentor and adviser to numerous students of color (including one of these authors).

Within the wider society, Ada Deer's struggles and perceptions of power imbalances led her to seek state and national office. She ran for secretary of state in Wisconsin and for the U.S. Congress. In 1993 President Clinton named her director of the Bureau of Indian Affairs, the governmental agency with which she had so often been in conflict during the Menominee's struggles for empowerment.

◆

This example of Ada Deer's work demonstrates ways in which community-level approaches, based on individual critical consciousness-raising, connection, and confidence through skill building, can be critical if we are to improve the status of women of color. Ada Deer first focused her energies on working within the Menominee nation to develop community-based projects. She then reached out and joined with other groups of color to effect change in a second community sphere: that of an educational institution. Eventually, she enlarged her vision of community to include the wider society and a reformulation of the laws governing First Nation and non-First Nation peoples at the state and national levels. Action in one sphere led to broader actions on a number of other levels as the linkages between injustice on one level were critically analyzed in relation to injustice on other levels and with other populations.

Ada Deer focused her energies on working with her people to develop autonomy through skill development, which ultimately led to community development. This strategy for community development is but one method of community practice. In this chapter, we present a framework for carrying out community work with women of color. An important theme will be how empowerment methods of education, participation, and capacity building can be used for community change.

Understanding Community Practice

The goal for community practice is to create social environments that support human development. This will often require the transfer of power from more powerful to less powerful groups. Community practice can result in changes in social policy, program development, or local governance, as in the case of the Menominee. Although the target of change is the community, the forum for change can be individuals, families, groups, or organizations. For example, efforts to reduce violence in the community may begin with a series of dialogues and small-group meetings that result in the development of a social action organization (Lewis, 1993). This social action organization can then work to influence policy affecting economic and social institutions. Community change tactics can range from short and focused activities, such as the 1953 Menominee march to the Wisconsin state capital, to long and sustained projects, such as the Menominee Restoration Project (Kettner, Daley, and Nichols, 1985; Mondros and Wilson, 1994).

Models for community practice in social work have attempted to identify methods that facilitate this type of change. In his classic chapter on community intervention, Rothman (1994) identifies three approaches to practice: locality development, social planning, and social action. These approaches differ in their orientation to goals, assumptions, strategies, and roles for organizers. In practice, the community context should dictate the method used. For example, locality development methods such as those used by Ms. Deer may be most effective within relatively homogeneous communities. Although Rothman describes these approaches as discrete "ideal types," they are often combined in practice. With regard to working with women or communities of color, Rothman suggests that this may involve strategies that link locality development with social action. The goal would be to build community among women or people of color with the intent of challenging structures of power.

Although organizing has always taken place in communities of color, relatively little attention has been paid to the ways in which gender, race, ethnicity, or social class affect the organizing effort. This oversight has prevented organizers from working effectively with women or communities of color

(Bradshaw, Soifer, and Gutiérrez, 1993; Burghardt, 1982; Rivera and Erlich, 1995). By ignoring how issues of oppression affect their work, organizers can perpetuate the objectification and exploitation of women and people of color (Burghardt, 1982). For example, organizers who view communities of color in stereotypical ways will be ineffective in building leadership or working in partnership (Bradshaw, Soifer, and Gutiérrez, 1993; Rivera and Erlich, 1995). In this way, community practice can prolong the problems it was designed to solve.

The U.S. government's moves to relocate young adult men and women from isolated tribal lands to urban areas in the 1960s and 1970s illustrates this issue. This mass relocation to several cities was done without considering the past forced removal of native peoples by the government or the consequences of the move on the young adults, the extended family systems they left behind, or their children. While urban Indian health and mental health centers were developed during this period to meet the needs of the new urban dwellers, little attention was paid to the tribal group backgrounds of counselors hired relative to the varied tribal backgrounds represented in the urban community.

Only recently has the field of community organization begun to address this problem in practice. The literature on multicultural organizing has emphasized ways in which organizers can develop cultural competence for working in partnership with communities. The emphasis has training organizers to use their own self-awareness to build bridges for work within communities. Organizers are encouraged to take the role of the learner in approaching a community and looking into their problems and strengths (Burghardt, 1982; Bradshaw, Soifer, and Gutiérrez, 1993; Rivera and Erlich, 1995; Solomon, 1976).

Rivera and Erlich (1995) contribute to practice with communities of color by identifying appropriate roles for the organizer. They stress that the organizer's role should be determined by his or her relationship to the community. If the organizer is a member of the community, as Ada Deer was, then primary contact is appropriate, involving immediate and personal grassroots work with the community. In contrast, an organizer who is of a similar ethnic or racial background but not of the community, such as Indian Health Center staff members who represent none of the many tribal backgrounds served by the center, would be involved on the secondary level. This level would involve participation as a liaison or linkperson between the community and the larger society. The tertiary level of contact would be most appropriate for those who are not members of the group, who can nonetheless provide valuable contributions to the community through consultation and sharing of technical knowledge. For example, individuals interested in participating in community work with Ms. Deer would first establish relationships with key individuals in the Menominee communities. Their responsibilities would be those defined by the community, no matter how insignificant these might seem to the professional organizer. In this way, the tribe would come to recognize the organizer's willingness to use the culturally competent perspective of noninterference, and more opportunities for work with that community might then be revealed (R. Lewis, 1993; Attneave, 1982).

In their work organizing communities of color, Bradshaw, Soifer, and Gutiérrez (1993) focus on the integration of approaches. Of particular importance are skills to develop cultural competence to learn from the community. This involves self-awareness regarding one's own understanding of the community, finding ways to learn more about the local community through key informants, working as partners to develop local leadership, and concentrating on means to build cohesiveness within and between ethnic communities. The critical role of the organizer is that of a learner who approaches the community to understand and facilitate change.

An example from Ada Deer illustrates this cultural competence. During the years following her selection as leader of the Menominee Restoration Project, Ms. Deer often had to represent tribal interests at the state and federal levels. Able to develop a critical analysis that viewed governmental officials as forming policy communities, she could use the tertiary approach to entering these new communities. She then formed alliances with key governmental officials, educated them about the realities of her community, helped them develop their leadership roles so that they could effectively represent and support her community when she could not be present, gained new skills through information about the policy process on these various levels, and used these new connections to facilitate social change.

Feminist Perspectives on Organizing

Organizing with women has often been written about from a feminist perspective. This method of organizing can contribute to community work with women of color by its emphasis on integrating personal and political issues through dialogue. Feminist organizing assumes that sexism is a significant force in the experiences of all women and at the root of many of the problems they face. Therefore, a major focus for organizing with women of color is to identify ways in which sexism, racism, and other forms of oppression are affecting their lives (Bricker-Jenkins and Hooyman, 1986; Gould, 1987; Hyde, 1986; Kopasci and Faulkner, 1988; Morell, 1987; Zavella, 1986). Common methods for feminist organizing include the development of consciousness-raising groups, the creation of alternative services, and social action that incorporates street theater and other holistic methods (Hyde, 1986).

An important focus of this method is a concern with ways to work across differences. All women are thought to be a part of a community of women, as well as members of their own specific communities. Therefore, organizers should make efforts to bridge differences among women stemming from such factors as race, class, physical ability, and sexual orientation, applying the principle that diversity is strength. According to this model "feminist practitioners will not only strive to eliminate racism, classism, heterosexism, anti-Semitism, ableism, and other systems of oppression and exploitation, but will affirm the need for diversity by actively reaching out to achieve it" (Bricker-Jenkins and Hooyman, 1986, p. 20). This goal for feminist organizing has been most effective when carried out from a multicultural perspective (Gutiérrez and Lewis, 1994).

Very little literature has looked specifically at methods for organizing women of color. Yet organizing by women within ethnic communities in the United States has a rich and diverse history. For example, the organization of Black women's clubs more than a century ago by leaders such as Ida B. Wells Barnett were instrumental in developing nursing homes, day care centers, and orphanages within African-American communities. These clubs also organized to promote for social change, particularly by conducting antilynching and rape campaigns, and founding organizations such as the National Urban League (Hill-Collins, 1990; Macht and Quam, 1986; Smith, 1983).

Women of color have always worked to improve conditions within their communities and in society in general, and they have been more likely than European-American middle-class women to see community activism as a natural outgrowth of their gender role (Ackelsberg and Diamond, 1987; Gilkes, 1981). They have played important roles in the movement for equality and civil rights within ethnic minority communities during the middle and late twentieth century (Evans, 1980; Muñoz, 1989; West, 1990; Withorn, 1984). In Detroit and other urban communities, women such as Clementine Barfield have focused on neighborhood violence, economic, and environmental issues ("Fighting Back," 1988; Hirsch, 1991). With this backdrop, it is not surprising that Ada Deer was involved in running for public office at the state level in Wisconsin.

Effective community empowerment efforts respect these traditions. By looking at these historical and contemporary efforts, we can identify ways to expand the strengths and strategies that already exist. As suggested by Erlich and Rivera (1995), the role of the organizer can vary according to his or her relationship to the community or the issue being addressed. In order to determine the appropriate role, we must involve the community in defining the issues and the strategies they would prefer to take. For example, Ada Deer was able to use her role as a member of the community and designated leader to work on the primary level with the community to change structures. A very different role could have been taken by a Native American organizer from another community who could have provided important technical assistance or research skills. Although we emphasize the importance of participation by community members in primary roles, this does not overlook the important roles that are played on the secondary and tertiary levels.

Methods for Community Empowerment: Practice Principles

What does this suggest about working with women of color on the community level? Working within the framework of education, participation, and capacity building, we can develop methods for community practice. These methods build on those described in previous chapters; however, when used on the community level they can present new challenges and opportunities. Many of these methods are equally relevant for organizers and community members. Many traditional community-organizing efforts focus on community-level change, but we propose that organizers, too, embark on a process of intrapersonal change, involving education, participation, and capacity building. These reciprocal process methods, or practice principles, for empowering community organizing are summarized in table 7.1.

Interviews with three women engaged in organizing efforts in a community illustrate some of these practice principles. One of the women is from a European-American ethnic group; the other two are African Americans. At the time of our interviews with them, all three women were single parents and integrated their parenting with an intense commitment to doing community work. This commitment to community social work has not resulted in high

---

TABLE 7.1 Practice Principles

Education

    1. Learn about, understand, and participate in the women's community.

    2. Serve as a facilitator and view the situation through the lens or vision of women of color.

    3. Use the process of praxis to understand the historical, political, and social context of the organizing effort.

Participation

    4. Through participation, learn about the women's ethnic community.

    5. Begin with the formation of small groups.

    6. Recognize and embrace the conflict that characterizes cross-cultural work.

Capacity Building

    7. Recognize and build on ways in which women of color have worked effectively within their own communities; build on existing structures.

    8. Involve women of color in leadership roles.

    9. Understand and support the need that women of color may have for their own separate programs and organizations.

---

salaries, but each woman has been able to realize some of her dreams about cross-racial and ethnic work and women's empowerment.

Organizers who wish to work with women of color must be willing to recognize whether they are insiders, partial insiders, or outside the communities of color with which they hope to work. Cues about position can be gleaned from a knowledge of the historical, social, and political forces influencing the community of color or specific communities of women of color. An excerpt from the interview with Ella, the European-American organizer, illustrates this.

◆

Every six months or so, Ella gets asked about her role as a White woman working with families of color. According to her, "People's attitudes range from 'Why are you doing this?' to 'You shouldn't be doing this!' to 'We admire what you're doing.'

"Certainly, you change your interactions based on who you are talking to and interacting with. I try to be culturally sensitive and I think I am accepted by most of the African-American women that I work with. Being White, I will never be accepted or trusted totally. And I accept that. I also get very pissed when people question my intentions in a negative way when they have made certain assumptions. There is a balance between appreciating people's history and how they view me as a person.

"I am a single mom, and I have been poor in my life but not to the same level or intensity as the women I work with. The women will go to [her cofacilitator], and they'll share things with her that they won't share with me. So she does get more involved with personal issues than I do; there's a trust factor there."

For organizers who are themselves women of color, raising their own critical consciousness about the dividing as well as uniting dimensions of their interactions with other women of color is necessary. Patrice, an African-American woman organizer in the community who had been through experiences similar to those of the women with whom she was working, also addressed the issue of trust.

"When others say, 'You don't know what its like to be homeless,' I am glad that I can say, 'I do know what it feels like.' Knowing the human side of what they went through lends more value and trust, especially to women of color. We are not just relating to each other, but the women can see that another person went through it, and they achieved something despite all the odds against them. Because as women of color we have a lot of strikes against us in the United States: being a woman, being Black, and whatever else.

"Black women cannot always relate [to other Black women] because we've been taught within our own culture not to trust other Black women. [It's] harder to open up the doorway with another Black woman than with White women; the trust barrier is harder to get past because of the way society has dictated that Black women feel inferior. We always feel inferior."

Another area in which education, capacity building, and participation must occur reciprocally for both the organizers and the community participants who are building leadership skills is the involvement of women of color in leadership roles. Monica, the other African-American organizer, who has worked for over ten years with Ella, discussed her experiences in this regard.

"It is sometimes hard to recognize who the leaders are within a community, and it is hard to recognize different skills one has (which can be potential leadership qualities)."

"When you work in an area like [the organizing community] you don't always want to be there because you want to empower people to become self-sufficient and be able to take over their own lives and make decisions about what they want to happen within their own community. You want to leave it behind; you don't want to be something they can always hold on to. You want people to take their skills and build on them and become their own community, their own leaders and assets."

Monica's coworker, Ella, had different views about leadership development issues in the context of the human service organization where she worked.

"Monica was one of the key leaders in the community when I first started working here. There is leadership everywhere. There is a strong Black community here, represented by the churches as well as by a network of neighborhood women who are not recognized as leaders: they don't have as much status or education, but they are real movers and shakers."

◆

"When I first went into [the community], one of the real focuses was to see who the real community leaders were and to tap into their energy and interests. That's definitely Monica. [Ella was able to hire Monica at first part-time and later, when she got off AFDC, full-time.]

"I have run into situations where people think that Monica is my assistant, and I wonder if I have treated her in some way in front of people that would show hierarchy. We've also had questions from the staff about who is in charge. Although we have different titles, we are both equal. Actually, most staff members are directly accountable to Monica as she is the one who is out there running the program. Some people don't understand our relationship [which Ella believes also happens because she has an MSW and Monica has a GED, and thus their academic credentials differ in a place where academic credentials are viewed as important to fund-raising]."

◆

These excerpts from interviews with three empowering organizers illustrate some of the practice principles utilized in the organizational effort. The following sections address other conceptual and practical applications of these principles.

EDUCATION

Community organizers have most often recognized the impact of powerlessness on women of color from the perspective of institutional racism, overlooking the role of gender inequity in influencing their life chances.

The field has also often ignored the history of community participation by women of color. When women of color are viewed solely as members of their racial or ethnic group, and gender is not taken into account, community organizers may alienate women of color and reinforce ways in which sexism, both in the larger society, and within ethnic minority communities, is a form of oppression (Aragon de Valdez, 1980; Hill-Collins, 1990; Weil, 1986; Zavella, 1986).

An important first step for community work is to define the community. Women of color can be members of multiple communities and hold multiple identities. This presents both a challenge and opportunity for organizers. In working from a community perspective, we can define the community as a locality, such as a neighborhood, or as a community of interest, such as gender, ethnic identity, religion, or something else. In working within higher education, for example, Ada Deer's definition of community included not only American Indian students but other students of color who were experiencing an alienating climate at the educational institution.

Often the central issue around which the organizing is taking place will define the community (Netting, Kettner, and McMurty, 1995). For example, if the issue is toxic waste dumping in a community, the neighborhood or city may be an appropriate level for work. If the issue is sterilization abuse and reproductive rights, then gender may be the focus. Being aware of these memberships in multiple communities can be helpful when building coalitions or alliances between different groups.

An organizer whose racial, ethnic, or class background differs from those of the women with whom she works must recognize how her life experience has colored her perceptions and how her status has affected her power relative to the political structure. Her beliefs and perceptions should not dominate the organizing effort. She must work toward serving as a facilitator and view the situation though the lens or vision of the women in the community. This requires allowing their vision to alter the way she views her own work and sharing that new information with others hoping to organize and work within the community. Another excerpt from Ella's interview best illustrates this shifting of visions or lenses.

"I used to write grants that were fairly condescending (disempowering) to the community. I am now really convinced that we have to write things using positive, strong, and powerfully focused language about the community we are trying to get money for. For example, the federally funded Youths Experiencing Stress program is a name I had to come up with overnight. I am definitely not into the 'Just Say No' stuff. The kids aren't, and it's just plain stupid. It's a focus on the negative and you can't do this and you can't do that. We want to focus on and celebrate people's strengths."

When organizing with low-income women in a housing project, one of the authors initially attempted to separate individual from community concerns. Her initial plan was for group members to work on individual problem resolution for eight weeks and then, having established a pattern of interaction within the group, to work cooperatively on analysis and resolution of community concerns. It became clear within the first two meetings that the group *could not* separate and sequentially work with individual and community concerns. As one participant put it, "My individual problems *are* the community's problems." The flexibility to alter the design based on the realities of the community allowed the group to continue to work toward resolution of its identified goals, not those of the facilitator/researcher. This example points up the importance of understanding the community's lens of reality and applying the process of praxis to unravel the salient historical, social, and political forces at work. To have insisted on separating the individual from the community problem would have resulted in the loss of committed community activists who proceeded to make change on the individual and community levels (Lewis and Ford, 1990).

Using the process of praxis to understand the historical, political, and social context of the organizing effort means that the organizing process as well as the outcome will inform both the organized community and the community of the organizer. In analyzing the process and outcome of organizing efforts, the outcome of a tactic may emerge as less important than what the community and organizer learn about the nature of the problem being addressed. In this way, community issues are often redefined (Freire, 1973; Lewis, 1993). Empowering organizers and communities must constantly reflect on the question, "What have we learned from this last action"? Or, to paraphrase Kazdin (1982), "What works, for whom, under what conditions, and at what costs?"

Two examples illustrate how this principle operates. The involvement of women of color in the battered women's movement has been of concern to feminist shelter programs and organizing efforts for some time. When many feminist shelters observed that they were unsuccessful in reaching women of color, they defined the problem as that of inadequate outreach. When this outreach was unsuccessful, women of color in some localities provided feedback to many shelter programs that their approach was alienating and foreign to communities of color. They often identified the lack of women of color in administrative or permanent staff positions as one way the programs indicated a lack of commitment to their communities. It was through critical consciousness-raising about the the organization's own processes that feminist shelter organizers could then understand the outcomes. Programs that have been most successful with women of color have been those that addressed their own racism, classism, and ethnocentrism in the development of alternative models (Schechter, 1982).

The women of Four Corners, Louisiana, offer another glimpse into the importance of focusing on processes rather than simply outcomes. Lorna Bourg, an organizer with the Southern Mutual Help Association, developed a relationship with a self-help community development group within the town. The women in the group, who had not had prior training in economic development and housing development prior to the organizing effort, had learned these skills and helped to rebuild at least twenty-six houses in the community between 1989 and 1992. Then tragedy struck. In August 1992, Hurricane Andrew swept through the area, completely demolishing most of the work the women had done over three long years. The destruction could have been viewed as the end of their effort, and the community would have disintegrated. Instead, Bourg helped one woman remember the skills and knowledge she had developed in those three years simply by placing a hammer in her hand as she sat on the grounds of her destroyed home. Together they went house to house to other members of the self-help association and began the rebuilding effort with donations from regional churches. Moreover, the women of Four Corners committed themselves to organizing others in surrounding communities so that they could use the processes the group had developed to effect change in their own locales.

PARTICIPATION

Participating in the women's ethnic community is an important step for educating the organizer and building bridges for future work. This participation can result in an analysis of societal institutions, including the one represented by the organizer, and how they might ultimately benefit or hurt the community. Churches, community centers, schools, and social clubs can be avenues for reaching women of color and effecting change within the community. Reading and participation in community events can provide knowledge about specific communities of color (Kopasci and Faulkner, 1988). As the interviews quoted above indicate, working with women of color requires an understanding of their cultural context.

In an effort to become involved in the community, one organizer participated in activities sponsored by the local community center. She worked for
several months in enrichment programming for the community's children
before proceeding to work with women. During this time, she became aware
of community members' patterns of interaction, their relationships with
agencies in the city, and other potential issues in the community. Community
members and group participants had the opportunity to meet and talk with
the community worker and to watch her interact with their children. Many
of the initial participants later mentioned that their decision to participate in
the work was directly related to their approval of the facilitator's work with
their children and presence in the community (Lewis and Ford, 1990).

Effective organizing often begins with the formation of small groups. The
small group provides an ideal environment for exploring the social and political aspects of personal problems and for developing strategies for work
toward social change (Gutiérrez, 1990; Hyde, 1986; Pernell, 1985; Schechter,
Szymanski, and Cahill, 1985). It can also be a forum for identifying common
goals among diverse groups of women. Chapter 5 identifies ways in which
these issues can be effectively explored with women of color.

Organizing should begin with small groups of individuals brought
together to work on specific problems and later go on to coordinating these
small groups so that they can work in coalition with others on joint issues. On
the community level, the small group, or house meeting strategy, has been the
primary way in which women of color have been organizing movements to
improve conditions in ghettos and barrios (Hirsch, 1991; "Fighting Back,"
1988). For example, Clementine Barfield's work with sosad (Save Our Sons
and Daughters) in Detroit began with discussions in a small group of individual mothers who had experienced the loss of a child through violent death
in the inner city.

Building these alliances to develop community efforts can be particularly
challenging when more than one ethnic group or European-American-domi-
nated groups are involved. The United States is a highly segregated society in
which very little meaningful interaction takes place among people from different races, classes, ethnic groups, or sexual orientations. Effective organizing
requires breaking down societal boundaries to build alliances. To begin with,
we must recognize and embrace the conflict that characterizes cross-cultural
work. Conflicts will inevitably arise both within those organizations that have
been successful in reaching a diverse group and between the organization and
a larger community that may be threatened by the absence of expected
boundaries. In some respects, the emergence of conflict is an indication that

meaningful cross-cultural work is taking place. The sources and resolution of conflict will affect the outcomes of the organizing effort, however. The extent to which the organizer anticipates conflict related to group interaction, the effects of internalized oppression, strategies within the wider society to destroy the community change effort, and similar issues will often determine whether the efforts are successful (Ristock, 1990; West, 1990).

Some of this conflict arises from the discomfort many organizers feel when they find themselves the only person from a particular ethnic or class background in a group of women of color or when they attempt to participate for the first time in a community event that has previously been attended solely by members of the community. It is important for organizers to recognize that they will be tested by community members to determine whether they, like others who came before, are present only to take. The excerpts from Monica, Patrice, and Ella's interviews are examples of the testing process experienced by someone attempting to enter the community.

It is our experience that European-American organizers are often less comfortable than women of color with the conflict engendered by the development of multicultural organizations. Conflicts are a part of our everyday lives. They reflect choices about facts, values, and strategy alternatives that we face intra- or interpersonally (Lewis, 1989). Too often women have been socialized into avoiding conflicts. Such behavior only temporarily delays conflicts, however; they will resurface when issues are not addressed appropriately. Addressing a conflict has often been misconstrued as being synonymous with confrontation, another conflict resolution strategy. They are, however, quite different. Confrontation often means the minimization of or attack on a party with whom there is conflict rather than a dialogue about the nature of the conflict itself (Weingarten and Leas, 1989).

Addressing conflict directly means employing interpersonal skills such as engagement, active listening, and consensus building, as discussed in chapter 2. It means looking at the situation through various views or lenses and then reaching some consensus about how to work through it. The process of reaching this consensus will often mean being candid about differing conflict styles and managing to hear the content of the messages being presented rather than only the affect with which they are presented. This requires openness and a strengths or capacity-building perspective on the part of those who have only been privy to one way of handling conflicts in the past. In this way, conflict avoidance techniques may be valued for their ability to focus immediate attention on the conflict.

Conflict resolution that results in genuine dialogue and analysis on the basis of difference will have a direct effect on the outcome of an organizing effort. For example, only until they involved women of color in their organizations did many European-American women encounter a different view of gender constructions and how these translate into different strategies and goals. Once women of color were included in their organizations, work on sexual assault had to recognize and deal with the fears of many European-American women concerning men of color. In one organization, it was only when they as a group began a campaign confronting "The Myth of the Black Rapist" did women of color within the organization and in the community believe that the organization represented their needs.

Dealing with such conflict is difficult but valuable. Certainly, the inability to do so has resulted in the death of some organizations and has minimized our ability to work in coalition. If we are to work toward a more equitable society, this vision must be integral to the work of our organizations. This requires us to have the stability to know ourselves and be open to knowing others. Dealing with community backlash and conflict also requires taking risks in order to speak out in support of our vision.

CAPACITY BUILDING

Contemporary organizing by women of color has often taken a grassroots approach based on existing networks of family, friends, or informal and formal ethnic community institutions. In this way, individual, family, and community systems are viewed as compatible and integrated with one another. Many African-American women, Latinas, and other women of color describe themselves as motivated to engage in activism because of their commitment to their communities and ethnic group (Hill-Collins, 1990; Barrera, 1987; Gilkes, 1981, 1983; Lacayo, 1989). Women have also been active in mutual aid societies within ethnic communities such as the Hui among the Chinese, the Ko among the Japanese, and the tribal councils among Native Americans. These organizations have all served as vehicles for assisting individual ethnic group members, families, and entire communities by establishing business loans, subsidizing funerals, and setting up community groups. The establishment of the Menominee Restoration Project is but one example of a mutual aid society.

Organizers must recognize that women of color have been involved in advocating for women's rights since the beginning of the feminist movement. For example, many of the first shelters for battered women were founded by women of color responding to the needs in their communities (Schechter, 1982). Recognition of the contributions of women of color to feminist causes can help to break down some of the barriers and difficulties that exist in this work.

The project, however, may involve an even broader perspective than the one initially envisioned by the organizer as work with communities of color recognizes ways in which race, gender, sexual orientation, class, and ethnicity are often intertwined. This makes it impossible to separate the needs of women from those of their families and communities (Gutiérrez and Lewis, 1994; Neighbors and Jackson, 1996). For example, the role of women in the civil rights movements of the fifties and sixties indicates the importance of gender in mobilization efforts. The successful Montgomery, Alabama, bus boycott is usually credited to African-American male ministers who were in public leadership positions; however, the impetus for the boycott was a group of African-American women who persuaded the ministers that the cause was just and that they themselves would launch the boycott if the ministers would not take a public stance (Robnett, 1997). The women contributed to social action by raising the consciousness of the ministers in this way; however, they were willing to take work behind the scenes rather than spearheading the boycott themselves because they thought it was imperative that African-American men's leadership be supported (Robnett, 1997). This delicate interaction of race, ethnicity, class, sexual orientation, and gender must be in the forefront of the organizer's praxis perspective.

Too often organizing with women of color has taken the unidirectional outreach approach, in which communities of color are targets of change rather than active participants and collaborators. When this method is used, women of color often resist the organizing efforts or even undermine them (Schechter, 1982; Kopasci and Faulkner, 1988). It is crucial, therefore, to involve women of color in leadership roles from the outset, as in the case of the cofacilitator relationship of Monica and Ella. Predominately European-American organizations wishing to collaborate with women of color will need to include women of color as leaders and active participants before taking on this type of work. Such collaboration may require redefining the kind of work they do and their attitudes toward institutions such as the church and family: the history of attempts at collaboration suggests that those interested in cross-cultural work must identify how racism may exclude women of color from leadership roles (Burghardt, 1982; Schechter, 1982). Successful collaboration will require that European-American organizers change their interactions with women of color and be capable of sharing power and control of their programs with them, as illustrated by Ella and Monica's relationship. This type of organizational work embraces the tenet of feminist organizing that "diversity is strength."

Issues of perceived or actual class differences must also be taken into account, even when the organizer is from the same ethnic or gender background as the community in which he or she is working. As noted earlier in this chapter, the definition of community may be psychological as well as geographic. Those entering or reentering communities should be aware that their economic or educational backgrounds may be perceived as making them somehow different from other community members. Backlash may be experienced as a result. As in other conflict situations, a process of dialogue and action can be used to work through this problem. This can result in participation in the community on its own terms. Perhaps one of the highest compliments paid to one of the authors was in a community meeting in which she was introduced to others as "not an educated fool."

Some examples from Monica and Patrice's experiences as women of color organizers illustrate the potential for backlash in doing organizing work.

PATRICE: Yes, I do experience backlash! When I do something for a Black woman, I get static from White women, and vice versa. Either way I'll experience backlash. I can't please everyone.

MONICA: God yes, I experience a backlash! Some people say, "You don't live out here. How can you know what it's like?" It's hard to take care of yourself and not bring things home with you. I always think about what's going on. What keeps me going is the resources from the church, especially the inspiration from the women ministers. [It is important to note here that Monica was indeed a long-term resident of the community, who only relocated years after beginning work with the community organization.]

One method for building effective coalitions is the incorporation of informal debriefing groups for community workers. These groups should include all members of the community and provide opportunities for input and clarification of the organizing process. Those in key leadership positions should model their ongoing praxis experiences by being open about the choices made in the organizing effort and the assumptions on which these choices rested. Debriefing sessions should allow for community members who are not an integral part of the organizing effort to share additional strategies and to evaluate the impact of the design on the community. Some groups have used the house meeting strategy to provide debriefing opportunities, while others have relied on formal written materials such as community newsletters to keep community members informed. Consistent, ongoing debriefing efforts need to be built into the organizing design and expanded as needed.

Within the realm of organizing, there is room for multiethnic organizations, organizations developed by and for women of color, and cross-ethnic coalitions. Organizers need to understand and support the need women of color may have for their own separate programs and organizations. For women of color, a separate group or organization in which to explore who they are in relation to the communities in which they live can often provide the basis for creating a vision for future work (hooks, 1994; Boyd-Franklin, 1989). A separate organization is one means to build strengths within a community. In work with women of color in an educational setting, the formation of a women-of-color caucus had a positive impact on the ability of a women's studies program to hire more faculty of color and develop courses that were more racially and ethnically inclusive. Although the formation was initially viewed by some as divisive, all participants in the program ultimately recognized that the caucus was a critical element in empowering women of color and nurturing their capacity to work for positive change for all.

Conclusion

If we are to have a positive impact on the overall status of women of color in our society, community work will be necessary. Community work has the exciting potential for institutionalizing the changes we make on the individual or family levels. In the conceptual model guiding this book, community organization is seen not as separate from other types of work but as flowing from the empowerment process. In this chapter, we have identified critical skills and methods for engaging in community work and illustrated some of these with the experiences of three dynamic women of color organizers and one marvelous European-American organizer who demonstrate what is possible when empowered practitioners integrate education, capacity building, and participation.

EIGHT

◆

Endings: Evaluation and Termination

◆

Emily Sato is a twenty-two-year-old Nisei attending community college. She currently lives with her partner, Amanda Reyes, a Filipina, in a sunny apartment in a multicultural neighborhood. She and Amanda have been together three years, having met during their first semester in college.

Although Emily had felt attracted to other women for some time, it took her many years to explore her identity and begin to develop relationships. This development of her sense of lesbian identity has taken a toll on her relationship with her parents. When she came out to them during her senior year in high school, they reacted with shock, horrified by the shame they felt her life choice brought on them and the family. They told her that they did not want to hear anything more about it.

At the time, Emily was lucky enough to be involved in a program for gay, lesbian, bisexual, and transgendered youth. She had called the program a few weeks before approaching her parents to discuss her fears about her sexual orientation and get ideas about how to talk to her parents about it. The sponsoring organization invited her to visit their program.

Emily was very nervous when the time came for her first visit to the organization, but this anxiety was quickly transformed into excitement when she saw that the building where it was located was just a big house in an urban neighborhood. When she went inside, it felt like a home to her. The youths there greeted her and told her about their programs. She decided to attend a support group on exploration and coming-out issues. During that first visit she saw no one over the age of about twenty.

These experiences in a setting run for and by gay and lesbian youth helped Emily to develop the courage to talk with her parents. After her first conversation with them, she was able to go back to the group and discuss her feelings. The support and skill building she received there gave her the tools to continue the dialogue with her parents.

Five years later, Emily looks back on her experiences and credits the youth program as having made a big difference in her life. She has remained involved in the program, no longer as a consumer or recipient of services, but as a volunteer and active participant. Emily now serves as a peer counselor, participates in community education panels, and is on the program committee. She is particularly helpful to other young Asian-American women who are interested in exploring their sexual orientation.

Traditionally, the processes of evaluation and termination have focused on ways to assess the degree of change that has occurred during the helping relationship and to negotiate its ending. But Emily's story suggests that it is important that we look at these processes as collaborative and ongoing. Although the helping relationship may end, the client's development and change will continue. In many empowerment-based programs, this may involve them in different roles in the service program or in their lives in general. In order to prepare for this, social workers need to begin thinking about termination from the onset of change.

The challenge of any social work process is developing ways to maintain positive change. When empowerment practice is carried out on multiple levels, mechanisms for maintenance can be built into the intervention plan. For example, by encouraging the involvement of clients in self-help or support networks, we are helping them to create a support system for the maintenance of change. Similarly, if skill development is a critical part of social work, counselor and client together can develop a plan for maintaining and updating skills. Most importantly, if the social worker carries out the process by collaborating and sharing power with clients, clients will more readily recognize their role in the change process and their ability to maintain the level of power they have gained.

Evaluation methods should be built into the ongoing helping process. From the beginning of work together, practitioners should join with service consumers to determine effective strategies for intervention and timelines for termination. In this way, clients and consumers will develop the means to evaluate their own change processes and to monitor their direction.

In this chapter, we present a framework for developing methods for collaborative processes in termination and evaluation. It is important that all the dimensions of empowerment practice—education, participation, and capacity building—be incorporated into this phase as well. As is clear from Emily's example, these can be strategies for developing skills for lifelong living.

When Emily first began counseling at the center, she and her counselor, Marie, worked to set goals and objectives for their work together.

MARIE: Now that we have gotten to know each other better, let's spend a little while talking about what you would like to get out of counseling.

EMILY: Well, first of all I'd like to feel more comfortable with who I am. This is all so new to me. It's scary and exciting.

MARIE: Feeling more comfortable with who you are. How will you know when you are feeling more comfortable? What will that be like?

EMILY: I don't know. I'll be able to say that I'm a lesbian and not feel embarrassed. I won't care if people know or not.

MARIE: So that could be a goal. Being able to tell others and feel good about it.

EMILY: Yes . . . but maybe not even feeling good, maybe just not caring what other people think.

In this example, Marie is helping Emily to begin to see her goals in specific and observable ways. They are working together through dialogue to understand what she would like to get from their work and how they will know that they have accomplished their goals. This is a skill that Emily will be able to develop, internalize, and take into other settings. Through the participatory process of empowerment, Emily as client will be an active participant in measuring her progress and the process of change.

Empowering Methods for Evaluation

Evaluation of social work practice has often been viewed as an objective process divorced from the reality of practice. Recent work on evaluation, however, suggests ways in which it can be an organic method for improving and understanding our work. The model for evaluation we present here is client centered, educational, and participatory. A key consideration will be the client's perception of success and satisfaction in the process (Hernandez, Jorgensen, and Parsons, 1988). To that end, goals and methods for evaluation will take place within a participatory framework (Hernandez, Jorgensen, and Parsons, 1988; McMahon, 1990).

When evaluating the outcome of empowerment practice with women of color, the primary issues are whether the initial concerns of the client were addressed and whether the client became more powerful on the personal, interpersonal, or political levels. Some outcome measures for personal empowerment tap into the client's perception of her own power and ability to make choices. Measures of interpersonal power would include a look at the degree to which the client has gained the ability to influence others in socially acceptable ways. In assessing gains in political power, the counselor and client could look at how effective the social work relationship has been in increasing the involvement of the client in mutual aid groups, neighborhood groups, or political activities that could improve the status of women of color.

The evaluation of empowerment practice should take into account the facts (did the client gain in power?) and the feelings (how is the client experiencing change?) of the process (McMahon, 1990). The overall goal of evaluation in this context is to enhance the progress of work, so both formative and summative methods should be included. Formative methods provide information on the usefulness of the process and the degree to which it is being followed. Summative evaluation determines whether initial goals were met. At the end of a working relationship, an impact evaluation can establish the degree to which social conditions have been improved (Hernandez, Jorgensen, and Parsons, 1988). An overarching goal of integrating evaluation into practice is the development of skills to improve the system's ability to evaluate its own progress and use feedback from the environment to assess change. In this way, individuals, families, and communities can internalize the skill of engaging in change (McMahon, 1990).

The process of participatory evaluation should be empowering (Brown, 1994). By engaging together in the research process, both the client and practitioner will develop their knowledge of research methods and methods for change, as well as their abilities to make change (Brown, 1994). This method assumes that all people are capable of understanding and defining their particular worlds. Through collaborative dialogue, the evaluation of practice can enhance the capacity of all involved in the process (Brown, 1994).

◆

Through their dialogue together, Marie and Emily identified the goal of feeling more comfortable as a lesbian. The next step was to design some way to keep track of how well they were meeting these goals.

MARIE: Now that you have set this goal to feel more comfortable about being a lesbian, how will we evaluate whether you have met this goal?

EMILY: You know, it would mean not caring what other people think.

MARIE: Right. And it can be helpful to find a way to keep track of what is going on, so that we can know if you are feeling comfortable enough. At that point we might want to move on to working on different things.

EMILY: Oh, I see what you mean. Do you mean something like filling out a form or something? That would seem silly.

MARIE: Some folks like forms, but it sounds like they're not for you! We need something that would work for you. What might work for you and who you are?

EMILY: Well, I really love to write in my journal. Sometimes that is the only thing that keeps me going. I could write in my journal every day about how comfortable I feel. I could then bring it with me and share with you what has gone on each week.

MARIE: Sounds like a log could work for you. How would you feel about writing a brief summary each week of how you feel each day? Then we can discuss it each week and keep a copy here. After a few weeks we can review your logs and see how we're doing.

EMILY: Could be interesting. Let's just give it a try and see what happens.

---◆---

In this example, Marie is working with Emily to develop an evaluation method that works for her. Emily is an avid journal writer so an ongoing log might work for her. Another client might prefer a form in which she could rate her level of comfort on a preset scale. A different client might want to role-play different situations each week and then evaluate her level of comfort. Any number of methods could meet the goal of evaluating progress. What is critical is working with the client collaboratively to develop and implement the method.

Our discussion here has focused on methods for evaluation with individual clients. But evaluation is equally helpful with families, groups, communities, or organizations. Evaluation with families will often involve measures of family functioning. For example, if the goal is to improve parent-child communication, a mother could keep track on a daily basis of the number of times she has been able to sit down and discuss things with her child. She and the child could then self-evaluate at the end of each discussion their evaluation of the process (feelings) and outcome (facts) of their interaction. In other cases, eco-maps, which reflect family interaction, could be used to evaluate family processes. In Emily's example, as she began to discuss her family situation with

Marie, she kept a running log of how comfortable family members were with her sexuality. After three months of counseling, she was able to look at her log and see how far she and her family had come (see table 8.1).

Through this process of tracking family reactions to her sexuality, Emily learned that her circle of support was increasing. She could now bring her partner to many family activities. Although her mother was still unsupportive and distressed that her daughter would not follow the traditional path, all other members of the nuclear family were supportive. Through creating a genogram, Emily was also able to identify the members of her mother's family as being less supportive. In discussing this with Marie, she gained some insights into how her maternal family norms seemed less open to difference in

TABLE 8.1 Recording Reactions Over Time

Log of Family Reactions: January 1997	Log of Family Reactions: June 1997
People Who Are Positive About My Sexuality	
Cousin Jeff	Cousin Jeff
Sister Diane	Sister Diane
	Dad
	Aunt Yoko (Dad's sister)
	Uncle Sato
	Aunt Izumi
	Sister Jean
People Who are Negative About My Sexuality	
Mom	Mom
Dad	Uncle Jake
Aunt Yoko	
Uncle Jake	
People Who Don't Know About My Sexuality	
Sister Jean	Grandma
Grandma	Grandpa
Grandpa	
Uncle Sato	
Aunt Izumi	

general. This process helped Emily and Marie learn more about the dynamics of Emily's family and to focus their problem solving on ways in which she could work with experiences of nonsupport.

Evaluation of group intervention should also involve multiple methods and tools, such as software that, during a group session, could assess the number and intensity of interactions among group members (Dodd, 1994). During the past ten years, the Consortium for the Study of Empirical Contributions to Group Theory and Group Research has been formed. This group has identified new measures for analyzing group effectiveness that can be adapted for use in practice.

As in other kinds of practice, it is important to include multiple assessment periods to gain knowledge of the impact on the group and its individual members (Rose, 1989). Individual and group improvement are not identical outcomes, so both should be assessed. Measurements of individual change can include strategies such as the Network Utilization Analysis discussed in chapter 2. A weekly reporting method within the group setting can assess individuals' goals and objectives, while weekly round of pencil-and-paper evaluation of the benefits and drawbacks of the particular group session can obtain measurements of group change. Figure 8.1 illustrates a possible brief evaluation form that may be used to gain feedback on perceptions of group process.

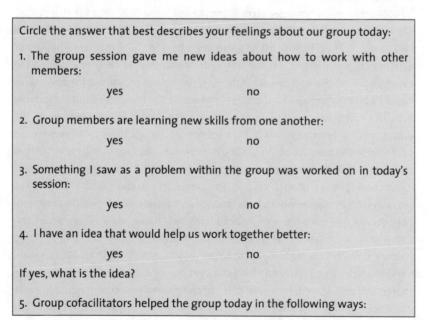

FIGURE 8.1 Sample Session Evaluation Form

Repeated assessments of individual and group outcomes can be planned by professional cofacilitators throughout the group duration. For long-term therapy groups, these assessment periods may be more numerous than in informational or self-help groups. The number of assessment periods may be discussed with group members or professional colleagues and modified if the sessions seem to be interfering with group process.

Involuntary group programs mandated by courts or social services can be particularly challenging.

In the fifth year of her involvement with the program, Emily participated as a coleader of a mandated group for young offenders convicted of hate crimes. This group was established as a partnership between the organization and the county attorney's office to provide an avenue for education and rehabilitation. While those participating in the group had chosen to attend rather than being incarcerated, most still harbored long-standing hatred of lesbians and gay men, Jews, and people of color.

Emily and Paul, a gay White male, met with the group for eight weeks in two-hour sessions. During the first three weeks, they showed films depicting the outcomes of hatred on the basis of difference, how this hatred had been reinforced by societal forces, and the legal consequences of these behaviors for all involved. These films were followed by discussion among the group members. For the next two weeks, Emily and Paul asked group members to share their own individual experiences with hatred on the basis of difference and then role-played the experiences. At the end of each role play, the coleaders used a fishbowl technique to identify group members' feelings about the situation depicted and the activities engaged in to discuss alternative behaviors to those exhibited by the group member reenacting his or her experience. The last three weeks were used to reinforce the practice of alternative behaviors in the face of trigger situations that group members might experience in the future.

At the beginning of each session, Paul and Emily used a "round" strategy to check in with group members. In the rounds at the end of each session, the members shared one new piece of information each had gained either about the group or him- or herself as a result of the preceding meeting. At first, group members' remarks were likely to be hostile or sarcastic: "I don't think I can learn anything from this group, and I want to get out of here." As experiences were shared and role-played, however, some of the ending-round comments became more neutral or positive, such as: "If Charlie can walk away from this type of situation without worrying about his manhood, then I guess I can, too."

The cofacilitators used two other forms of evaluation. First, Emily and Paul mapped the seating arrangements of group members throughout the eight weeks. At the beginning, all the group members were trying to sit as far away from the facilitators as possible; by the end of the group, all the participants but one were sitting nearer to both one another and the facilitators. The lone exception had refused to participate in group exercises voluntarily and had been isolated by the other group members, who had become more interested in the process. The eleven other group members continued to meet after the end of the formal group setting.

The second tool Emily and Paul used was a short paper-and-pencil test to ascertain both the degree of group cohesion and ways they could improve their cofacilitation (see figure 8.1). At the end of the mandated group, four members were interested in continuing their learning about discrimination on the basis of sexual orientation and doing their mandated hours of community service with an organization focused on the issue. Emily and Paul referred them to the local P-FLAG (Parents and Friends of Gays and Lesbians) chapter in their community.

◆

As with other kinds of practice, it is important to include multiple assessment periods in involuntary groups to gain knowledge of the impact of the group on individual and group processes and outcomes (Rose, 1992). Individual and group improvement are not identical outcomes, and Emily and Paul wanted to make certain that both were assessed. The paper-and-pencil and mapping activities monitored group cohesion throughout the eight weeks, while the weekly rounds helped to identify individual learning outcomes. The overall design of this group, based on the empowerment strategies of critical consciousness-raising, confidence through skill building (to foster alternative behaviors), and connection with others facing similar life circumstances could be used even with this involuntary population. Referrals to P-FLAG provided an avenue for this continued development. In addition, periodic follow-up assessments of program participants could be undertaken to determine whether the gains measured at program termination were maintained.

In cases where change is meant to occur at the organizational or community level, some measurement of change is warranted as well. This can be accomplished by simply gathering feedback from community residents, family members, or organizational representatives. For example, in Emily's program, members systematically collected information from workshop participants on what they had learned about the issues of gay, lesbian, bisexual, and transgendered youth. This process can provide immediate feedback as to how the workshops were successful and in ways in which they could be modified.

One afternoon, Emily and other participants from the program presented a panel at a local conference sponsored by the School of Social Work to educate mental health professionals on the experiences of youth in their community. After each panelist had spoken and there had been a question-and-answer period, the youth facilitators broke the workshop participants into small groups to answer the following questions:

1. What did you learn today about gay/lesbian/bisexual/transgendered youth?
2. How will you use this information in your work?
3. What else would you like to know about gay/lesbian/bisexual/transgendered youth?

After each group had discussed and completed the questions, they were invited to post their answers on pieces of newsprint that were placed around the room. One sheet of newsprint was designated for each question. After the responses were posted, group participants and panelists walked around and read them.

As a final part of the process, each question was discussed. The discussion involved a lively interchange about what people had learned and what more they wanted to know. From this process, participants were able to enhance their learning from each other, and the panelists were able to identify new topics for future workshops.

This brief discussion illustrates that methods of evaluation can vary widely. Selecting the best evaluation strategy for empowerment practice is dependent on first identifying the goal for evaluation. In tracking the progress of work with a specific client or family, individualized measures selected by the client are most appropriate. If the goal is to look at an entire program, then more elaborate procedures might be used. For example, if the director of the program for gay/lesbian/bisexual/transgendered youth was interested in looking at ways in which her program empowered youth, she could look at such things as youths' reports of their feelings, counselors' assessments, community perceptions, and the level of youth participation in running the program. To measure these different dimensions, both quantitative (e.g., survey data) and qualitative (e.g., focus-group discussion data) could be used. If youths and the community in general were involved in designing, developing, and implementing the evaluation process, the process of evaluation would contribute to empowerment as well.

The Termination Process

As discussed earlier in this chapter, termination refers to letting go of a particular helping process. The goal for all social work practice is for termination to signal the achievement of a capacity for ongoing functioning and growth (Miley, O'Melia, and DuBois, 1998). In empowering practice, effective work will result in continual growth and change in the individual, family, or community long after the work is done. In this respect, the empowering worker is simply a catalyst for lifelong change.

Termination should focus on ways of planning for ongoing change (Miley, O'Melia, and DuBois, 1998). A clear termination plan is important so that both the worker and client understand how professional helping can be phased out (McMahon, 1990). Such a plan can be developed whether the ending of the relationship is anticipated or not (Miley, O'Melia, and DuBois, 1998). It should be linked to evaluation: as goals are met and new ones set, it is important that long-range plans be kept in mind. Throughout the process, methods will focus on institutionalizing change and developing different ways to continue the process of consciousness, confidence, and connection. In some cases, this can involve referral to other organizations or support systems. And as in all other empowerment methods, termination plans are developed collaboratively with clients.

◆

When Emily first came to see Marie, her focus was on feeling comfortable as a lesbian. In their work together, much of their effort involved managing Emily's anxiety and identifying social supports for her sexual orientation. Each week, Emily remained involved in the counseling, bringing in her log and discussing her progress and pitfalls.

After six months of counseling, Emily described herself as more comfortable with her sexual orientation. Support groups, discussions, and reading helped her to understand that much of her discomfort was related to homophobia in the larger society. This new consciousness helped her to feel more comfortable with herself and led her to become more active in the program. She became particularly concerned about the experiences of other Asian-American lesbians.

Periodically, Marie would check in with Emily about their progress and need to continue. At each point, they were able to identify new goals and issues to work on. Initially, they had contracted for six months of work, so it was time to again talk about termination.

MARIE: It sounds as if your work with the support group has been important to you.

EMILY: If it hadn't been for the group—and you—I just don't know what I would have done. This should be here for everyone who needs it. But in the Asian-American community, we have almost no information about this.

MARIE: We were talking at the beginning of the session about whether to continue the one-on-one counseling. In looking over the logs, it's clear that you have accomplished a lot. What more could the counseling do for you?

EMILY: Well, I can always use the support. Someone to talk to. But I also feel kind of like moving on. At least for a while.

MARIE: We can start to plan for ending counseling. Let's say we meet another four times and focus on how to keep up the good changes you have made.

EMILY: Like staying with the group. I am thinking about being trained as a facilitator. And maybe joining the community education panels. I feel nervous talking to groups, but they really need more Asians—and lesbians—involved!

◆

With this dialogue, Marie and Emily began to make a termination plan. They set a time line (four more weeks) and tasks for maintaining and continuing change. Emily would continue with the drop-in support group indefinitely and perhaps train as a facilitator in the future. One of the termination tasks would involve finding out more about what facilitator training would require. Another task for termination would be exploring Emily's comfort in working in community education and perhaps conducting some stress management exercises around speaking in front of groups.

Certain activities can be helpful during the process of termination. As with all phases of empowerment practice, the feelings involved in the work are as important as the facts. The feelings of termination will involve recognizing and working with the powerful emotions that can arise (Germain and Gitterman, 1980; Miley, O'Melia, and DuBois, 1998; McMahon, 1990). Both clients and workers can experience feelings of excitement and exhilaration as well as anxiety and anger. These feelings—and their effect on the work—are part of the work of termination.

◆

Two weeks into their termination process, Emily began to have some second thoughts. There was a big family gathering coming up—her sister's wedding—and her mother had asked her not to bring her partner. Emily was not sure what to do.

EMILY: If I don't take her, then I'll be giving into *her* idea of who I am, but if I do, then am I showing disrespect for my family? I may not go at all!!!

MARIE: Sounds like a real no-win situation. How can we work on this?

EMILY: I don't know. That's why I need you! It's all coming at once: the wedding, and then I won't have you to talk with in two weeks. What if I fall apart?!

MARIE: Wow, some scary feelings. Let's work on those a while and then get back to the wedding.

At this point Marie needs to monitor her feelings as well. Perhaps the plans for ending are premature. Maybe Emily isn't ready to be on her own. If a crisis emerges during termination, it is important to assess it and determine how to proceed; a renegotiation of the termination contract might be appropriate. In this case, through their work together, Marie and Emily recognize how Emily has developed skills to recognize, express, and manage her intense feelings. On her own, Emily suggests a role play to try out different ways of talking with her family about the wedding. After trying out some different scenarios, she decides to discuss this with her more supportive family members before she makes a final decision. Through this process she recognizes that she is not all alone.

One element of the termination plan can involve reviewing the life cycle of the work (McMahon, 1990). An individual, family, group, or community organization can discuss and chart out their work together. One element of this process involves looking at the past and at what has been learned. This can be particularly important in recognizing ways in which individual's efforts have been effective (Germain and Gitterman, 1980). For example, parents in a parenting group were asked in the final session to write down what they felt they had gained from the group and what more they would like to learn in the future. They were then distributed a similar form that they had completed in the initial session. With a partner, each discussed the initial goals and how they related to what had been learned. These goals, and the process used to meet them, were then charted on newsprints posted on the wall. The exercise helped participants recognize the progress they had made and see how a variety of activities both in and outside of the group had contributed to positive change.

So-called futuring or visioning exercises, which involve imagining a desired state, can be used in termination to begin work on thinking about ways to sustain efforts.

In their community education programs, the gay/lesbian/bisexual/transgendered youths always ended with what they called a visioning exercise. The lights were turned off, and participants were led into a state of relaxation. They then were told to think about the following things:

1. Think about a world without heterosexism and homophobia. What would it look like?
2. See yourself in this world. How would you feel? Who would your friends be? What would your workplace be like?
3. How do we get to this world? How will you help us all get there?

After twenty minutes of visualization and thought, the lights were turned back on, and each participant discussed his or her visions with a partner. The observations were then shared with the group and summarized. From this exercise, participants developed ideas for ways in which they could continue the work and learning they had obtained from the panel.

◆

Visioning exercises can be helpful for maintaining an image of what clients want and what changes can involve. Such guided imagery can thus help them anticipate new challenges and consider how their new skills might help them meet these challenges on their own. The exercise does not minimize the challenges of the future but helps to make them more manageable. This cognitive rehearsal is a skill that clients can then draw on when facing new challenges.

Throughout the process of termination, it is important that clients see how the ending is also a beginning (Germain and Gitterman, 1980; Miley, O'Melia, and DuBois, 1998). While recognizing feelings about this particular ending—and endings in general—is important, it is crucial that the main focus be on future life paths. Rituals can be an important way to acknowledge the achievement of a transition point. All cultures recognize significant development through rituals such as weddings, bar mitzvahs, graduations, quinceñeras, and so on. Completing work through the empowerment process can involve similar ways of recognizing change. These should be worked out collaboratively with clients.

◆

Recognition rituals were an important part of the programming with gay/lesbian/bisexual/transgendered youth. For example, when each community education group finished its training, the ending was marked with a celebration in a local restaurant, when each member received a T-shirt designed by the group. Each group also put together a memory book, copies of which were distributed to all members.

In individual counseling, each counselor and client worked together to decide how to mark the transition from counseling. Emily and Marie began discussing this as part of the termination plan.

MARIE: I was wondering if we might want to develop a way to recognize the work we have done together.

EMILY: Well, I feel as if this counseling has helped me so much with coming out. That's been the biggest thing for me. I feel like a new woman!

MARIE: How can we mark the ending of this phase and the beginning of the next one?

EMILY: How about my logs? We've been keeping a set here. What if we get them bound or put them in a nice notebook? Then I can have them on my bookshelf to read over when I am down. I'll be able to see that *anything* is possible!

MARIE: Sounds as if that would mean a lot for you. Let's work together on designing a cover, and I can have them bound here. At our last session, you can take them home with you.

By turning the logs into a document of Emily's change process and binding them, Emily and Marie created a way to recognize the work they had done. Though the gesture was simple, it symbolized the way in which Emily had become a new woman. Other rituals can involve creating art, exchanging photographs, or printing up certificates. Certain ethnic or nationality groups may develop rituals that are culturally significant and involve specific songs, art, foods, or customs.

In this chapter we have reviewed ways in which the processes of evaluating and ending practice can be conducted from an empowerment perspective. As with all practice, we are most successful when clients can move on to more effective living. An empowerment approach puts additional emphasis on ways in which increases in power can lead to change on different levels. Emily, for example, moved among individual, group, and community-level changes, and even when her individual sessions ended, she continued to gain support from the group and engage in community-level change. In evaluating and ending our work with all clients, we need to consider ways in which multidimensional change can be built into the termination process.

PART II

Understanding Women of Color

NINE

The Sharing of Power: Empowerment with Native American Women

Christine T. Lowery (Laguna-Hopi)

It is the circle, and all that it represents, that feeds the spirit of Native America and defines the power of the people. Despite the diversity evident in Indian country—representing only 1 percent of the U.S. population but over five hundred tribes and over two hundred languages—our individual and collective power emanates from our place on the earth and is fortified within our people, our community, our tribe. Power from a Native American perspective draws on environmental and spiritual forces that shape our being. Empowerment with Native American women emanates from the spirit of the individual and expands the circle, for the strength of a people is determined by how well they share their power.

This chapter discusses three examples of empowerment with Native American people by Native American women. Each example is framed within a specific area of service: a reservation empowerment project, an urban Indian library, and an urban domestic violence project. To provide a context within which to view contemporary Indian life, however, the first section outlines a historical, sociopolitical perspective of Native American life in this country.

A Sociohistory

Native Americans are often included in descriptions of the so-called powerless populations. This depiction reframes the Native American existence.

The Native American is not powerless. The powers that she/he carries are simply not valued in the dominant society. These powers are the fuel of the spirit. When they are not allowed to burn, the spirit is snuffed out. Assimilationist policies and genocidal practices have eroded the sense of power for many of us. Meaning and power, under these circumstances, are hard to recognize.

To understand the present, one must have some understanding of the past. The impact of colonization continues to be a direct assault on the environmental/spiritual power, health, and sustenance of Native Americans in contemporary battles over water, fish, game, forest, minerals, and land. And in the process of forced relocation, many Native Americans were removed from the power-centered place of the tribe or group.

The acquisition of wealth and domination was a goal in the conquest and colonization of the peoples of the New World. McNickle (1973) outlines the realities of the time and "the surge for strategies of colonial exploitation and profit." Competition for raw materials "allowed no latitude for concessions to humane principles. Any political power that was not prepared to override scruples where native people were concerned might find itself out of the race for preeminence in the market" (p. 46).

Aristotle's doctrine of natural slavery outlined a life of servitude for "one part of mankind" as being set aside by nature to "masters born for a life of virtue, free of manual labor" (Hanke, 1959, p. 13). This doctrine was followed in the conquest of peoples, and slavery became the first European policy introduced in the New World (Hanke, 1959). Forced labor of indigenous peoples worked the gold and silver mines of South America (Hanke, 1959), the colonial system of Columbus's island discoveries (Sanderlin, 1971), and the fields of the Catholic priests in the Southwest (Kessel, 1987; Hanke, 1959).

The displacement of peoples from their homelands in the name of progress was racially motivated. From 1815 to 1850 the Native American was rejected by White society, as the United States shaped policies that "reflected a belief in the racial inferiority and expendability of Indians, Mexicans, and other inferior races" and a world dominated by a "superior American Anglo-Saxon race" (Horseman, 1981, p. 190). By 1850 U.S. expansionism meant the extinction of races that lacked the ability to transform their ways of life (Horseman, 1981). The stress of survival in the face of this violence imposed by the White man in his goal first to eliminate an entire people and later to mold them into the likeness of himself has cost indigenous peoples greatly. The role of Native American women has not remained untouched.

THE PLACE OF WOMEN

Before contact with White men, Indian women had a strong place in tradi-
tional Native American cultures and in the survival of their groups. Women
"have always formed the backbone of indigenous nations on this continent"
(Jaimes, 1992, p. 311). The cosmology of Native America sings with the power
of the female: Mother Earth, Spider Woman (Hopi and Dine), White Buffalo
Calf Woman (Lakota), Sky Woman (Seneca), Thought Woman (Laguna),
Corn Woman (Cherokee), Changing Woman (Dine), First Woman
(Abanaki), Hard Beings Woman (Hopi) (Gunn Allen, 1986; Jaimes, 1992).

Women's ability to give birth ties Indian women to the spiritual realm and
designates woman's special power. Her power is not limited to childbearing
but includes political power and, in some tribes, power as a warrior. After contact with the White man, imposed Christianity and federal policies reconstructed the egalitarian nature of Native American life to conform to European patriarchal models. Such policies resulted in the loss of the female role
in governance and the ritual and political relationships between Native American men and women (Gunn Allen, 1986). For example, the early selection of
males only as representatives of reconstructed tribal governments displaced
not only traditional leaders but females who may have had long-standing
sociopolitical power, as among the Iroquois and Cherokees (Jaimes, 1992).

When Indian women were studied by anthropologists and historians of
women, their findings maintained the stereotype of the Indian woman originally shaped by the views and interpretations of White men (Powers, 1986).
For example, they interpreted some tribes' isolation of women during menses
to mean that menstruating women were considered somehow unclean. The
real reason was the belief that women's power was enhanced during menses
and might interfere with powers for hunting or medicine ceremonies. Isolation of women at this time protected these other powers (Gunn Allen, 1986).

In the late 1960s and 1970s, about the same time Indian women were being
involuntarily surgically sterilized by the Indian Health Service (Jaimes, 1992),
another distortion was being manufactured: the political redefinition of the
"Indian problem." The early twentieth century saw machinations of colonial
policy such as the General Allotment Act of 1887, the Indian Citizenship Act
of 1924, and the Indian Reorganization Act of 1934. These policies established
control of Indian land, Indian resources, and Indian lives (Jaimes, 1992). No
longer seen as barriers to settling the frontier, Native Americans ceased to be
the problem; now they *had* the problem: alcoholism.

Alcoholism, among other social problems, is a function of genocide and oppression by the dominant society. Since the early 1960s, however, alcoholism has been blamed as the active culprit in the breakdown of traditional ways, a breakdown directly attributable to White man's diseases, policies, domination, and greed. Ironically, Native American tribal leaders, as well as health professionals, have perpetuated this scapegoating, as if alcoholism were the cause and not a symptom. The alcoholism issue has driven the policy of Indian health care. Dr. Everett R. Rhoades, former director of the Indian Health Service (IHS), reported that changes in personal and community behavior, rather than intensified medical services could decrease or eliminate much of the existing burden of prevalent illnesses, including alcoholism, among Native Americans (Rhoades et al., 1980). This assessment ignores the sociopolitical realities in which many Indian people live.

The Native American woman faces powerful elements in her environment that maintain a heightened psychological vulnerability and contribute to social problems. These may include racism, marginal economic existence, high unemployment, intergenerational alcoholism in her family and her community, and the consequent losses as a result of accident, suicide, and cirrhosis (Westermeyer, 1977; Peluso and Peluso, 1988). Her community is fractured by historical federal legislation and current state policies, conflicting political groups, and outside religious groups whose goals have been conversion and the historical suppression of indigenous religious practices. Her community is dominated by bureaucratic agencies, including the Indian Health Service and the Bureau of Indian Affairs. Tribal governance, established by the Indian Reorganization Act of 1934 and based on imposed patriarchal models (Jaimes, 1992; Gunn Allen, 1986), struggles to compete in a non-Indian, violent, knowledge-and-wealth-based business arena (Toffler, 1990). The Indian woman faces the never-ending, legally sanctioned oppression by non-Indians for resources on Indian lands (Churchill and LaDuke, 1992). Finally, she endures the appropriation of Indian tradition and spirituality by White shamanism: a subset of a much broader assumption within the matrix of contemporary Eurocentric domination holding that non-Indians always and inherently know more about Indians than do Indians themselves (Rose, 1992, p. 406).

In her autobiography, Mary Crow Dog (Crow Dog and Erdoes, 1990) describes the supposed place of Indian women in her chapter "Drinking and Fighting":

> If you are an Indian woman, especially in the ghetto, you have to fight all the time against brutalization and sexual advances. . . . Many of these brawls

are connected with drinking, but many occur just because you are an Indian. . . . I have often thought that given an extreme situation, I'd have it in me to kill, if that was the only way. I think if one gets into an "either me or you" situation, that feeling is instinctive. The average white person seldom gets into such a corner, but that corner is where the Indian lives, whether he wants to or not.   *(p. 51).*

Native American Empowerment

Empowerment among Native Americans differs from the feminist empowerment model. First, power, from a Native American perspective, is the ability to contribute rather than the ability to get what one needs. Power is also the ability to understand how others think, feel, act, or believe, not the ability to influence these. And, finally, power is the ability to bring and share resources into a family, a community, an organization, or society instead of the ability to influence the distribution of resources in a social system. Thus personal power is evaluated by how well it serves the group.

To work with Native Americans, the social worker must recognize what powers each person carries. These are not necessarily esoteric or spiritual characteristics. They can, however, be extensive in their contribution: for example, the power to cook and make people feel good through the preparation and sharing of food; the power to make people laugh with a constant and creative wit; the power to set broken bones and find the source of sprains; the power to feel and understand and speak consensus; the power to pray, to entreat the spirits of the other world on behalf of the humans in this world.

So how does this influence social change? Social change exerts power at another level and moves the tribe/nation/urban center into the larger societal context. Here we may use the contribution that the feminist model makes. The power of the group in the political sphere becomes the ability to get what the organization/tribe needs, the ability to influence the resource holders on behalf of the group, and the ability to influence the distribution of resources on its behalf.

The strengths of Indian people in facing adversity are woven into the stories that follow. Each of these stories comes from a Native American woman who, as part of her empowerment, recognizes her obligation to share that power. A second theme is the democratic characteristic of the work of each woman. For how can we be separate from our people?

Native American Empowerment Project

Emily Salois is a Blackfeet woman working in Missoula, Montana. After almost a lifetime on her reservation in Browning, she returned to school and completed a bachelor's degree at the University of Montana. She then successfully negotiated a transition to Seattle and completed a master's degree in social work. Emily has since returned to work with her tribe and the seven Indian reservations in Montana. At a time when many workers are retiring, she is beginning her social work career. An elder of fifty-five, she sees her age as an asset in her work.

Emily has been a natural helper for many years; she knows Indian leaders and "grassroots people." She understands the politics of the reservations, the historic rivalries among tribes, and the history of the state's attitudes toward its tribes. She was there in the 1950s and 1960s, when Indian children were being transported out of the state "by the trainload" for placement and adoption. This policy had a direct effect on Emily and her community. As Emily describes it:

> As part of the education process, I took quite a few classes in Native American studies and never really realized the impact that policies had on me as an individual and on my family and those people I had grown up with. For example, I was raised by grandparents and as a young child—I think about six years of age—went to a boarding school. I just always thought that was something I had to do, until I had grandkids. [One morning] I picked up one of my little grandkids that was six years of age, took him out of bed, and was holding him in my arms. He didn't want to get up, but he had to because I was going to work. I began to cry because I thought, "This was how old I was, when I had to leave home and go to a boarding school."

The impact of this oppression is stamped on Emily's current work, and her self-knowledge is put to use. The goal of the part-time work she does with the Native American Empowerment Project—funded by the USDA's Extension Services—is to reach high-risk youth. Early in the project, Emily identified the need for healing and connected this to her community.

> If it's looked at from a parenting perspective . . . empowerment would [include] becoming the kind of parent I would like to be. I think anybody who is a parent would like to be an adequate parent, a parent who provides not only a child's basic needs, but . . . provides love and nurturing. But it's really hard to give something you don't have.

You asked why I identified a need for healing. I was visiting with other people who were raising grandkids, like I am, and talking about how difficult it is to raise teenagers. One of the guys [suggested] that it's probably more difficult for us as Native people to parent teenagers, because we don't have role models. It was like somebody threw a dipper of cold water in my face!

I'm a third-generation boarding-school person. I spent my teen years in boarding school. So, consequently, I tried to parent my kids like a [boarding school] matron parented me. As long as their basic needs were met and everything was clean, I thought these kids should just be really thrilled! What else could they want? So, if we are like that [even] with the education and training that we have, why wouldn't other people be affected the same way?

The recognition of the need of healing for herself and others who experienced the same type of oppression—boarding schools, removal from their tribe—was key to Emily's ability to structure the intervention strengthening families and communities. The method Emily uses is a small-group, community-training process focusing on parents and facilitated by trained community members. The goal of the empowerment project is to initiate parent-training groups on each of the seven reservations in Montana. The parenting groups are guided by a curriculum developed by "reservation people" at Fort Belknap and recently revised by Emily and two Fort Belknap women. The "Parenting: A Native American Perspective" curriculum incorporates a contemporary piece on child development; however, behavior management is minimal. There are chapters on traditions and culture that guide participants as they look at the history of their tribe and the oppression they have endured as a people in an effort to understand themselves.

Group processes significant for Native Americans are demonstrated: the incorporation of a spiritual component and emphasis on cooperation; the issues of confidentiality in a community where everyone knows one another; and, of course, the use of humor and acceptance to make these sessions safe enough for disclosure and healing, the primary emphasis. At some point, elders are invited to talk about parenting, usually during the first hour of one session. This validates the contributions of the elders in the community and provides those parents who have no elders in the family "with someone to learn from." The elders are asked to leave before the second hour, which is reserved for group discussion. "Parents were reluctant to share at a real gut level, because they didn't want these elders to know what they were doing and what they've done—out of respect," explained Emily. It is good to ask for advice from elders but not necessary to burden them with things for which shame is felt. There are other ways to work through shame with understanding, and the "training" provides one such opportunity.

The empowering transfer of information and experience exemplifies the role of the elder in Native American society. Emily uses her role as teacher in the empowerment of others. "Although I see direct services as really important," she explained, "I think that by doing training and teaching and community organizing, I can reach larger numbers of people. It was a luxury for me to go to school, so I want to be able to pass that along."

There is respectful groundwork in the preparation of the training. The tribal councils for each reservation are advised of the empowerment project and their sanction is sought. Work with extension agents—primary resources in rural areas—and site coordinators on each reservation helps to develop advisory committees for the project on each reservation. The advisory committee selects the people who will be trained as facilitators for the groups. "What we do is a lot of collaborative effort, so that this will go on after the five-year grant period is up," explains Emily. "The goal is community ownership. Another thing is that the other trainers are not young people. We speak in a language that everybody can understand [jargon is prohibited], and we really pay attention to the process of the training."

Because their children spend a large part of their day in school, parents are informed about recent laws concerning special services for their children and parents' rights to access these services. "In so many instances these parents don't feel like they have a right, let alone a responsibility, to be a part of their children's education," Emily observed. Instruction focuses on good communication skills, body language, tone of voice, and self-esteem to "bring [parents] to a place [where they can] realize that . . . their children may feel the same way they did in the school system. For the love of their children, they usually have been really willing to begin to work on those feelings." They identify their strengths and take the steps toward accomplishing these tasks.

The empowerment project has produced latent and direct outcomes. Extension agents, two of whom are Native American, report increased contact with people who have participated; the agents are eager to provide their services in agricultural advising. Non-Indians and human service workers have taken these classes and become more aware of cultural and historical issues. Some who have completed the training are returning to see how they can help with the next training session. One family has used the empowerment project as a springboard for sobriety. The children of parents who attended training groups have increased their school attendance. Attendance at the training helped one father from the Crow reservation regain custody of his children.

Almost an equal number of men and women attend the groups, and it is heartening to see these young fathers [in their thirties] willing to risk being vulnerable. The empowerment they feel through the parenting groups lets them know that they have something to contribute, and it isn't necessary to have money, or education, or even a title, to do it.

THE MINNEAPOLIS INDIAN WOMEN'S RESOURCE CENTER LIBRARY

The sharing of power is a cultural concept for American Indian women and has no professional boundaries. It is not just the domain of social work or education or nursing and so is not limited to social workers, teachers, or nurses. The sharing of power is a state of mind and emanates from a heart that understands (1) the significance of being a human being and (2) the power that comes from knowing how to treat another human being. Anyone in the community can contribute their power, their strengths, and their knowledge. One of these community members is Shelley McIntire, an Ojibwa, a one-woman show.

Since 1988 Shelley's space in the moderate-sized library at the women's center has been reduced to maneuvering room only, its space tumbling with books about Native Americans and file cabinets heavy with data and copies of single articles not collected elsewhere. Shelley is the librarian at the Minneapolis Indian Women's Center. "It's both worse and more wonderful," she says as she simultaneously comments on both her current project and the space in the library.

The current project has her enthralled. In an effort to present a complete picture of the Native Americans in Minnesota, Shelley is gathering "tons of data that other organizations around here should be doing, but no one [else] is." She is pulling together statistics on housing, health, poverty, chemical dependency, pregnancy rates, and so on. "Conditions got much worse for Native Americans living in Minneapolis in the last ten years: poverty levels increased 40 percent, income dropped $300 per capita, to $5,600. Minneapolis is the worse place in the whole United States to be an Indian," Shelley continues. The statistics stand stark in comparison because "Minnesota is such a well-to-do, middle-class kind of state." For example, 17 percent of Indian households have no telephone, compared to 1 percent of White households; over half of Indian households have no vehicle, compared to 19 percent of Whites; 42 percent of Native Americans pay 30 percent or more of their income for housing. "I'm looking for a title for this, and I've come up with 'read this and cry, then get to work' or 'still suffering in our own homeland,' " she says with a serious laugh. She moves on to her view of empowerment:

When I first heard about this term "empowerment" I ran over to this white women's organization and bought their book on it. I work in an Indian women's organization and recognized something familiar about what their book was saying and that had always been there. . . . Without romanticizing it, it is there. What we connect empowerment with is things that have already been going on for fifty thousand years. It's already built in: the respect of women's right to congregate and discuss and organize among themselves. This does not deny internalized oppression. But what appears to be a social scenario will actually involve sorting out community values, problem solving, making one's mind up about something and deciding to take action or not take action, all in the company of others.

The threads of empowerment are woven into the fabric of a healthy society, one unhampered by "boarding schools, forced starvation, horrid poverty." Critical to empowerment is democracy. "For example, on the surface, our tribal council governments are arranged in a hierarchy. But if you look at how things operate in our communities, everyone is on an equal level. Even the people everyone hates in the community will come in and have their say and people will listen with respect, even if they are getting yelled at."

She moves on to the significance of her work, the result of purging years of persecution as an Indian female in the educational systems of a dominant society. "Book learning is a tool, and we have a right to use it. In Ojibwa culture, extreme democracy is reflected in an access to information. Nobody should be denied this. Consider this, if we lived three hundred miles north of here, we could be denied the opportunity to work with birch bark because only experts can do this. Think of the logic of that! We must have access to tools, information, the ability to think freely; we [Indian people] carry these kinds of urges."

Shelley flips through her log of requests for information, starting in July. She gives information to a social work intern wanting information on case management with Indians, a county social worker wanting information on Native American battered women, some commercial firm wanting information on the Indian legend of the snow man. "I told him that according to Ojibwas, we weren't suppose to build snowmen, because they might be evil spirits!" Shelley exclaims. A student in a university class has read that Indians don't experience eating disorders. Shelley stops this misinformation and sends statistics from Indian youth studies indicating that young Indian males and females are at risk for eating disorders. Someone from Sweden wants a list of all the tribes in the country. Shelley provides education by explaining that there are "tribes of cultural entities and tribes of political entities" and refers the Swede to anthropological resources for cultural lists and to the Bureau of Indian Affairs for the names and addresses of tribal governments. A chemical dependency counselor is seeking information about five different drugs an Indian client in recovery has been prescribed; this knowledge will inform advocacy strategies for this client. A publishing company wants film footage for a CD-ROM chapter on Indian politics. Shelley recommends a computer network where "real Indians" are talking. A major complaint about so-called Indian networks, she explains, is the takeover by White shamanists.

BIA EASTERN AREA

One of the visible elements of change in the Bureau of Indian Affairs (BIA) is the appearance of Native American women both in the ranks and in leadership positions. For example, Ada Deer, a Menominee from Wisconsin, now serves as the assistant secretary of the bureau. The next story, however, focuses on the leadership, influence, and activities of Evelyn Roanhorse, a Navajo woman, and her role with Native American tribes in the eastern part of the country.

Evelyn is the lone social worker in the BIA Eastern Area office (Virginia) where she responds to twenty-seven federally recognized tribes in twelve eastern states, from Maine to Florida, South Carolina to Texas, and to Indian child welfare requests in a twenty-five-state area (five Department of Health and Human Services regions). She has no assistant, no secretary. Instead, the money that would be used for their salaries is funneled into quarterly, one-hour conference calls. The calls provide a forum for the twenty-seven tribes to create an agenda for their training meetings. These quarterly meetings are hosted by different tribes on their reservations. Alternating between north and south, the meetings allow geographic distances to be bridged and relationships to be developed among widely scattered tribes. Lawyers from the Native American Rights Fund (NARF), regional state people, and local people have presented topics ranging from program development to legal issues: child protection, alcoholism, tribal courts, development of children's court codes, tribal-state agreements, criminal background checks, and more.

The Bureau and IHS have formed a strong working partnership in this area. Memoranda of agreement on alcohol and substance abuse, child abuse, and domestic violence outline their complementary roles. Conference call costs (about $700 each) are alternately shared by both governmental entities.

A volunteer tribal committee serves as a third partner. The committee monitors the progress of the written plans for the eastern area and makes suggestions; for example, using jail time to educate Native Americans about substance abuse, child abuse, or domestic violence in structured small-group sessions.

Several positive strategies are working in the Eastern Area. BIA and IHS recognize the competence of the tribe: "[Tribes] run a better program than the BIA can," acknowledges Evelyn. Tribal input is valued, and tribal expertise is exercised in training. Training is based on practice experience and the perceived needs of the tribes and covers a variety of related problem areas, such as substance abuse and domestic violence. Most importantly, the quarterly calls and conferences provide a viable and consistent method of obtaining this information. There is an atmosphere of shared responsibility: the tribes take responsibility for organizing the conferences, and BIA/IHS share responsibility for costs. The democratic theme is evident. "We're open about problems, we listen to everybody, and we respect everybody," says Evelyn.

This chapter has explored the individual approaches of three Native American women: their personal styles, their communities, their attitudes and beliefs, and the activities involved in their work. Empowerment must work in both individual and community spheres, with awareness of how each influences the other. Crucial to empowerment is an individual's identification as a contributor within the community; respect for the people, their strengths, and their contributions to their community; the prudent use of social work tools; and the recognition of how one's own value is complemented by others in that community.

The history of the community is crucial to the way one works within a community setting. Emily's common history with other Native Americans in her state, the shared pain, and the need for healing in her community (Montana Indian reservations) is one example. Shelley's documentation of her community in Minneapolis lays the groundwork for others. Facilitating resources for her regional community provides Evelyn with fuel for her endeavors.

A democratic frame of mind is required: recognition of the wisdom and value not only of the visible people in the community but of all its members. Emily Salois demonstrates democracy and respect in the preparation of the community for the parenting groups in Montana, just as Evelyn Roanhorse recognizes respect for the tribal contribution as the Eastern Area training agenda's lifeblood. Shelley McIntire explains democracy within a cultural context.

In the 1970s I was struck by the crabs-in-the-bucket metaphor.[*] If you turn this metaphor inside out and look at the crabs in the bucket in a positive way, you'll recognize that it is democracy in a basic kind of Indian sense. Why should my cousin make two million dollars, when I can't buy shoes for my children? That's Indian values! This kept us in good shape for centuries before European contact. It ties into Ojibwa values: we are here to help each other . . . to give moral support, to give love, and if possible, to give material support to each other.

Understanding context is required. The individual, especially the Native American woman worker, is a part of the community. Evelyn Roanhorse has identified her community not as one but as one of many Indian people scattered over a wide distance and connected by a common sense of service. Emily marvels at the sense of community between the Crow and the Blackfeet, traditional enemies, and their work in the parenting groups. As she receives electronic mail, Shelley McIntire stands on the brink of creating a new community.

As Indian women within our community, our sense of place is defined, and our spirits are fed. Without our community, we experience spiritual ennui, and we become undernourished. Those entering Indian communities must see their role as one of contribution not domination, as being one of many with power, not the only bearer of knowledge.

The circle of empowerment is the interplay of the spirit of the land (our sense of power and place), the spirit of the people (our community)—including those who have gone before us and those coming after—and, finally, the responsibility and obligation to share our power with our community as it exists now. What we must remember is that we carry the seeds of empowerment right here, in our spirits.

[*] An Indian and a White man were walking on the shore, each carrying a bucket of crabs. The White man's crabs kept climbing out of the bucket, but the Indian's did not. The White man queried the Indian about this. "Oh, these are Indian crabs. Every time one starts heading for the top, the others reach up and pull him back!"

TEN

Staying on the Path: Lessons About Health and Resistance from Women of the African Diaspora in the United States

Edith Lewis

> Resistance is the secret of joy!
> —*Alice Walker*

In many social work textbooks, health and mental health are treated as independent constructs. No one can convincingly determine, however, where mental health begins and health ends or vice versa. If health and mental health can only be measured along an imprecise continuum against an imprecise external standard, then who is to create that standard? For too many years, it has been created by people who have divorced their very core selves from the process in order to appear whole. Forcing people to work eight continuous hours, including afternoons, when evidence has shown us that the body needs a rest period in the afternoon in order to function maximally (other industrialized nations have figured this out and incorporate strategies like the midafternoon siesta) is but one example of this divorcing of self from the natural rhythms of life. Other examples include delivering babies in horizontal rather than more natural vertical positions, subjecting White skins to the summer sun to become darker in spite of the severe health risks associated with doing so, and building dwellings over flood plains when the potential for the waters to seek their former natural courses is high. Yet all these activities are considered normal in this modern age.

This perspective is quite distinct among Western industrialized people and has been termed a "mastery-over-nature" ideology (Spiegel, 1982; R. Lewis, 1993). A mastery-over-nature perspective recognizes that power exists in the universe and can be harnessed to do the will of human beings, who are the most important life forms on the existing planet. To be sure, a mastery-over-nature perspective has guided people to the expansion of medical services, the exploration of other parts of the universe, and the construction of the concept of the global village, supported by sophisticated communications devices and technology. Yet the mastery-over-nature perspective also has a flip side, even for each of the great achievements just identified. Our ability to create medications and procedures that will allow children and adults to live longer has resulted in a great flurry of medical ethics discussions on who should be treated with the new technology and who should be made to pay for it, a debate that is leaking into public policy formulation (Fuchs, 1983; Gilder, 1981). The other side of exploration of the universe is that the amount of money invested in this exploration may be displaced from other programmatic efforts that could have a more direct and lasting influence on the current and future populations of the planet. And another side of our vast communications linkages is that we have exported to other countries the idea that to live prosperously is to live with the "basic necessities" of air conditioning (when the amount of power needed to do so would annihilate global resources), multiple-vehicle transportation (when the overdependence on oil has made slaves of industrialized nations), and excessive consumption of durable goods (simply for the sake of a lifestyle in imitation of that depicted on the television show *Lifestyles of the Rich and Famous*) (Mason, 1998).

The mastery-over-nature perspective exists in the field of mental health as well. There is a strong dedication to curing or conquering whatever interferes with the individual or family's ability to function in the wider society. Power is viewed as a finite resource available to those entitled to it by exhibiting societally accepted norms of behavior. Other patterns of behavior, even those that might be considered quite life enhancing (such as delivering babies in the vertical rather than horizontal position), are considered odd or indeed punished by societal institutions. Mattis (1995) argues that the very attempts by the social sciences to adopt concepts about health from the physical sciences lead those using contemporary mental health constructs such as homeostasis and equilibrium to misunderstand other forms of mental health not based on a mastery-over-nature worldview. This chapter will provide some examples of these.

Seldom do we as a nation consciously explore the double-sidedness of the mastery-over-nature perspective, although it is becoming increasingly difficult not to do so. In fact, many of us do not even recognize that a mirror image even exists, we have been so socialized to believe that a mastery-over-nature perspective is responsible for civilization.

So how do those who have adopted other perspectives explain their place in the universe? What are the implications of these other perspectives for the health and mental health of women of color? Are there lessons to be learned about empowerment as a form of resistance to a health-detracting way of life?

This chapter examines the ways in which one group of individuals in the population of this universe has developed an empowering perspective on their own health issues. "Women of the African diaspora" has been chosen as the operant term herein—rather than "African-American women"—in order to pay homage to the women who have roots in Africa but also in the East or West rather than the Americas. I also include in this definition those who live in the United States but claim their African homeland of origin as their primary home, as well as those Black women from the Caribbean and South and Central America. For some of us, the gap between those of our ancestors born in Africa and succeeding generations born elsewhere is vast. For others of us, it is simply a generation. We speak many different languages, have many different customs, have different rates of life expectancy, mother and infant mortality, educational achievement and access to Western forms of privilege (Mattis, 1995; Ceballo, 1995). Yet, in some ways there are connections among us that recognize our ability to be bicultural or even multicultural people, that is, people who can live in several cultures simultaneously, finding ways to identify via our daily work lives, romantic relationships, or children and parents the flip side of the culture we find ourselves temporarily planted in.

In this chapter, the lessons from those linkages will be portrayed as they have been discussed by women from the African diaspora and other writers so that they might serve as examples to other women and reminders to us. Even those of us who work in mental health careers need such reminders in order to avoid the danger becoming divorced from our true selves. I was reminded of this in 1994 as a woman of the African diaspora making my first trip to Costa Rica. As I prepared to disembark from the airplane, a man made his way through the line until he was standing behind me, tapped me on the shoulder, and said, "Are you from Limón?" I gave him a puzzled look—I had not done enough homework on the country to know where and what Limón was—and then he smiled. Apparently, his wife was from Limón, a city on the western side of the country where many African peoples had settled after slavery in Central and South America was abolished. He then said, "You must go to Limón while you are here. You will find yourself at home there." He was quite right.

This chapter is divided into four sections. The first provides some basic demographic and social information about the women discussed, while the second, third, and fourth connect the lessons of an empowerment framework to the experiences of these women. The chapter concludes with some recommendations for integrating an empowerment perspective into healing work with women from the African diaspora in the United States.

Some Background on the Women of the African Diaspora

To suggest that the history of women of the African diaspora began with the slave trade discounts a rich and quite diverse set of prior experiences. Yet many records of African peoples in the West begin only in the 1600s, with the forced importation of people as though they were animals, to fill the labor needs of the European colonialists. Feminist women of color griots and writers paid homage to the oral histories they had heard of the experiences of African peoples in this hemisphere (Bambara, 1970; Giddings, 1984; Smith, 1983; Giovanni, 1994; hooks, 1994). The oral tradition may be the only major source of documentation of the experience of women from the African diaspora. These oral traditions have been handed down from generation to generation and entrusted to those who will take the responsibility of conveying the story of a people seriously.

One of those people is my Aunt Arthurlee. She inherited the task of serving as the family's oral historian at the time of my mother's death more than twenty years ago. Even before that, however, she could tell the stories of several generations of Donaldsons and Stephens, and she dutifully made certain that her nieces and nephews heard those stories. Out of respect for her role in the family, she has been honored with the secrets of successive generations of the family and has held them close to her heart. With these secrets, she helps to heal the new generations by sharing the stories of how family members overcame trials and interactions through the years. As she ages, she shares the stories with two women members of the next generation, entrusting them with the secrets with an expectation that they will continue to be used to foster health among the family members.

Other methods have been developed to contain the history and herstory of peoples from the African diaspora. Today, demographers and others rely heavily on survey research projects, such as the U.S. Census, to provide information about people. Yet these forms of information are criticized for their lack of precision and their inability to collect data about people who do not have access to permanent homes, telephones, or mainstream employment. Sadly, people from the African diaspora fall disproportionately into these categories, and thus information collected through these channels must be used cautiously.

Standardized national data collection methods also fail to identify the diversity within the African diaspora in the United States. The term "Black" may include people from the Caribbean, Africa, or Europe. In recent decades, the term has also come to include those from Puerto Rico or Cuba who may or may not have listed themselves as both Black and Hispanic, to use the Census Bureau's categories.

As many forms of data as possible must be collected when attempting to understand the paths particular women or groups of women have taken to reach their present lives. Using only one method may lead to incomplete information (for example, the accuracy of the oral tradition depends on the willingness of individuals to learn data and to transmit it *completely* to others). Using only survey research methods yields instruments that may be understood by researchers but may not accurately reflect the reality of the respondents (Lewis 1993a, 1993b). With that caveat, we will discuss some of the demographic data available on women from the African diaspora.

STORIES FROM THE SURVEY DATA

According to the 1990 census, individuals identifying themselves with the designation "Black (not of Hispanic origin)" constituted 13 percent of the United States population (U.S. Bureau of the Census, 1992). This population, found in all areas of the United States, made up 11 percent of the total northeastern population, 9.6 percent of the total in the Midwest, 19 percent of those living in the South, and 5.4 percent of those living in the West. Women from the diaspora accounted for 53 percent of the total diasporan population. This discrepancy between the number of Black men and Black women has been consistent for several decades and is particularly evident among men and women between twenty-one and forty-five years of age, when women outnumber men significantly (Lewis, 1988).

While the totals are not consistent from summary data file to summary data file in the census and much of the available data is not disaggregated by sex, some broad themes can be determined. People from the African diaspora ranked third of six racial groups in per capita income in 1989 (U.S. Bureau of the Census, 1992), with an average figure of $8,859. This is due, in part, to the number of dual-earner families in the population. Much has been made of income parity between White and Black Americans in the latter half of the twentieth century; however, there are very few places in the country where this parity is realized, and even there it is restricted to certain occupations such as the arts, teaching, and the helping professions (Jansson, 1997).

Census data were disaggregated and sorted by sex with regard to poverty and employment statuses at the time of this writing. These data are represented in table 10.1.

Those listed as "not in the labor force" in table 10.1 include children under the age of eighteen, and those listed as "unemployed" may include the disgruntled workers who have tired of unfruitful job searches. As holds true for most ethnic and racial groups, the percentage of men's salaries is higher than women's, and the percentage of women in poverty is higher than that of men.

Thirty-seven percent of the total diasporan population over age twenty-five responding to the U.S. census had not completed high school. Twenty-eight percent of this group had completed high school, 19 percent had attended college without receiving a degree, 5 percent held associates degrees, 8 percent had completed bachelor's degrees, and 4 percent had earned graduate or professional degrees. Women, particularly women with children, are more likely to be living in poverty, and these rates have been steadily climbing in the past thirty years (Gutiérrez and Lewis, 1994; Crosbie-Burnett and Lewis, 1993b). This means that large numbers of the children in these families are poor, and an alarm about their life chances has been raised by numerous scholars and researchers (Danziger, 1995; Ceballo, 1995).

TABLE 10.1 Selected Income and Employment Characteristics by Sex from the U.S. Census

	Men	Percentage	Women	Percentage
Living above poverty line (per 100,000)	10,534	71.5	10,537	63.5
Living below poverty line (per 100,000)	4,197	28.4	6,044	36.4
In labor force (employed)	5,657,112	57.8	6,068,997	52.3
In labor force (unemployed)	855,024	8.7	832,354	7.2
Not in labor force	3,276,516	33.4	4,696,340	40.4

With all these reports of the dire constraints faced by women from the African diaspora, why would any rational human being want to learn lessons of healing and reintegration from them? Perhaps a look at some of their other experiences would be helpful here to fill out the picture.

OTHER STORIES OF THE AFRICAN DIASPORA IN THE UNITED STATES

Nikki Giovanni, in her poem "Nikki Rosa," cites the arrival of researchers to her neighborhood to study poverty among the residents. While listing the supposed drawbacks living in the neighborhood entailed, according to the residents, Giovanni (1996) ends her poem "all the while, I was quite happy" (p. 42).

While poverty is not a joyous affair, and racism and discrimination, combined with sexism and classism, have made life quite difficult for women from the African diaspora, an increasing body of scholarship is now tracing the strengths of these women historically and contemporarily and registering their ability to forge ahead even when faced with the types of obstacles illuminated by the demographic data above. Giddings (1984), Macht and Quam (1986), and others have traced the emergence of mutual support and aid networks developed by women from the African diaspora to meet the needs of their communities. In chapter 7, we discussed the Black women's clubs of the 1880s and their impact on drawing attention to issues of child care, care for the aging, lynchings and other violent acts against Africans from the diaspora, and the like. Moreover, a rich tradition of settlement houses built by and for members of the African diaspora at the beginning of this century served individuals and families excluded from the White movement as a result of legal segregation. Such is the rich foundation of social work practice among people of African descent.

Forms of resistance to the extensive segregation and discrimination experienced by people from the African diaspora have remained constant, and the role of women here has been stellar. It should be noted that the instances of women splitting off from men from the diaspora to form their own organizations are rare and more recent. The choice of the women has been to work together with men to foster change, a reality with which the Western feminist movement still has difficulty (Lorde, 1984; hooks, 1994). But viewing racism and sexism as equal acts of violence against people makes a great deal of sense to women of the African diaspora, who may daily experience both. Documentation of the role of women as central, although behind-the-scenes actors in the civil rights movements of the 1950s and 1960s (Robnett, 1997), is grounded in the oral histories from this period. Forms of women's resistance are also visible in the literary tradition of diasporan writers, including Zora Neal Hurston, Alice Walker, bell hooks, Angela Davis, Audre Lorde, Bebe Moore Campbell, and the Nobel Laureate Toni Morrison (Mattis, 1995; Randle, 1994). These acts of resistance may be overt, such as the stories of African women killing their children during the middle passage rather than submitting them to the ravages of slavery, cooks placing ground glass in plantation owners' food, or using spells to right some wrong. The acts may also be covert, as in the coming together of women in prayer to change the heart of a wrongdoer or the positive self-statements of faith in oneself and one's people made in the face of a world that daily denigrates them.

Recognizing these overt and covert acts of resistance helps us to understand that the women of the African diaspora are not passive victims of the social, political, and historical circumstances they are born in. Instead, social work practice has a long and rich herstory in the mutual aid and support networks and public and private institutions of Black communities across the United States. Social workers who would be part of the Black empowerment movements in the United States would do well to seek out the wisdom of the community's griots and hear their stories of support, mutual aid, and resistance. These are chronicles of forces that have contributed to the health of a diverse and adaptive people. Other forces, however, have worked against the maintenance of holistic health for women from the African diaspora, and I will examine them in the next section.

Forces That Contribute to the Lack of Health Among Women from the African Diaspora

Sadly, the literature on women from the African diaspora also abounds with information on how difficult it is to live our lives as whole people. This ability to find the negatives in our lives evokes the admonitions of Andrew Billingsley (1968), who once wrote that if one wanted to find material on the then-called Negro, one simply had to look up topics such as crime, poverty, and teenage pregnancy. When he was writing, it was much more difficult to find literature listing the strengths of Black families. Even now, it is more common to find scholarship that takes a deficit perspective on women from the African diaspora rather than a strengths perspective. This structuralized negativity in focus contributes to a lack of knowledge about the strengths of these women. Three major factors contribute to the life-destructive experiences of women from the African diaspora: institutionalized racism, the interactions among race, gender, and class for women of African descent, and the wider society's superwoman image of the population. Williams (1990) and Pinderhughes (1989) poignantly discuss the first factor. The experiences of people from the African diaspora in the United States have not been those of full citizenship and personhood. From the origins of the U.S. Constitution, which listed Black *men* (ignoring Black women) as three-fifths human, this has not been the case. Discrimination was more overt and sanctioned within the wider society in past decades, but even today the helping profession literature abounds with examples of how biased assessment, treatment, and diagnoses can be when practitioners are aware of clients' racial backgrounds (Thompson and Jenal, 1994; Lewis, 1993a, 1993b).

The legacy of having been considered not even three-fifths of a person in the eyes of the constitution governing the land they live in has taken a toll on women of the African diaspora. Contemporary arguments against affirmative action ignore the lasting effects of this legacy in economics, employment, and education. While stating that affirmative action provides preferential treatment for women and men of color and White women, the data ignores the reality that at least 90 percent of those in decision-making capacities, regardless of type of job, are White men. Comas-Díaz and Greene (1994) discuss the ongoing psychic pain that can result from institutionalized patterns of discrimination based on race. They document the ways in which professional women of color are often called on to teach all their White coworkers about people of color or to answer stoically the questions about things everyone always wanted to know but were afraid to ask.

To that experience must be added the institutionalized patterns of discrimination based on sex, sexual orientation, and/or class. These create at least a double-whammy for those experiencing them, because this is an interactive model, not an additive one. There is no hierarchy of oppressions, and for those struggling with the multiplicative and interactive experiences of multiple forms of discrimination, no hierarchy need be established (Lorde, 1983). While individually any form of discrimination is life- and health-detracting, a combination of them can, in Gitterman's words, be "life-derailing" (personal communication, 1995).

For example, diasporan women had difficulty fighting for the civil rights of all African peoples in this country during the 1950s and 1960s because of the lack of support for gender equity and the end of sexism within their own communities. Women involved with White feminist organizations may also feel torn between loyalties to their communities of origin and those of White feminist organizations that may not understand their particular histories/herstories and the reasons for their involvement in coalition building (Reagon, 1983; Yamada, 1983; Andersen and Hill-Collins, 1995).

Women of the African diaspora are extremely good at caretaking, often at the expense of their own health (Boyd-Franklin, 1987; Pyant and Yanico, 1991). Within the family, the myth of the Black superwoman has loaded a great deal of responsibility on women from the African diaspora (hooks, 1981, 1994). We are held responsible for diasporan men's economic and social conditions, for the number of children living with the economic support of only one parent (remember the disparity between the numbers of men and women, particularly those of childbearing and childrearing ages), and for our inability to meet our chronic life stressors without complaint. These factors contribute to the poor mental health of women from the African diaspora.

Yet all these factors also provide opportunities for empowering practice to build on the existing strengths of these women. The maintenance and support of acts of resistance are the foundation of the physical, mental, emotional, and spiritual health of women from the African diaspora. An empowerment framework in practice encourages these women to celebrate their struggles and triumphs, gives credence to their formal and informal networks, and provides a basis for the healing of others. Some illustrations of the lessons learned from the women of the African diaspora follow.

Some Teachings from the Women of the African Diaspora for Those Who Would Do Empowering Practice

LESSON I: CRITICAL CONSCIOUSNESS-RAISING EXISTS IN THE HERSTORIES AND TRADITIONS OF THE WOMEN

This chapter has already outlined some of the forms of resistance used by women from the African diaspora to offset the chronic stressors of life in the United States. Among these were the use of the oral tradition to pass on the stories of triumph so that children know their heritages in ways that might be unavailable to them in written documentation. The oral tradition, in this instance, serves as a form of critical consciousness-raising for the population.

Dr. Mildred Pratt, a professor from the Department of Sociology, Anthropology, and Social Work at Illinois State University in Normal, Illinois, has been using her oral history project to inform younger members of the Normal, Illinois, and Bloomington, Indiana, communities of social, political, and historical storms navigated by earlier Black residents. For almost fifteen years, she has met with the older men and women in the community and collected their stories, preserving them in written form. These stories may now be used in rites of passage ceremonies for adolescents (discussed in more detail later in this chapter), foster grandparent programs, and women's support groups.

Another strategy for influencing the development of critical consciousness is the honoring and reading of both verbal and nonverbal signals from the environment. Social work students are introduced to these strategies when they learn about interpersonal styles of communication; however, many women and men from the diaspora have had to learn these strategies at much earlier points in their lives. They must know, for example, that calling people by their nicknames without their prior permission is inappropriate. For example, I have chosen to be called by the nickname Edie but know of few other women from the diaspora who have made a similar choice. Edith was a common name among women from the African diaspora who were born before 1955, including Edith Sampson, the first woman to graduate from Loyola University Law School and one of the first women of African descent to serve as a judge. Nonetheless, the several Ediths I know are constantly having to correct people about their true names and how they wish to be addressed. They note, for instance, that it is a short distance from mislabeling a person by applying an unchosen nickname to other mislabels that are more denigrating—such as "gal" or "Auntie"—and connote closeness when none exists.

Other examples of the nonverbal development of critical consciousness are the silent marches and candlelight vigils held by diasporan women to draw attention to the escalating violence in some of their neighborhoods. Ida Barnett-Wells's antilynching campaigns extensively utilized this method of drawing attention to the slaughter of men from the African diaspora. These acts offset the internalization of racism and sexism (as well as classism) that can face women of the diaspora, and they have served as examples for other women around the world as well.

Prayer, meditation, and other forms of calling on the universal life force for assistance or presence in the face of seemingly insurmountable problems can be considered yet another form of critical consciousness-raising. Recognizing one's membership as one of the children of God or part of the universal spirit, particularly in concert with others, can serve as a mechanism for more thoroughly examining the painful elements and experiences faced by women of the diaspora. It is no wonder that many movements for the rights of women have started in spiritual gatherings: meditation, reading, church, prayer, or renewal groups.

The empowering practitioner's use of lesson 1. Those incorporating an empowerment framework into their practice with women from the African diaspora will be cognizant of the various ways critical consciousness can be fostered. They will actively seek to listen to the wealth of knowledge present in the oral tradition through stories, songs, poems, and plays and to benefit from the insights these can provide into the messages that have been handed down from one generation to the next. They will support the growth of such data collection and knowledge development through the use of oral histories, whether audio- or videotaped or transcribed. Use of the oral tradition will be particularly useful for those women whose educational attainment or writing ability may preclude their use of more paper-and-pencil-driven methods.

As the stories are told, empowering practitioners will help women link them to the realities of their contemporary lives. What problems are they currently facing that were faced before by women like them? What heroines might they have or develop as a result of making these types of linkages? To what extent are their family compositions like those of others who have overcome similar obstacles? Who might they call on for help?

Several groups in the southeastern Michigan area, including the Detroit Urban League and Ann Arbor's Community Action Network, have championed rites of passage programs for young women (or men) of African descent. The programs, based on their counterparts in traditional African communities and countries, are geared to twelve- to fifteen-year-olds and usually run several weeks. During this time, the young women are exposed to herstories of African and Black women who have made a difference in their communities and are provided with opportunities to address some of the challenges they face as young women, including maintaining health, thriving in the face of racism and sexism, and developing self-loving identities. At the end of these programs, a formal rite of passage ceremony is held, attended by parents, peers, and friends, and culminating in the welcoming of the new young adult woman into her community.

Social work practice should also become more receptive to an ecological perspective in understanding family diversity. What might happen if, in addition to the use of genograms in the intake process, empowering social workers actually asked consumers during intake to tell stories linking their current situations to those of their own heroines? Currently, practitioners commonly use the question, "What would your world be like if suddenly a miracle happened and everything now troubling you was all right?" Another set of questions to be used by empowering practitioners who incorporate linked critical consciousness exercises in their engagement process could be, "What would your heroine have done about this situation? What other examples do you have of others who have faced what you have faced? What have they done about it? Who or what did they need to accomplish their goals? What did they do when (not if) they were opposed?"

Another method of raising critical consciousness, as I already noted, is for the practitioner to understand and appreciate the spiritual life of these women and incorporate that appreciation into practice. We are aware, for example, that meditation can help people lower their blood pressure, that the use of relaxation techniques similar to the quiet centering of some religions can be very calming. The use of prayer as a method of "turning it over" may help reduce unuseful ruminations about certain situations. Some empowering practitioners regularly employ a period of centering for both themselves and those with whom they work at the beginning and end of each session. This may allow all parties to focus on the present situation rather than other possible distractions. Empowered social workers will not hesitate to link women of the African diaspora with spiritual activities in their home communities, such as women's day programs at local churches or informal support or self-help groups. As discussed in chapter 3, attention to the spiritual life of the practitioner will also be a focal point of empowering practice.

LESSON 2: CONFIDENCE DEVELOPMENT THROUGH SKILL BUILDING

Formal opportunities to learn and practice new skills have long been a part of African traditions. The goal of these activities, whether battles of the choirs from numerous churches or the Saturday Freedom Schools of the 1970s, is to increase the participants' confidence through teaching new skills. These same formal and informal opportunities operate today within and across numerous families from the African diaspora. While these may vary by economic class (as in the annual debutante balls put on by several African-American social clubs, or the summer day camps and breakfast programs for low-income children), they all serve the function of preparing others to take on tasks deemed necessary by the host community. Sometimes these tasks may not be immediately open to a person (as in the case of Mae Jemison, the first woman from the African diaspora to become a NASA astronaut), but skill building will help the person prepare for opportunities that may eventually present themselves.

Their traditional roles as caretakers, cited in an earlier section of this chapter as one of the factors that may limit the health of women from the African diaspora, may also serve to build skills, if used properly. While people often expect women from the diaspora to be the healers in their families and communities, and this burden can be overwhelming, the process of healing can be shared with others so that many have responsibility for the skill. In order to achieve this, women have to tell their healing stories to a wider audience, as in the case of Sojourner Truth's brilliant "Ain't I a Woman?" speech before an audience of White suffragists. In other instances, women will have to be open about the healing arts available to them, be they words, or herbal remedies, or knowledge about the human body and spirit. Increasingly, younger women from the diaspora are seeking the counsel of older women from their communities so that they can keep alive the knowledge embedded in African traditions (Greene, 1994a). Luisa Teish, Iylana Vanzant, and bell hooks have all produced texts for regular use by women of the African diaspora, some in the form of daily meditations, some as lessons of healing, and some as rituals to enhance growth.

The empowering practitioner's use of lesson 2. This type of confidence development through skill building is difficult even for empowering practitioners, because often the skills being developed are new to the practitioner as well. While many of us have been trained in mastery over nature, few of us have had the rich backgrounds to allow us to work comfortably in concert with nature. Although there may always be a desire to step in and guide the process away from discussions of more natural forms of healing and informal methods of skill development, we must guard against these if we are to use effectively the experiences of those with whom we are working. Hooks (1990a) has called this "choosing the margin as a space of radical openness" (p. 145). Even some of the seemingly most nonsensical acts or stories often contain the grains of wisdom. Learning to give speeches at every gathering of their social clubs has helped prepare people for public speaking before large groups. The battles of the choirs alluded to above have also helped people establish a public presence. Learning how to still oneself and provide an open heart and hand to others in pain can be used in numerous situations, with oneself as well as with others. In other words, while those with whom we practice are engaged in skill building, we as empowering practitioners are doing the same. Those lessons we learn and skills we build in individual sessions may be passed on to others, and this in turn allows us to be part of a larger healing movement. We need to be careful, however, to make certain that we understand the lessons that we have received. Mis-understandings of the nuances of language and our own positions as women trained in nonholistic forms of practice may result in our misuse of the lessons with which we have been entrusted (Latting, 1993).

As empowering practitioners, therefore, we must continually be engaged, even those of us who are women of color, in self-examination and analysis of the congruence and discongruence of our lives and those with whom we work. Are we asking people to build skills that will enhance their interactions with the wider society at the expense of their health in their home communities? Are we able to believe sincerely that the use of a mantra meditation with a deep muscle relaxation can enhance the process of anxiety management (Cormier and Cormier, 1998)? Can we learn something in each session from those with whom we work and then communicate that new piece of learning to the consumer as well as our colleagues? Skill building is a two-way venture for empowering prac-titioners, who must become colearners rather than simply teachers. Indeed, to guard against relying solely on the teaching role in developing a viable working environment for empowering practice, a third set of lessons is required.

LESSON 3: FORMS OF CONNECTION

Women from the African diaspora are recognized worldwide for their skill at developing forms of connections among themselves and others (Reagon, 1983; hooks, 1993). Nagel (1994) notes the propensity among peoples of the African diaspora to build individual ethnic identities through group involvement. For the women of concern in this chapter, this is accomplished in intimate set-tings, family settings, within both their own home communities of origin and the wider society.

Within the family, the observance of occasions such as elders' birthdays, the birth of new children, and the deaths of loved ones are often celebrated in group settings. Birthdays, funerals, and other rituals serve to foster the con-nection among family members, and those who cannot be part of these cele-brations often suffer deep pain. Lesbian or bisexual women whose sexual ori-entation is not openly known to family members, for example, may often feel unable to participate fully in family events because part of their identity can-not be shared with other family members. After an elder family member dies, relatives accustomed to celebrating that person's birthday may find themselves in distress when the next birthday arrives.

Naming ceremonies, weddings or commitment ceremonies, and other similar events are ways that families share their intimate relationships with members of their home communities. In traditional West African cultures, the birth of a child is a community celebration (known as an "outdooring" in Ghana, for example), as the entire community takes responsibility for the child. Most people of the African diaspora living in the United States are descendants of West African communities (Greene, 1994c) and have continued these traditions in this country. While the church has served as one focal point for the public mechanisms of connection, community centers, private homes filled with neighbors and friends, and other types of gatherings also serve to foster connection among people. Further, while the intent of these occasions is to provide a public witness to a particular issue, the connections developed also become useful organizing tools, as was discussed in chapter 7. For example, many of the social justice movements developed by people from the African diaspora were begun in churches or local community gathering places.

Other methods for connection among peoples of the African diaspora include using printed materials such as books, magazines, and electronic mail groups to maintain relationships. The use of other media sources, including television and radio programs, has also been on the increase during the last two decades, particularly since the advent of cable television local access stations and the Black Entertainment Television network. These more expansive forms of connection allow information about situations to pass much more quickly within and between communities.

Many nonmembers of these African diasporan communities are unaware of the range and depth of forms of formal connection within this population. For example, in seeking to provide health information regarding lupus, which strikes many women of African descent, the Bay Area chapter of the Lupus Foundation of America (based in Rockville, Maryland) developed a special pamphlet on the effects of the disease on women of color and brought public attention to it in an issue of *HealthQuest* magazine geared specifically toward articles about Black wellness (Womack, 1994). While many in the wider society have celebrated the strength of *Ms.* magazine, few are aware that *Essence*, a magazine for women from the African diaspora, has been published since 1971.

The empowering practitioner's use of lesson 3. The empowering practitioner should seek to gain a true appreciation for the vastness of connection among people of the African diaspora. Like the husband whose wife was from Limón, empowering practitioners can further such connection in the practice setting by recognizing and legitimating the interfamilial, intrafamilial, and community mechanisms that maintain it. Entire new networks do not have to be developed for women of the African diaspora. They may simply need to move from those that have been life distressing to those that are more life enhancing. Becoming familiar with the various resources available to women from the diaspora is a critical part of empowering practice.

How can empowering practitioners accomplish this? First, they can periodically review the numerous journals, magazines, and pamphlets created by and for women of the African diaspora. They can now also cruise the Internet and find numerous on-line magazines and discussion groups on topics of interest to Black women. Further, linking women with ongoing rituals such as the annual Kwanzaa celebrations closest to their homes will help strengthen their connection to the Black women's community.

Conclusion

This chapter has addressed some of the opportunities for doing empowering practice with a group of women who have already helped to create and maintain many of its elements. For every challenge to engaging in empowering practice with this population, there are many more opportunities. Table 10.2 outlines some of these.

The road to health is a constantly evolving process. These illustrations of health, strength, courage, and resistance will be useful to those who wish to become more empowering practitioners, as well as those of us who are attempting truly to live with joy as members of the African diaspora.

TABLE 10.2 Empowering Practice with Women from the African Diaspora

Challenges to health for women of the African diaspora	Opportunities for empowering practice based on strengths	Role of the empowering practitioner
Institutionalized racism	Critical consciousness-raising	Facilitating storytelling and information sharing
Interactions among race/class/gender/sexual orientation	Confidence expansion through skill building	Providing opportunities for practice of new skills
Superwoman expectations	Connection with others to share the responsibilities	Awareness of linkages for women

ELEVEN

Empowerment with Latinas

Lorraine Gutiérrez and Zulema Suarez

◆

Yolanda is a young woman of Mexican descent living in Texas. Her family has been living in the Rio Grande valley as long as anyone can remember. For generations, her family has engaged in migrant labor work, traveling from Texas north to Michigan to follow the crops.

For the past four years, Yolanda has worked as a camp health aide (CHA) with the Midwest Migrant Health Council. Camp health aides are members of the community trained to provide simple medical care and health education to other members of the migrant community. Yolanda became a CHA because she enjoys helping people and saw the job as a way to further her education. In her work as a CHA, she has advised her fellow workers and neighbors on nutrition, prenatal care, AIDS, and the importance of regular checkups. As part of her training, she has learned basic information about health, nutrition, and counseling methods.

When she first began working as a CHA, Yolanda enjoyed the one-on-one work and the ability to help other migrant workers. As the years have gone by, however, she has used her experience to become more active in her community. Before becoming a CHA, Yolanda often saw situations in the camps that bothered her, but she rarely spoke up. Now, she will speak out in the workplace when things bother her. For example, last year she learned that migrant children would not be allowed to attend schools in one of the host communities. Many of the other workers were upset, but they did not complain. It was Yolanda who pulled together the migrant community to confront the local school board and make sure their children received a proper education.

Yolanda is one of many examples of Latinas who have gained the power to work to improve their communities. In Yolanda's case, her involvement with the CHA program provided her with the means to increase her personal, interpersonal, and political power. In other cases, empowerment work with Latinas will involve only one of these levels. Whatever the case, effective work with Latinas places empowerment at the center.

Yolanda is one type of Latina: a Mexican American or Chicana. However, under the umbrella term "Latina" we include all women whose lineage originates in Latin America. We reject the term "Hispanic" because its entire focus is on Spain and the European roots of our people. It does not recognize the multicultural roots of Latin America or the ways in which the interactions of Latinos and Latinas in the United States have characterized our experience (Hayes-Bautista and Chapa, 1987). The term Latina also emphasizes our multiracial background. For example, most Mexican Americans, such as Yolanda, are mestizos: a combination of Native American and European backgrounds. In some parts of Latin America, such as Puerto Rico, the most common mixture is African and European. By emphasizing our Latin American roots, we recognize that we are a a very distinct type of American.

We begin by discussing some of the characteristics of Latinas in the United States: new immigrants and descendants of some of the original inhabitants of this continent, aliens and U.S. citizens, English and Spanish speakers, people of national origin or another, and those who identify closely with their ethnic heritage and those who do not. By using the single term "Latina," we do not mean to diminish or ignore the very important ways in which we differ. Still, increasing contacts between different Latino and Latina subgroups have led to perceptions of similarity, and we recognize that political efforts may be more effective through coalition. Moreover, others perceive cultural and phenotypic similarities among Latino subgroups, so a blanket term makes sense on that level. Finally, the U.S. government has attempted to move beyond purely racial categorizations of the population (Hayes-Bautista and Chapa, 1987; Padilla, 1985; Portes and Truelove, 1987), and "Latina" is a step toward that goal.

Sociohistory and Demographics

What do we, as Latinas, have in common? As a group, we are more likely to live in poverty than non-Latino Whites. An analysis of census and other governmental statistics reveals that Latinas lag behind all other groups in terms of median years of education and participation in higher education. Our median income is only slightly higher than that of African Americans. We are concentrated in the secondary labor market, and our rate of poverty is more than double the national average (Garcia and Montgomery, 1991; Moore and Pachon, 1985).

A single pattern does not characterize Latina migration to the United States (Bean and Tienda, 1987). The pull to migrate and the circumstances of migration vary among the different Latino groups. Most of the research on immigration has focused on men; recent work has found that Latinas may seek to migrate for different reasons. For example, experiences with family violence or gender exploitation may cause Latinas to seek employment in the United States (Arguelles and Rivero, 1993).

Mexican Americans make up 63 percent of the Latino population (Garcia and Montgomery, 1991). The original population of Mexican Americans did not enter the United States voluntarily but were conquered during the Mexican War. Mexican Americans have experienced over a century of domination, oppression, and exploitation by Anglo society. In the Southwest, this domination has taken the form of school segregation, housing discrimination, political gerrymandering, job discrimination, and other direct forms of oppression (Acuña, 1988). Throughout the nation, Mexican Americans are targets of prejudice, stereotypes, and discrimination (Acuña, 1988; Estrada et al., 1982). Although subsequent waves of Mexican immigrants have entered this country voluntarily, they, too, have been subject to this same discrimination, which has restricted their access to jobs, housing, and political participation. This experience of domination can explain why Mexican Americans have been present in U.S. society for over one hundred fifty years and yet have relatively little economic and political power (Acuña, 1988; Estrada et al., 1982).

Despite increases in legal Mexican migration to the United States, slightly more than a quarter of Mexican Americans were foreign born in 1980, unlike other Latino groups (U.S. Bureau of the Census, 1992; Bean and Tienda, 1987). Because of the geographic proximity of the United States and Mexico, Mexican Americans also appear to have the largest number of undocumented entrants to this country (Bean and Tienda, 1987). More than seven out of ten people who applied for legalization under the Immigration Reform and Control Act (IRCA) of 1986 were from Mexico (U.S. Bureau of the Census, 1992).

When Yolanda was a little girl growing up in the Rio Grande valley, she knew no Mexican Americans who had gone to college and very few who had graduated from high school. Her parents told her that when they were small, they were required to attend "Mexican schools" that were poorly staffed and had few supplies. When they were in school, they were sent to the principal's office and paddled if they were caught speaking Spanish. If they wanted to attend high school, there was no bus transportation, so they had to find their own way to the high school five miles away, in town. By the time they reached the eighth grade, most saw no purpose in going anyway, because there were no jobs for "educated Mexicans" in their town. By the time Yolanda was in school, civil rights laws had eliminated the "Mexican schools," and bus transportation was provided into town. However, the dropout rate for Mexican-American kids remained high. Many of her friends did not finish school because there still were not very many jobs for educated people in her community.

◆

Puerto Ricans make up 11 percent of the Latino population and have a history similar to that of Mexican Americans in relation to the United States (Garcia and Montgomery, 1991). Puerto Rico is a commonwealth that was acquired by the United States at the end of the Spanish-American War, a century ago. Commonwealth status has allowed the U.S. to exploit the island economically and to transform it from a plantation to an industrial economy. High rates of unemployment, a consequence of this transformation, have contributed to large waves of Puerto Rican migration to the mainland since the 1950s. Racial and ethnic discrimination, the low average education and poor job skills of Puerto Rican migrants, and a declining manufacturing sector in the Northeast have contributed to the marginal economic position of this group. Of the three major Latino subgroups, Puerto Ricans are the most disadvantaged economically (Moore and Pachon, 1985; Nelson and Tienda, 1985, Portes and Truelove, 1987).

Unlike other Latino groups, Puerto Ricans are U.S. citizens. This enables them to move easily back and forth to the island and renders them, technically speaking, migrants rather than immigrants. Because Puerto Ricans often return to the island after living in the United States for a while, they have been characterized as having a pattern of circular migration.

The Cuban subgroup, 5 percent of the Latino population, presents a different socioeconomic picture (Garcia and Montgomery, 1991). Their educational and economic demographic profile mirrors the national averages (Portes and Truelove, 1987). Cubans' relative success has been attributed to three factors: their status as political refugees and the resulting federal economic benefits and positive reception; the average high educational and professional status of the first wave of immigrants; and the development of an ethnic enclave economy by the initial immigrants that has provided jobs and support for more recent immigrants (Nelson and Tienda, 1985; Portes and Truelove, 1987). Although they have achieved economically, Cuban Americans most recently have become targets of ethnic discrimination and stereotypes, manifested in political conflicts regarding bilingualism and the perception that they are involved in drug trafficking and organized crime (Portes, 1984; Queralt, 1984).

Central and South Americans constitute 14 percent of the Latino population (Garcia and Montgomery, 1991). Among Central American immigrants, those from Guatemala and El Salvador made up the largest percentage in 1990, while immigrants from Colombia, Ecuador, and Peru formed the largest foreign-born South American groups (U.S. Bureau of the Census, 1992). These newest Latino immigrants, like the Cubans, have been pushed to leave their countries by political turmoil. Very little is known about this population, which is the second largest and most rapidly expanding subgroup. This incredibly heterogeneous grouping includes Central American refugees and white-collar and professional workers from South America. Depending on their job skills, education, and mode of entry, they can either resemble the Cubans or the more economically disadvantaged Latino groups in terms of their socioeconomic status (Melville, 1988; Portes and Truelove, 1987).

In her work as a camp health aide, Yolanda is meeting more and more women from Central America. Some of them have worked very hard to get to the United States. Many of them are fleeing violence and poverty in their families and communities. For example, Herlinda came to the United States from Honduras to escape sexual abuse by her father and older brother. There were no legal protections for young girls in her village, and she had no way to support herself economically if she moved away from her family but stayed in her village. Thus she felt that flight to the United States was her only means of escape. She was sponsored by a family who wanted to hire her as a nanny. When she got to her new job, she found herself working sixteen hours a day, seven days a week, for seventy-five dollars a week plus room and board. Yet, because the family sponsored her, she had to remain in this job for fear of being deported. One night, she heard a public service announcement on the Spanish-language radio station that provided information about a group that helped people with immigration problems. She called and got help with keeping her green card. After leaving the job, she joined the migrant stream.

The majority (87 percent), of the Latina population resides in just ten states: California, Texas, New York, Florida, Illinois, New Jersey, Arizona, New Mexico, Colorado, and Massachusetts. Particular groups cluster within each state: Mexican Americans are most likely to live in California, Texas, Arizona, New Mexico, and Colorado; Puerto Ricans in New York and New Jersey; and Cuban Americans in Florida, New York, and New Jersey. Illinois is one of the few states that has substantial percentages of each major Latino group (U.S. Bureau of the Census, 1992).

Although the majority of agricultural workers are Latino, about 90 percent lived in a metropolitan area, in contrast to 76 percent of non-Latinos (U.S. Bureau of the Census, 1992). Nearly five million Latinos lived in the Los Angeles Consolidated Metropolitan Statistical Area (CMSA), while nearly three million lived in the New York CMSA. About a million Latinos reside in the CMSAS of Miami, San Francisco, and Chicago, with three-quarters of a million living in the Houston CMSA. Other CMSAS and Metropolitan Statistical Areas (MSAS) with a high concentration of Latinos include San Antonio, Dallas–Fort Worth, San Diego, El Paso, McAllen, Texas, and Phoenix. Within these areas, Latinos are more likely to live in central cities (52 percent) than are non-Latinos (U.S. Bureau of the Census, 1992).

This brief sociohistorical and demographic description of the Latino population demonstrates both our unity and our diversity. Although we are represented on all levels of society, Latinas tend to have low incomes and fewer than average years of education and to live in urban environments. In addition, the legacy of racism and ethnocentrism in our society has maintained our lower socioeconomic statuses. Latinas are thus likely to experience problems related to poverty and discrimination based on both their gender and ethnic status. Even for those Latinas who have gotten ahead, the overall status of our group has an impact, directly or indirectly, on our life experience.

Cultural Roles and Values

Although Latinos and Latinas originate in many countries, core values characterize our group. Latinas have been described as familistic: they have a strong cultural tradition and commitment to the extended family. In the traditional family, the basic social unit is characterized by "a bond of loyalty and unity" that includes nuclear family, extended family, and fictive kin (Bernal and Flores-Ortiz, 1982). Individual needs are often set aside in favor of the needs of the family. Yet, according to some researchers, this cultural tradition changes with the process of immigration, which tends to entail critical shifts in behavior and a redefinition of kinship obligations (Marin and Van Oss Marin, 1991). Also, although the familistic system can be a source of support, it can also be a significant source of stress as not all that goes on in Latino families is supportive and harmonious (Rogler et al., 1983).

In addition to familism, a configuration of other cultural variables influences help seeking and the use of social services (Rogler et al., 1983). These include *confianza*, the value of trust in self and others; personalism, a concern for personal dignity, together with a person-oriented approach to social relations and a distaste for impersonal relationships (Queralt, 1984; Rogler et al., 1983); and *verguenza* and *orgullo*, a sense of shame and strong pride. These values arise from and reinforce interactions in a culture based on close social relationships (Rogler et al., 1983).

While Yolanda was growing up she hardly ever saw a doctor. Most of the health care she received was from the public health nurses, who gave her vaccines, or from the *curandera* in the community. Her mother preferred to go to the curandera because she would take the time to get to know the whole family. The public health department seemed too impersonal.

The *curandera* used her knowledge of the mind, body, and spirit to help people with health problems. She would prescribe herbs, prayers, and other treatments. Yolanda still remembers vividly a time when she was eight years old and experienced *susto*, a sense of paralyzing fright. She developed the problem after she saw her younger cousin run over by a tractor in the fields. The *curandera* worked with her family to carry out a ritual, which involved prayers and an egg, for one week. After the week was over, she was cured.

Yolanda has used her background with folk medicine in her work as a camp health aide. For example, she will suggest *yerba buena* (mint) tea for people with digestive problems or *manzanilla* (chamomile) for people who are feeling nervous. These two herbs are used throughout the world as folk remedies.

Another salient, and often misunderstood, cultural orientation among Latinas is fatalism (locus of control), the belief that events are determined by forces outside one's control. Latinas also endorse a subjugation-to-nature orientation (Szapocznik, Kurtines, and Fernandez, 1980; Rogler et al., 1983). Latinas adhering to fatalistic cultural orientations may view themselves as being unable to control natural forces or modify detrimental environmental conditions. This value orientation is thus in conflict with the mainstream cultural belief that human beings are capable of exerting mastery over nature.

The traditional Latino family is commonly viewed as patriarchal in structure and rigidly organized around hierarchies based on age and gender. Older family members and men hold more formal power within the family than do women and younger people. Yet gender role dynamics within Latino families are more complex that this. Acculturation, education, and informal norms affect how gender roles are structured in Latino families (Beckman, 1979; Kranau, Green, and Valencia-Weber, 1982; Moore and Pachon, 1985; Vasquez-Nuttall, Romero-Garcia, and De Leon, 1987).

Latinas, in comparison to other ethnic groups, are more likely to hold traditional attitudes regarding women's roles (Fischer, 1987; Moore and Pachon, 1985); however, many of these differences become less significant when one controls for education, age, class, or generation (Cromwell and Cromwell, 1978; Vasquez-Nuttall, Romero-Garcia, and De Leon, 1987). Less restrictive attitudes toward women are found to be associated with acculturation (Kranau et al., 1982; Vasquez-Nuttall, Romero-Garcia, and De Leon, 1987), education (Kranau, Green, and Valencia-Weber, 1982; Vasquez-Nuttall, Romero-Garcia, and De Leon, 1987; Soto, 1983), marital status (Kranau, Green, and Valencia-Weber, 1982), age (Kranau, Green, and Valencia-Weber, 1982), and labor force participation (Vasquez-Nuttall, Romero-Garcia, and De Leon, 1987; Ybarra, 1982). In general, younger working women with more education have more egalitarian attitudes toward women than do their older, less educated counterparts. Education has a particularly strong effect on sex role attitudes. This suggests that the classic depiction of Latinas as endorsing a very traditional view of women's roles represents a subgroup within the larger population.

Although birthrates in Latin America are declining, Latinas in the United States maintain higher fertility rates than do other ethnic groups (Darabi, Dryfoos, and Schwartz, 1986; Ortiz and Casas, 1990). This is particularly true of Mexican-American women, for whom the high birthrate is associated with low rates of contraceptive use (Darabi, Dryfoos, and Schwartz, 1986; Mays and Cochran, 1988). This has been attributed to both cultural values and barriers to health care.

Sex role attitudes among Latinas may have less influence on fertility preferences than they do among Anglo or African-American women (Beckman, 1979). Traditional attitudes toward women may affect contraceptive use among more traditional Latinas (Ortiz and Casas, 1990); however, studies of reproductive beliefs found that Mexican-American women had more modern beliefs regarding women's role, preferred family size, and contraceptive use than previous studies had suggested (Amaro, 1988; Jorgenson and Adams, 1987). Unfortunately, service providers persist in viewing Mexican-American patients as holding traditional beliefs that prevent the use of contraceptives (Jorgensen and Adams, 1987). Thus access issues may be more important than traditional sex role attitudes on reproductive beliefs and behaviors in affecting the fertility of Mexican-American women.

Despite the Latino culture's strong familistic orientation, the number of Latino female-headed households has increased at a rate faster than that of African- and European-Americans. Although the number of single-parent families has risen for all racial and ethnic groups in this country, the number of Latino single-parent families increased by 7 percent from 1980 to 1990, as compared to an increase of 3.1 percent for European Americans and 3.8 percent for African Americans (Marin and Van Oss Marin, 1991). In 1990, 29 percent of Latino families were supported by a woman on her own; the rate was 19 percent for European Americans and 56 percent for African Americans. Of the three major Latino groups, Puerto Rican families are more likely to have female heads (33.7 percent) than are Mexican-American (15.6 percent) or Cuban (15.3 percent) families (U.S. Bureau of the Census, 1992).

Latino female-headed families are more likely to live in poverty, with almost half (48.3 percent) living below the poverty line (Baca-Zinn and Dill, 1994b). Mainland Puerto Rican households had the highest poverty rate (64.4 percent). Female heads of households are confronted by numerous factors that relegate them to persistent poverty, among them, a weakened family support structure and social policies that prevent them from exiting from poverty. Having limited education, Latinas often lack employment options, and those available to them usually have restricted or no benefits. Because of these economic factors, as well as the lack of child care, many single mothers are forced to seek public assistance to support themselves and their families (Baca-Zinn and Dill, 1994b).

Yolanda's Aunt Mercedes is one of the few people in her family who receives public assistance. Mercedes quit school in the eighth grade because her family needed her income. She married another farmworker, Rudy, and even when their children were babies, the whole family picked crops. But two years ago Rudy left Mercedes for another woman while they were on the road. The children were aged eight, six, and three. Mercedes found it almost impossible to stay in the migrant stream as a single parent with small children: she was constantly having to find someone to watch the kids, and she was very tired. Although her mother offered to keep the children with her in Texas, Mercedes did not want to burden her with the expense, and, besides, she wanted to be the one to raise her kids. So she applied for Temporary Assistance for Needy Families. She is now studying for her GED so that she can get a job in town.

Empowerment Practice with Latinas

Given the challenges and strengths of the Latino community, how can an empowerment perspective be brought into practice with Latinas? Looking at the concepts of consciousness, confidence, and connection that are outlined in chapter 1, a model for practice emerges. In this final section we discuss the integration of cultural and structural issues into work with Latinas, using Miriam Ocampo's example to illustrate how this work can be carried out. This case example is a composite based on Latinas we have worked with in community settings in New York and Chicago.

Miriam Ocampo is a twenty-six-year-old married Puerto Rican woman living in the Bronx, New York. She has two children, daughters aged six and eight. Ms. Ocampo has an eighth-grade education. At the age of fourteen she left school to marry a much older man, a friend of the family whom she had met during a visit back home on the island. When he met Miriam, his interest in her "swept her off her feet." After they were married, the couple moved into an apartment in the same building where Miriam's parents lived.

At first, their marriage was "like a dream." But after the birth of his daughters, Mr. Ocampo became physically abusive. He has never forgiven Miriam for not bearing a son, and he often brings this up during his rages. His most recent attack occurred when he learned that Miriam was looking into getting her GED. Then, his abuse was so severe that he broke Miriam's arm. When she arrived at the emergency room, she was seen by counselor, who referred her to a shelter for battered women.

CONSCIOUSNESS

Gaining consciousness in the empowerment process means beginning to understand oneself, one's environment, one's problems, and one's opportunities. Based on an ecological perspective, empowerment practice looks at the total person in interaction with the social environment (Germain, 1979; Rappaport, 1981). Therefore both the individual and the social context must be assessed. With the Latina client, the ecological assessment process is a good way to begin the work and to develop a working relationship.

The social worker must assess the client's present level of functioning and present sources of individual or interpersonal power (Pinderhughes, 1983; Shapiro, 1984; Solomon, 1976; Stensrud and Stensrud, 1981). Latina clients have been involved in a process of struggle against oppressive structures, and this has required considerable strength. By analyzing elements of the struggle, client strengths are more readily identified, communicated to the client, and then utilized as a basis for future work.

When Miriam arrived at the shelter with her two children, she was grateful for a safe place to sleep. She had not thought much about her next steps. The next morning she was surprised to meet Ana, who would be her counselor at the shelter. Ana was a Cuban American who had immigrated to New York at the age of six. Ana had struggled hard to get an education and had been working at the shelter since getting a bachelor's degree in social work.

Ana began her work with Miriam by talking casually with her. First she offered her a cup of coffee or tea and some coffee cake and asked Miriam if she would like to meet in her office, in another room in the shelter, or in a coffee shop. Miriam chose Ana's office. Ana then started off by asking about Miriam's family, her background, and where she had grown up. She also shared a good deal about her own background. In this interaction, she learned a lot about Miriam while establishing a good rapport.

Assessment also focuses on exploring the power issues in the client's ecosystem. Eco-mapping assesses a client's relationships with the social environment (Hartman and Laird, 1978; Holman, 1983) and can identify the relative power of the individuals and systems in that environment. Once completed, this assessment tool can then suggest to the social worker and clients areas in which an increase of personal, interpersonal, or political power may be crucial.

Another form of power analysis involves a discussion of how social status, race, ethnicity, or gender is having an impact on the situation (Garvin, 1985; Keefe, 1980; Mathis and Richan, 1986). This involves dialogue about the social-structural origins of the current situation (Keefe, 1980; Longres and

McLeod, 1980; Solomon, 1976). Involving the client in identifying power blocks and sources of potential power in her situation is crucial if the social work relationship is to contribute to achieving empowerment on all three levels (Gutiérrez, 1990; Pinderhughes, 1983; Solomon, 1976).

The social worker must also work with Latinas to assess their level of acculturation and sense of ethnic identity. Understanding acculturation and identity helps to uncover possible problem areas and suggests ways in which the ethnic community can be a source of resources and strength (Ruiz, 1990). Several instruments and guidelines are available for assessing ethnic identity among Latinos (Comas-Diaz and Griffith, 1988; Marin and Van Oss Marin, 1991; Silva, 1983). At the very least, the worker should consider the client's specific national origin, place of birth, immigration or migration experiences, preferred language, preferred ethnic label, perceptions of the importance of her Latina identity, and the value (positive or negative) she attaches to that identity.

Assessing cultural issues should also try to evaluate the degree to which they can interfere with or contribute to solutions. For example, the belief that the only positive roles for women involve marriage and children may discourage a young woman from pursuing an education or leaving an abusive relationship. Latinas are in a position to evaluate critically what they think is working or not working for them in terms of culture. It is crucial that the social worker stand back and let them decide this for themselves.

---◆---

In their first meeting, Ana asked Miriam to share something about her cultural identity. How did she think of herself ethnically? What language would she like to speak in the interview? What had being Puerto Rican meant to her life? Here is a piece of that discussion:

ANA: You mentioned before that you were born and grew up in the Bronx. How was your upbringing? Was your family very traditional or more Americanized?

MIRIAM: Oh, even though we lived here, my family is very traditional. My parents have been married forty years! Every summer we were sent to our *abuelitos* in Ponce. My parents wanted us to be *bien educados*. That is where I met Juan.

ANA: You met Juan in Puerto Rico. What brought him to New York?

MIRIAM: He needed work and thought there would be something for him here, and we were in love. He wanted to marry me the day he met me. I was only fourteen.

ANA: And how did you feel?

MIRIAM: I thought I was too young, but there were no other choices. It is very important to my parents that we girls get married and have kids. That is our purpose in life. Marriage is a sacrament with God. I was lucky to find a man who had a steady job to support us. But I never thought anyone could be so cruel. Maybe if I had had a boy he would have been a better husband.

From this discussion Ana learned that Miriam and her family had very traditional views of women and families, based in their devout religious beliefs. This could have contributed to Miriam's life choices. At this point in the working relationship, Ana chose not to explore this subject further but to consider it in future work.

◆

Latino culture is collectively oriented and focused on ways in which individuals can experience harmony with their social environment (Triandis, 1983; Delgado, 1983). Thus eco-mapping, network utilization, and analysis of the social elements of the client's situation work well with Latinas. Similarly, work concerning ethnic identity is often welcomed by Latinas, who may experience much confusion and pressure to reject or mute their bicultural status (Ruiz, 1990). The desired outcome of this cultural assessment would be *conocimiento* (understanding) of the person, her identity, and the surrounding environment.

CONFIDENCE

Building confidence in Latinas means helping them to identify ways in which they can have a positive impact on their social world. This begins with a helping relationship based on collaboration, trust, and shared power. The social worker assumes the role of enabler, organizer, consultant, or compatriot with the client to avoid replicating the powerlessness the client experiences with other helpers or professionals. As stated by Leigh (1985): "[We] will have to face giving up that 'expert' power and share skills with those who have more 'expert' power derived from their perception of their own communities. To me this factor is the essence of empowerment techniques" (p. 54).

The transaction between social worker and client is characterized by genuineness, mutual respect, open communication, and informality. It presumes that the social worker does not hold the answers to the client's problems but instead that in the context of collaboration the client will develop the insights, skills, and capacity to resolve the situation herself (Germain, 1979; Keefe, 1980; Pinderhughes, 1983; Schechter, Szymanski, and Cahill, 1985; Solomon, 1976).

Accepting the client's definition of the problem is an important step in building confidence. By accepting the client's definition, the helper communicates the belief that she is capable of identifying and understanding her situation. This technique also places the client in a position of power and control over the working relationship. The social worker is not precluded from bringing up issues for exploration, but the focus of work begins only with those issues that interest the client (Garvin, 1985; Shapiro, 1984).

When Miriam first came to the shelter, she knew that she wanted only one thing: safety for herself and her children. But she was not sure how she would be able to be safe. At the end of their first meeting, Ana talked with Miriam about her goals and ideas about her situation.

ANA: When we first started talking, you said that you came to the shelter because you wanted to be safe. I'd like to get a better idea of what safety would mean to you. What do you think of when you think of being safe?

MIRIAM: I think of feeling secure. Knowing that I will not be hurt. Knowing that my kids will be okay. I feel safe now that I am here at the shelter and Juan can't get to me.

ANA: What will we need to do here for you to stay safe?

MIRIAM: I'd like to get help for Juan and me so he will not try to hurt us again. I would not feel safe if I had to live on my own. This is not a safe neighborhood for a woman living alone. And how could I support myself and the kids?

ANA: Getting help for Juan is something we can look into. It sounds as if it is important to you to stay married.

In this interview, Ana accepted Miriam's perception of her situation and began to explore what it meant to her. She learned that Miriam has sought safety from Juan but that she also saw Juan as a source of safety from a hostile world. In order for Miriam to feel secure, she would need to develop the confidence and skills to take care of herself and her children.

This orientation to engagement is culturally responsive to the concept of *personalismo*, developing a personal relationship and understanding before beginning work (Applewhite and Daily, 1988; Laval, Gomez, and Ruiz, 1983). The helper also communicates *respeto* (respect), another important element of

Latino social interactions, by taking the time to become familiar with the client and her understanding of the situation (Applewhite and Daily, 1988).

Latino cultures are structured around hierarchies, which requires individuals to give proper respect to those with more power (Mizio, 1981), so for open communication to take place in the helping relationship, a reduction of the power imbalance may be necessary. If the client experiences personal power within the social work relationship, this may be generalized to feelings of power in the larger social environment. Specific means for accomplishing this transferability include role playing and practicing powerful behaviors; engaging in roles in which clients help others; and clients' taking control of the helping process by setting the agenda, coleading groups or meetings, and researching resources (Pinderhughes, 1983; Schechter, Szymanski, and Cahill, 1985; Shapiro, 1984; Simmons and Parsons, 1983a).

Ana saw Miriam twice a week for counseling at the shelter. After their initial interview, she focused more on exploring the strengths within Miriam and her social environment. She also discussed with her plans for the future: how could Miriam remain safe?

Whenever Miriam had a question about a program or service, Ana did not provide the answers but worked with her to get the information she needed. For example, in their work together Miriam realized that Juan usually beat her after he had been drinking. She wondered if he had a drinking problem. Ana suggested that she might want to join a support group for wives of alcoholics. Miriam was interested in this, so together they came up with a plan to talk with other women in the shelter about resources and look up Al Anon in the telephone book and call them.

Although Miriam felt shy about discussing Juan's problem, she felt that she needed support. First, she called Al Anon and got the name of a group that met at a local parish. Then she asked some of the women at the shelter about the group. One of the women, LaTira, was a member and offered to take her that week. When LaTira talked about her husband, Michael, he sounded so much like Juan.

Actively involving the clients in the change process can also build confidence. These activities range from the exploration of a problem to the development of alternative structures in a community (Checkoway and Norsman, 1986; Garvin, 1985; Hirayama and Hirayama, 1985; Kahn and Bender, 1985; Mathis and Richan, 1986; Pinderhughes, 1983; Solomon, 1976). The example of Yolanda, the camp health aide, suggests the powerful impact of this kind of work. As clients are actively involved in change, they also reflect on and analyze their experience (praxis). The knowledge gained from this analysis can then be integrated into the development of future efforts (Freire, 1973; Keefe, 1980; Longres and McLeod, 1980; Rose and Black, 1985).

Teaching specific skills is another way to help Latinas develop confidence and increase their social power (Mathis and Richan, 1986; Shapiro, 1984; Garvin, 1985; Keefe, 1980; Simmons and Parsons, 1983b; Solomon, 1976). In teaching skills, the social worker acts as consultant or facilitator rather than instructor so as not to replicate the power relationships that worker and client are attempting to overcome (Solomon, 1976).

The one thing Miriam worried about the most was talking with her parents about Juan. She had never said anything about the beatings to them. She was afraid that they would just tell her that she had married too young. Juan was always so nice to them that she knew they would not believe her. But she knew that her mother was probably worried about her and wondering where she was.

MIRIAM: I know I should talk to my mom about all that's happening. But I am so embarrassed. What will I say?

ANA: You feel embarrassed to talk to your mother.

MIRIAM: Yes, she will probably think that the whole thing is my fault. Maybe it was. But I don't make him drink. And I don't make him hit me.

ANA: What do you want to tell your mother?

MIRIAM: I want her to know that the kids and I are safe. And that we will need to stay away from Juan until he learns to treat us better. I don't want the kids growing up seeing me like this.

ANA: Why don't you pretend I'm your mom. Then you can tell me what you want to tell her.

For the next few minutes Miriam and Ana role-played a talk with Miriam's mother. They did the same role play many times, with Ana responding differently each time: first loving, then angry, then sad. In the role plays, Miriam was able to try out different approaches and responses. She role-played until she felt ready to talk with her mother. When it was time to talk with her later that week, she felt more confident to deal with the conversation.

CONNECTION

Building connection involves interventions on the individual, group, family, and community levels. Social workers must have the skills to move from one modality to another. Small groups have particular relevance for empowerment practice with Latinas because they offer an effective means for encouraging the psychological transformations and an ideal platform for introducing empowerment techniques. The group modality is the most effective environ- ment for raising consciousness, engaging in mutual aid, developing skills, solving problems, and experiencing one's own effectiveness in influencing others (Coppola and Rivas, 1985; Garvin, 1985; Gitterman and Shulman, 1994; Gutiérrez and Ortega, 1991). Small-group work is equally effective in empow- ering individuals and changing institutions. For example, the training and support that Yolanda received as a camp health aide occurred in group ses- sions. In these sessions, the CHAS were able to pool wisdom and resources to improve their work.

When Miriam arrived at the shelter, she felt that she did not belong there. She did not like the idea of being away from her family or taking her children into an institutional situation. She and her children had to share a room, eat meals com- munally, and meet many new people. She worried that she would never be on her own again.

One thing that made a big difference for Miriam was the support she received from the other residents. All of them had been abused and could understand where she was coming from. Miriam attended a support group every week where the women talked about common issues and concerns. The group's inter- action and collective knowledge were used to deal with the problems that were raised. For example, at each meeting a woman could bring up a problem to be discussed in a suggestion circle, where each woman would come up with alter- native solutions for her to select from.

At her fourth meeting, Miriam had the courage to bring a problem to the group.

MIRIAM: I have a problem to ask about. I know now that Juan is an alcoholic. As long as he's drinking, he'll beat me for sure. But I love him, and I don't want a divorce. What can I do?

MIKKI (the group facilitator): Let's all brainstorm ideas for Miriam. What can she do with this situation?

IRIS: Forget him. You can always get another man!

BETH: Take care of yourself and the kids. He can take care of himself.

LaTIRA: Keep going to Al Anon; get support for yourself.

DANIELLE: Take him to court; they can force him into treatment.

HYUN: Move out, but don't divorce. Tell him he can move back in when he is sober.

MARIBEL: Tell him he has to go to detox. Divorce him if he doesn't. No man is worth it!

The group generated ideas for Miriam until they had no more. Some were more realistic to Miriam than others. The group leader, Mikki, wrote them on newsprint. Then Miriam copied them all onto a piece of paper to think about, discuss with others, and focus on with Ana.

Mobilizing resources or advocating for clients is yet another way of building connections. In an earlier section of this chapter, we identified ways in which social and public policy have been oppressive to Latinas. By working with Latinas to develop the tools to confront and possibly change these policies, we can affect the status of all Latinos. In our work with Latinas, we should be involved in gathering concrete resources or information for the client as well as advocating on their behalf when necessary. Some have argued that advocacy may conflict with the goal of empowerment because it may reinforce feelings of powerlessness (Rappaport, 1981; Solomon, 1976); however, it can be carried out in a collaborative way that includes the client and involves learning new skills. Through advocacy and resource mobilization, the social worker and client together work to ensure that the larger social structure provides what is necessary to empower the larger client group (Checkoway and Norsman, 1986; Mathis and Richan, 1986; Pinderhughes, 1983; Solomon, 1982).

The Latino population has a rich history of working with one another to provide mutual aid (Gutiérrez, Ortega, and Suarez, 1990). Because most Latino culture is oriented more toward family and community systems than toward individual achievement, working within small groups often feels natural and might be more acceptable to some Latinos than individual social work (Acosta and Yamamato, 1984; Gutiérrez and Ortega, 1991; Hardy-Fanta, 1986).

Taking an active approach to social work with Latinas addresses their low status and power. By working with Latinas to increase personal, interpersonal, and political power, social workers make a lasting contribution to the entire Latino community. A professional focus on improving the condition of Latinos in general and linking personal and community problems and problem solving is quite compatible with the collective orientation of Latino culture (Triandis, 1983).

As part of their work at the shelter, Ana and the other counselors and advocates identify community needs and work with others to address them. For example, through their work at the shelter, they found that many landlords in their neighborhoods were illegally discriminating against families. After their initial attempts to advocate for their clients failed, they contacted the Fair Housing Center in the city. The paralegals there worked with them to document these cases of discrimination. By threatening legal action, they were able to change these discriminatory practices.

Conclusion

The Latina population in the United States continues to grow, and the areas of fastest growth are those communities and regions where the Latina population has till now been almost nonexistent. This suggests that the skills and understanding needed to work with Latinas should be a priority for us all. Working with Latinas will require an understanding of their culture and their unique experience in the United States. It will mean learning to work with women who come from a variety of racial, national, and class backgrounds. In this chapter, we have tried to provide some insights into empowerment practice with Latinas and examples to illustrate them effectively. However, it is only by active engagement with Latina clients and communities that we can empower ourselves to work with them effectively.

During her shelter stay, Miriam began to take control of her life. Individual counseling helped her to understand her experience with battering and to explore options. Together with Ana, she applied for public assistance and got an order of protection against her husband. Both of these experiences were frightening to her as she had never before been on public assistance or appeared in court. Role playing with Ana helped her to get through these experiences. The fact that Ana came from a similar background was inspiring to Miriam, helping her to see there were other alternatives for women like herself.

The group helped her to understand that she was not alone. She learned to share her feelings with others and get support. One of the most important things she learned from the group and from group living was that she could develop her own network of support. She would not need a man or even her family to survive.

Two years later, Miriam is still living a life without violence. She has legally separated from her husband and is in school to become an LPN. Although she still loves Juan, she has come to understand that until he gets control over his drinking and violence, she and the children will not be safe. At the back of her mind, she hopes that he will eventually sober up and get his life together, but she is not holding her breath.

At first, Miriam's family encouraged her to go back to Juan. She has had to work with her family members, especially the older ones, who believe that women should not confront abusive behavior. But she has received a lot of support from her mother and sisters. In fact, her sister and brother-in-law have been really helpful to her with child care so she can get through school.

When she left the shelter, Miriam was able to use her order of protection to keep the apartment in the building with her parents. The first year she had to call the police when Juan tried to come back in. She thought about moving but wanted to stay close to her family.

Miriam has come to realize that there are no easy answers, but whenever she has doubts, she remembers the long road that she has covered since the evening she arrived at the shelter.

TWELVE

◆

Empowerment: Asian-American Women's Perspectives

Gwat-Yong Lie

Contrary to popular impression, Asians in the United States are neither a monolithic nor a homogeneous group. Instead, at least twenty-nine distinct subgroups that differ in language, religion, and values are represented (Yoshioka et al., 1981). Even within each subgroup, there are variations based on attributes such as social class, migration experiences, and degree of assimilation or acculturation (Wong, 1985). Add to this chop suey the diversity of experiences emanating from gender-specific realities, and immediately the inequity of treating Asian Americans as a single sociocultural, economic, and political entity becomes apparent.

The issue of diversity within diversity as reflected in the convergence of ethnic and gender characteristics is especially cogent in a nation conflicted in its treatment of, for example, affirmative action and immigration policies and provisions. Given the vagaries of societal responses to matters of social justice and diversity, Asian women in the United States have found that they cannot afford to be dependent on society to provide the different and "dynamic combinations of human resources, opportunity structures . . . and public policies" (Yamanaka and McClelland, 1994, p. 832) necessary to address individual, familial, and community needs. Instead, they have had to take it on themselves to name and describe their realities and assertively to craft meaningful responses to enhance their own well-being and life functioning, as well as those of their families and community. This responsibility still persists.

This chapter attempts to describe not only large group attributes and behaviors but, where pertinent, also to address subgroup (i.e., national-, ethnic-, and/or gender-based) exceptions. Specifically, the chapter aims to do the following: (1) offer a demographic and socioeconomic profile of Asian-American women; (2) recount the historical context that shaped the destinies of Asian-American women today; (3) describe social-structural characteristics and distinctive beliefs and values; (4) identify challenges that Asian-American women in general face and the unique challenges posed by differences in nationality, ethnicity, gender, class, and culture; (5) document demonstrated strengths in the face of adversity; and (6) delineate ways that the empowerment perspective has been and could continue to be used.

Demographic and Socioeconomic Profile

According to the 1990 census, Asian Americans numbered 6.9 million, with roughly 1.6 million Chinese, 1.4 million Filipinos, 847,500 Japanese, 815,400 Asian Indians, 798,800 Koreans, 614,500 Vietnamese, 149,000 Laotians, 147,400 Cambodians, 91,200 Thais, 90,000 Hmongs, and 302,200 "Others" (excluding Pacific Islanders). Asians account for almost 3 percent of the total population in the United States. In a span of the thirty years stretching from 1960 to 1990, the numbers of Asian Americans increased by 800 percent, making this group the fastest-growing minority in the United States today (Fong, 1992).

Of the total number of Asian Americans in 1990, about 3.5 million, or 51.2 percent, were females. Slightly over two-thirds (66.8 percent) of Asian females were foreign-born. The median age for females was 30.9 years, as compared to 29.0 years for Asian-American males and 34.0 years for all women in the total population. The reported marital status of nearly half (46.7 percent) of Asian-American females in 1990 was "married." On average, just under two children were born per Asian-American woman aged thirty-five to forty-four in 1990. Among recent refugee and immigrant groups from Southeast Asia, however, the average number of children born to women in the same age group is higher. For Vietnamese women, the average is 2.5; for Laotian and Cambodian women, 3.5; and for Hmong women, 6.1 (Rumbaut, 1995).

Geographically, Asian Americans tend to be concentrated in six states, with over two-thirds living in California, Hawaii, New York, Illinois, Texas, and New Jersey. In fact, 54.6 percent of Asian Americans (as compared to about 27 percent of the total U.S. population) live in the West, where they account for roughly 7 percent of the total population. This concentration of Asian Americans in the West continues to intensify with the movement of recent refugee populations, such as the Vietnamese, Hmongs, Laotians, and Cambodians, from their sponsoring communities to areas in the West where there are established Asian-American communities (Knoll, 1982). This uneven distribution of Asian Americans is further illustrated by the census survey finding that in 1990 approximately 94.4 percent of all Asian Americans lived in metropolitan areas, especially in cities such as New York, San Francisco, Boston, Chicago, and Los Angeles.

A bimodal picture emerges with respect to educational attainment, according to data from the 1990 census. The majority of Asian-American women had at least a high school diploma or equivalent, and about 40.7 percent had completed at least four years of college. Subgroups with the highest proportion of women completing four years of college or more are Taiwanese American (58.9 percent), Asian Indian (54.8 percent), and Filipino American (50.3 percent). At the other end of the educational attainment continuum are women with less than a fifth-grade education, who predominate among the Hmong (71.2 percent) and Cambodian (50.9 percent) communities. Only about a third of refugees from Laos and Cambodia were high school graduates. Such disparities simply underscore "the rural origins and severe class disadvantages of many refugees" (Rumbaut, 1995, p. 248).

Although the majority was relatively well educated, only about 43.1 percent, or 2.1 million, women were in the workforce in 1990, and less than half of those women (40.6 percent) worked full-time and year-round. For this subgroup of women in the workforce, the median income was $21,335. The median income of those who worked less than full-time was $11,986. Approximately 11.4 per cent of all Asian-American families subsisted below the poverty line in 1989. However, poverty rates for Southeast Asian refugee groups were two to five times higher than for the U.S. population, and the disparity in welfare dependency rates was even higher (Rumbaut, 1995).

In the economic arena, Asian-American women have been portrayed as having distinguished themselves by their higher labor force participation and their above-average earnings relative to Anglo-American women. Wong and Hirschman (1983), for example, attribute this "earnings advantage" to Asian-American women's "superior educational qualifications, greater levels of full-time work, and geographic location" (p. 423). On the other hand, analysts such as Woo (1985) dispute this interpretation of the data. Woo contends that Asian women are in the workforce out of economic necessity, to help shore up family financial resources: Asian men in general had a lower earning capacity than Anglo males in 1970 and 1980, so it is highly probable that Asian women entered the workforce at a greater rate than Anglo women to make up the income discrepancy. Besides, as in 1970 and 1980, a greater proportion of Asian-American families lived below the poverty level in 1990 (11.4 percent) than did Anglo families (roughly 8 percent). It is reasonable to assume that Asian families cope by having multiple wage earners.

In spite of Asian-American women's "superior educational qualifications," the additional credentialing has not resulted in greater benefits (Woo, 1985; Yamanaka and McClelland, 1994). Instead, "the higher levels of education bring lower returns for Asian American women than they do for any other group" (Woo, 1985, p. 313). They gain far less for their efforts than either Anglo men or women. For example, when nativity status was statistically controlled for, and when regional rather than national comparisons were made, the findings showed that native-born women in 1970 were roughly on par with native-born Anglo women in terms of earning capacities. Asian-American women gained this parity, however, by working harder and for longer hours (Yamanaka and McClelland, 1994). Further, one cannot help noticing the income gulf between similarly educated native-born Anglo males and their female counterparts (whether Asian American or Anglo). Anglo males had a distinct advantage over females in general. Based on 1970 census data, native-born Asian-American women, depending on their subgroup membership, earned between 49 percent to 57 percent of what similarly educated Anglo males earned. This gap persisted in 1980 (Woo, 1985).

Contrary to the belief that geographic location contributes to the earning advantage that Asian-American women allegedly enjoy, census data indicate that Asian-American women tend to be concentrated in high-income states and metropolitan areas where income and cost of living are very high, whereas Anglo-American women tend to be more evenly dispersed throughout the country (Woo, 1985). Thus any additional economic advantage that Asian-American women may obtain by earning higher incomes is offset by their higher cost of living. In fact, when regional variation is controlled for, Asian-American women are frequently less well off than their Anglo-American counterparts (Woo, 1985).

Within the United States, "white Anglo males are critical as a reference group not only for capturing the nature and degree of sexual inequality (vis-à-vis Anglo females) but for determining the parameters of racial inequality" (Woo, 1985, p. 317). Within this frame of reference, not only do Asian-American women occupy jobs not commensurate with their training, but—in California, for example—they were underrepresented at the executive, administrative, and managerial level relative to Anglo men in both 1970 and 1980. Although some gains were made in the 1980s, these were not enough to close the gender gap (Woo, 1985).

Overall, the employment picture is bifurcated, with a large concentration of U.S.-born Asian-American women in "narrowly select, usually less prestigious, rungs of the 'professional-managerial' class," (Woo, 1985, p. 331) and another segment of college-educated women overrepresented in clerical or administrative support jobs. Foreign-born Asian women tend to concentrate in jobs such as service work and machine operation or assembly work (e.g., working as seamstresses or textile sewing-machine operators in garment factories or as operatives in the microelectronics industry) much more so than their Anglo female or male counterparts. Hossfeld (1994), citing California Department of Development estimates for 1983, believes that 50 to 75 percent of operative jobs are held by racial minorities, and these low-skill, low-pay, and low-stability jobs tend to be filled by Asian immigrant women, the preferred production workers of employers and managers in the semiconductor manufacturing industries.

For many Asian-American women, being labeled as the "model minority" has only served to oppress them further and alienate them from other racial/ethnic groups. For example, some Asian-American women in Chow's (1994b) study experienced great pressures to conform and to perform in accordance with the token image employers had created for them. Hossfeld (1994) offers more evidence attesting to the deleterious effect the model minority label has on those to whom it is assigned. She points to the racial division of labor in the high-tech manufacturing industry in California's Silicon Valley, arguing that it originated in the racially structured labor market of the larger economy and in the "racial logic" that employers use in hiring: "This 'racial logic' is based on stereotypes—both observed and imagined—that employers have about different racial groups. One of the effects of this racial logic, vis-à-vis workers, is to reproduce the racially structured labor market and class structure that discriminates against minorities and immigrants. Another effect is that within the workplace, racial categories and racism become tools for management to divide and control workers" (pp. 89–90). Hossfeld asserts that the hiring hierarchy must be challenged because "equality of opportunity, both at work and away from it, cannot be achieved unless we learn to recognize and reject practices that are based on 'simple formulas' about gender, race, and nationality" (p. 90).

Historical Legacies

The Chinese and Japanese communities share a history of immigration dating back to the 1800s, whereas Korean, Asian Indian, and Filipino immigration dates back to the turn of the century. The Vietnamese, Cambodians,

Laotians, and Hmongs represent more recent flows of refugee movements and immigration. Generally, the history of Asian immigration is marked by a history of discrimination and systematic exclusion from mainstream U.S. society.

From the 1820s until the turn of the century, only able-bodied Chinese males were allowed into the United States, primarily to meet the labor demands of railroads in the western parts of the country, on the farms and in the goldmines in California, and on the sugar plantations of Hawaii. Numbers of women relative to men were low because of laws that prohibited wives from joining their spouses. For instance, the sex ratio was one to nineteen among the Chinese in 1860 (Matthaei and Amott, 1990). A split-household family system (Glenn, 1983) developed, with some families remaining separated for several generations. Prostitution of Chinese women in the United States thrived, with women working in conditions far inferior to those of white prostitutes. However, "while many Chinese prostitutes were never able to free themselves, almost all found ways to keep their daughters out of prostitution" (Matthaei and Amott, 1990, p. 65). Laws to prohibit prostitution were enacted in the 1870s.

Although the majority of Chinese immigrants were wage earners, some managed to set up small businesses, such as truck gardens, tenant farms, and laundries. The unpaid labor of the few wives who were able to join their husbands in the United States was "crucial for the success of many of these small businesses" (Matthaei and Amott, 1990, p. 63). During the 1870s, the socioeconomic circumstances of women were described as follows: "More and more Chinese women were married and worked as homemakers. In cities, they also worked for pay at home, doing laundry or sewing, rolling cigars, making slippers or taking in boarders; in rural areas, they earned income from gardening, fishing or raising livestock. Chinese women were also servants, cooks and farm laborers, and a few fished, mined, ran lodging houses or worked on the railroads" (Matthaei and Amott, 1990, p. 65).

Unhappily, this was also the period of growing anti-Chinese agitation, which culminated in the 1882 Chinese Exclusion Act. In addition to stemming the flow of male Chinese immigrants, this act also served to prevent single Chinese women as well as wives of U.S. residents (except those of merchants) from coming to the States, thereby solidifying the extreme sex ratio imbalance. One effect that this sex ratio imbalance and the subsequent passage of miscegenation laws (which continued into the late 1960s) had on the community was the delay in the development of families (Yamanaka and McClelland, 1994). Another effect was the contraction of the Chinese-American community from 124,000 in 1890 to a low of 85,000 in 1920, rising only very gradually to 106,000 in 1940 (Matthaei and Amott, 1990).

In major U.S. cities, Chinatowns emerged "as segregated communities that sought survival and group protection in the midst of racial discrimination" (Lum, 1992, p. 13). Chinese women continued to work as seamstresses in the garment industry, in canning, as domestics, and, as in the 1930s, in "small producer" families. These family businesses emerged in response to the restricted labor market, and for them to make a profit, "super-self-exploitation of the whole family" was necessary (Matthaei and Amott, 1990). Every family member, young and old, worked long hours almost every day of the year.

During World War II, Chinese-American men and women served in the armed forces. The labor shortage created by the war resulted in the U.S. government's prohibiting the discriminatory hirings, and Chinese Americans found work in defense industries. As more job opportunities opened up, Chinese-American women found office work outside Chinatowns, in civil service, professional fields, and factories (Matthaei and Amott, 1990).

The Chinese Exclusion Act was repealed in 1943, although a racial quota of only 105 Chinese immigrants a year was allowed. Those immigrants who could prove that they had entered the country before 1924 or who came in under the new laws as permanent residents became eligible for citizenship. Matthaei and Amott (1990) further note that a later amendment to the War Brides Act allowed Chinese servicemen, once they had become citizens, to bring their wives and children to the United States. In fact, "many rushed to China to marry before the Act expired in 1949" (p. 68). For five years after the revocation of the act, immigrants from China consisted of primarily women and children.

The 1965 Immigration Act, referred to by Lum (1992, p. 14) as the "pivotal legislation that opened the U.S. to all countries," had a significant impact on the Chinese-American community. Between 1960 and 1985, the community increased fourfold, from 236,084 to 1,079,400 (Matthaei and Amott, 1990). Two very different communities emerged, however: an "Uptown" subgroup comprising elite professionals such as scientists and engineers and a "Downtown" subgroup largely made up of relatives of Chinese already settled in the United States.

Many of the "Uptown" Chinese were women "already educationally and socially elevated in Taiwan and China" (Matthaei and Amott, 1990, p. 68). The "Downtown" Chinese, in contrast, were primarily concentrated in Chinatowns, which were declining as second-generation Chinese moved out of the area. These Chinese might have been less privileged socioeconomically but were no less vulnerable to racism than their "Uptown" kin. The infamous underground economy, founded on garment sweatshops as well as laundries, restaurants, and grocery stores, continues today, still unprotected by labor laws (Matthaei and Amott, 1990).

Although there were many parallels between Chinese and Japanese immigration, there were also significant differences. Like the Chinese immigrants before them, Japanese immigrants were largely concentrated in Hawaii and on the West Coast and were overwhelmingly young and male, seeking economic improvement and intending to return to their homeland after their fortunes were made (Fong, 1992). Unlike the Chinese immigrants, however, would-be Japanese immigrants were carefully screened by the Japanese government so that most of those who left Japan were literate, including the womenfolk (Matthaei and Amott, 1990), whose emigration was promoted to encourage the establishment of families. The Japanese government adopted this policy in an attempt to avoid the pitfalls of "a bachelor society where prostitution, gambling and drunkenness prevailed" (Fong, 1992, p. 8, citing Wakatsuki, 1979). Despite the best intentions of the Japanese government to ensure the well-being of the mostly educated young single male emigrants, these men still ended up "as unskilled laborers on the railroads and in the mines, as gardeners or laundrymen, as 'houseboys' in domestic service or as field hands" (Matthaei and Amott, 1990, p. 69).

As in the Chinese-American community, the Japanese community was overwhelmingly male, with an estimated twenty-five men for every woman. Most immigrant women came as part of families and worked in agriculture, domestic service, or family businesses. And, again as in the Chinese community, prostitution became a thriving business. In the 1890s, there was public reaction against Asian prostitutes in general and Japanese prostitutes in particular. An anti-Japanese movement similar to the earlier anti-Chinese movement started to brew and was continuing to gather momentum at the turn of the century.

The Japanese government protested the treatment of its citizens. Because of Japan's stature as a world-class military power and diplomatic influence, the U.S. government reluctantly intervened (Fong, 1992). In 1907 a "Gentlemen's Agreement" was signed by both governments to restrict Japanese emigration to the United States. Interestingly, the agreement only restricted the flow of male immigrants; wives and female relatives continued to relocate to the United States. In 1900 there were 2,369 males to 100 females; by 1920 the ratio was 189 males to 100 females (Lyman, 1977). This improvement in the sex ratio transformed the Japanese-American community from a "bachelor society to a family society" (Fong, 1992, p. 10). This formation of families and the availability of unpaid household labor fostered the emergence of a household-centered mode of production, allowing first-generation truck farmers to compete effectively and to gain a dominant share of the produce market (Nee and Wong, 1985). Women and children played a key role in shaping the economic situation of the community (Matthaei and Amott, 1990).

Of the women who entered the United States between 1909 and 1920, over half, an estimated 23,000, were "picture brides" (Glenn, 1984; Matthaei and Amott, 1990; Moriyama, 1984). The practice was regulated by the Japanese government: men had to show evidence of stable employment and savings between $800 to $1,000, and laborers were ineligible until 1915. For their part, brides had to pass physical examinations and had to be no more than thirteen years younger than their prospective husbands.

These brides traveled to make homes all over the West. Glenn (1986) traced their destinations to sites such as remote labor camps in the mountain states, coal-mining areas in Wyoming, sugar beet fields in Utah and Idaho, lumber camps and sawmills in Washington state, fish canneries in Alaska, and tenant farms in California. It was not uncommon to find spouses working together, especially on farms. Glenn also describes the hardships that many of these women endured as they tried to make comfortable homes under very primitive conditions. Those who ended up in urban areas also worked long hours and lived in very tight quarters but were fortunate enough to have access to the ethnic community for social support. The picture bride practice ended in 1920, in response to a new wave of anti-Japanese sentiment.

The Japanese economic success provoked resentment, culminating in the 1924 Immigration Act, which limited immigration from southern and eastern Europe and stopped Asian immigration entirely (Ichioka, 1988). But as Nee and Wong (1985) note, Japanese small businesses continued to prosper in California until the infamous forced evacuation of Japanese Americans to internment camps beginning in February 1942.

Despite the extraordinary hardships of internment, camp life contributed to the emancipation of Issei (first-generation) and Nisei (second-generation) women (Matsumoto, 1984). Given greater opportunities to meet members of the opposite sex, Nisei women were less likely to enter into traditional arranged marriages. Further, the acute labor shortage of the time saw Nisei women moving into the workforce, taking on jobs in the domestic, clerical, manufacturing, and armed forces sectors. Differences of opinion as to how to deal with the government on the internment issue emerged during their confinement, and the issue apparently still continues to divide members of this generation of Japanese Americans, who were deeply affected by it.

The internment ended in 1945, and although many Japanese-American families remained on the West Coast, others dispersed across the United States. The task of reestablishing homes, businesses, and communities was formidable, and it was made more difficult in communities where there still lingered intense opposition and animosity (Fong, 1992). This animosity eventually dissipated, but Fong contends that the "vigor of the pre-war years" was never regained.

The ban on Japanese immigration ended in 1952. Replacing it was a quota system: only 100 Japanese a year were allowed into the States. This restricted entry ended with the 1965 Immigration Act, but unlike the Chinese-American and Filipino-American communities, which experienced a huge second wave of immigrants in the late sixties and early seventies, the Japanese-American community did not experience a similar surge in numbers or significant subsequent waves of immigrants from Japan (Matthaei and Amott, 1990).

Unlike their Chinese and Japanese immigrant counterparts, Filipinos are U.S. nationals (as distinct from U.S. citizens), a status gained through the U.S. colonization of the Philippines in 1898. Like other Asian immigrants, however, Filipinos were motivated to travel to the States by hopes of improving their socioeconomic circumstances and realizing their educational ambitions. Matthaei and Amott (1990) report that in the early 1900s, 14,000 young men came to study in the U.S., most working as domestic servants to pay their way. Others worked as laborers on farms, in canneries, on sugar plantations, in sawmills, and in industrial plants.

Members of the Filipino community were not exempt from acts of discrimination and harassment. They were also subject to the immigration quota system, and emigration from the Philippines was restricted to 50 people a year. Unlike their Chinese and Japanese counterparts, however, they could become citizens through military service (Cordova, 1983) and could intermarry (Posadas, 1981).

Prior to World War II, there were few women. For example, between 1925 and 1929, 24,000 Filipinos entered California, of whom only 1,300, or roughly 5 percent, were women (Rabaya, 1971). In 1930 the ratio of men to women was fourteen to one. Matthaei and Amott (1990) suggest that reasons for the sex imbalance included the preference of employers for young single men and the likelihood that, because of the continued close ties a Filipina tended to maintain with her own family, she might have been unwilling to move.

With the amended War Brides Act of 1947, Filipino-American servicemen began bringing wives in as citizens; in fact, many single Filipinos travelled to the Philippines to marry and then return (Matthaei and Amott, 1990). By this time, many Filipinas were eager to come to the United States. Matthaei and Amott note that most wives worked in agriculture or in the canning industries with their husbands, or in family businesses, or as domestic help in cities. Between 1950 and 1980, 63,000 Filipinas arrived in the United States, some as wives of servicemen stationed in the Philippines (Matthaei and Amott, 1990).

Following the 1965 Immigration Act, a third wave of Filipino immigrants arrived in the United States. As in the Chinese-American community, "bipolar income and job distribution" resulted (Matthaei and Amott, 1990, p. 76). One group comprised poor relatives reuniting with their families; the other was made up of highly qualified and well-trained professionals, many of whom were women.

New immigration from Asia since 1965 has been characterized by settlers from China (including Hong Kong), the Philippines, India, Korea, and Vietnam (Reimers, 1985). These immigrants tend to be either entrepreneurs or well-educated professionals and their families or less well-to-do relatives brought over to the States under the family reunification program. In the 1970s and 1980s significant numbers of refugees—Vietnamese, Cambodians, Hmongs, and Laotians—arrived from Southeast Asia. Many had survived multiple losses and other traumatic and difficult events in their flight from their home countries.

It is estimated that over a million refugees and immigrants from Vietnam, Cambodia, and Laos have arrived in the United States (Rumbaut, 1995). According to Lum (1992), the first wave, of over 130,000 refugees, in the mid-1970s consisted mostly of well-educated and affluent individuals, many of whom had left their homes suddenly and without their families or possessions (Sue and Sue, 1990). Later waves brought farmers, fishermen, and laborers, who tended to be less well educated, possessed fewer job skills, were from rural areas, and were less likely to be fluent in English (Sue and Sue, 1990). Most fled in boats, and many drowned or were killed by pirates. For this later group, the adjustment from a rural, agricultural, and nontechnologically oriented environment to the fast-paced, modern, and technologically progressive United States continues to be a struggle for many (Lum, 1992).

Gordon (1987) reports that roughly 42 percent of all Southeast Asian refugees were women. Refugee women faced particular hardships in some refugee camps (Sundhagul, 1981). Many Khmer women lost their husbands during the war or while fleeing from their home country. The proportion of single-parent female-headed households among Cambodian refugees in 1990 was 25 percent, as compared to the U.S. norm of 16 percent or the overall Asian-American index of 11.5 percent (Rumbaut, 1995). Suddenly finding themselves in the unaccustomed and unwelcome role of head of household and unprepared to cope with this new responsibility on their own, several Khmer widows entered into marriages of convenience, which did not last very long and added further to their anguish (Gordon, 1987). Similarly, young single women in the camps would also resort to hasty and subsequently unsuccessful marriages to protect themselves from the multiple sources of intimidation that were present (Ben-Porath, 1987). Yet another source of difficulty for women in the refugee camps was the lack of any resources to prepare them for their new lives. In contrast, there were specially designed educational activities to prepare men for future work opportunities, including English language preparatory classes (Kelly, 1978). Despite this, in 1990 about half of all Southeast Asian households were classified by the census as "linguistically isolated" or not fluent in English (Rumbaut, 1995).

In sum, the history of Asian Americans in general and of its womenfolk in particular was primarily shaped by hostile immigration policies. These policies and laws were often passed in response to the prevailing vicious racism. Yet Asian-American communities have thrived. This resilience serves as a testament to the fortitude and determination of its members, particularly its womenfolk. Their contributions included being willing to accept any part-time or full-time employment, regardless of their qualifications, both as members of an inexpensive but industrious pool of family labor and as co-procreators of future cheap laborers. In addition, these women were able to support and nurture stable families in spite of the impoverished and hostile circumstances in which many found themselves.

Structure, Status, Beliefs, and Values

Most Asian-American families are patriarchal in structure. In particular, traditional families from East Asian cultures, notably China, Japan, and Korea, are strongly influenced by Confucian philosophy and ethics (Ho, 1987; Shon and Ja, 1982). Within this framework, a woman has three pathways to follow, all of which demand subservience to a male. As Ho (1987) elaborates, in youth, the girl must obey her father, uncle, or brother; in adult womanhood and after marriage, she must obey her husband; on the death of her husband, she is under the protection and direction of her oldest son.

These pathways also reflect the hierarchy of authority based on sex, age, and generation that characterize Asian families (Chow, 1987), with young women at the lowest level, subordinate to father, husband, brother, son. Well-defined roles complement the hierarchal structure, with the father as head of the household—provider, decision maker, disciplinarian, and protector—while the mother serves as compliant wife, nurturer, caretaker of husband and children, and homemaker (Chow, 1987; Shon and Ja, 1982).

Chow (1987) contends that domination by men is a commonly shared oppression for Asian-American women. Women have been socialized to accept "their devaluation, the restricted roles for women, psychological rein-forcement of gender stereotypes, and a subordinate position within Asian communities as well as in the society at large" (p. 286). She adds that while their filial piety and obedience ensures protection by the family, these same qualities socially alienate Asian wives and daughters from their Asian sisters.

At the other end of the continuum are women from families that have acculturated to white, middle-class values. Such families usually consist of sec-ond-, third-, or fourth-generation American-born parents and their children (Ho, 1987). Alternative family forms, such as single-parent families (whether consisting of an unwed mother and her child[ren] or a divorced parent and his or her child[ren]) and gay or lesbian families are still relatively rare. Divorce rates are comparatively low, and more traditional wives are likely to turn to suicide rather than divorce when dealing with marital discord (Ho, 1987).

In between the traditionally raised woman and the Americanized woman are those who continue in their struggle to straddle both cultures and to chal-lenge those worldviews and values that are inconsistent and incompatible with the environmental circumstances in which they find themselves. These women tend to be either recent immigrants or members of the first genera-tion born in the United States, and they are relatively well educated and involved in the labor force. Despite this, their lot is by no means any less demanding. For example, Suzuki (1980) notes that foreign professionals are just as vulnerable to being marginalized as are their working class sisters and just as likely to encounter the so-called glass ceiling. Further, these women, despite their educational advantage, still have to, "struggle at work to ensure family survival and . . . cope with racist oppression, patriarchal domination, and economic exploitation within the work bureaucracy" (Chow, 1994b, p. 221).

The extended family structure is still a valued family form in the Asian-American community. Extended families, however, have had their own unique challenges. Differential rates and patterns of adaptation become sources of conflict, especially between generations where parents tend to adhere to traditional ways while their children adopt the American way. Moreover, because wives are willing to accept lower-status jobs (e.g., domestic work), they initially adapt at a faster rate than their husbands (Santopietro and Lynch, 1980). To complicate matters further, this role reversal, where wives serve as sole providers for their families until the husbands obtain employment, may exacerbate existing family tension.

Not all Asian-American families in the United States today are multigenerational or supported by a network of close kin. Many, in emigrating or fleeing from their country of origin, also left behind familial support networks, and these may not have been replaced. Some extended families, however, coped by creating new families. Distant relatives, friends, and even strangers who were also refugees have been incorporated into the creatively defined extended system (Ben-Porath, 1987), and women played an important role in this reconstruction process (Kibria, 1994). These social support networks served many of the functions that would have been assumed by the extended family system.

Challenges, Strengths, and Responses

Asian-American women have been politically invisible at the national level. Chow (1994a) attributes this invisibility to their relatively small numbers, the ethnic diversity within the group, and geographic dispersion. She adds that to some extent, "political participation may be a class privilege for women who have the luxury of time, money, and energy" (p. 184). Because over two-thirds of Asian women in the United States are foreign-born, many are generally preoccupied with the onerous daily task of subsisting, balancing domestic and workplace responsibilities with little time left over for community participation. Wei (1993) notes that working-class women have been the most neglected and least active sociopolitically among Asian-American women. Even when women have the time, money, and energy, some may be reluctant to be politically visible as a result of the anxieties associated with being recent immigrants. Wanting to fit in—that is, to be inconspicuous and accepted—these Asian women may elect not to participate sociopolitically even when presented with opportunities to do so. They are probably reluctant to rock the boat, fearful that this may place at risk their "landed alien" status, their employment, and their individual and familial socioeconomic and political security.

The disinclination to identify collectively with the feminist movement of the late 1960s and early 1970s was based on the perceived lack of congruence between the goals and vision of both groups of women. Chow (1994a) identifies several factors that she believes were responsible for limiting Asian-American women's participation in the feminist movement. These include the perception that the feminist movement did not address issues and concerns of primary importance to them (i.e., racial and class problems affecting people of color in general and Asian Americans in particular). Then there was the belief that affiliation with the movement would jeopardize the solidarity of the Asian-American community and induce an identity crisis by pitting ethnic identity against gender identity. Another factor was a preoccupation with economic survival, which limited the time and energy available for sociopolitical activism. Finally, an important factor was sociocultural barriers, such as the set of values that many Asian-American women subscribe to—obedience, family centeredness, fatalism, and self-control—values thought to be antithetical to political activism. Further, many recent immigrants lacked proficiency in English, which in turn limited their access to important information, restricted their ability to make demands clearly and coherently, and erected barriers to establishing contacts with women from other representative groups.

Some women activists "preferred to join forces with Asian American men in the struggle against racism and classism" (Chow, 1987, p. 287). But as Asian-American women became more active in their communities, they encountered sexism. They began to realize that equal participation in community organizations could never be realized as long as the traditional dominance of men and the gendered division of labor continued. While some changes in attitudes and treatment of women came about in response to protests and other efforts to sensitize their male counterparts (Chow, 1987), some women leaders remained skeptical that further changes allowing maximum participation by women in those organizations could result. These leaders opted for a separate organization to address issues and concerns specific to women (Chow, 1994a). In this sexist climate, Asian women's groups emerged spontaneously (Wei, 1993).

Two main types of groups have been identified by Chow (1994a): the radical group and the women's rights support group. The radical group espouses a Marxist-Leninist-Maoist approach to sociopolitical and economic reform. They advocate the building of a classless society in which sexism and racism will no longer exist. The women's rights support group seeks to "combat sexism and racism, to achieve social equality and justice in society, and to increase the social participation of women at all levels" (p. 185). Today, the leading Asian-American women organizations include Asian Women United–San Francisco (AWU-SF), the Organization of Asian American Women (OAW), the Organization of Pan Asian American Women (Pan Asia), Pacific Asian American Women Writers–West (PAAWWW), and an umbrella organization, the National Network of Asian and Pacific Women.

Socioeconomically, a challenge that continues to persist is the exploitation of Asian women through the mail-order bride industry. This thriving industry supplies Asian women as wives to non-Asian American and European men. Matthaei and Amott (1990) estimate that some two to three thousand U.S. men find wives this way each year. Most of the women come from poor families in the Philippines and Malaysia (Lai, 1986). Many brides complain of beatings by their spouses but fear deportation if they seek help (Matthaei and Amott, 1990).

In the mental health realm, Chow (1994b) asserts that for many Asians, immigration has had devastating effects on their labor processes and work experience. Asian women have encountered status loss, difficulties in searching for or changing jobs, and problems relating to skill transferability, language differences, unfamiliar work environments, and discrimination. True (1990) reports that despite their diverse cultural, ethnic, and socioeconomic backgrounds, Asian-American women share a certain commonality in the nature of stresses they experience. This is based on their shared experience as members of racial and sexual minority groups, who are thus subjected to the double jeopardy of discrimination. She also notes that Asian-American women have to deal with the conflicting values and belief systems of the family and community on the one hand and the dominant society's on the other.

One source of stress, and thus a potential issue in psychotherapy, is gender and ethnic identity definition. True (1990) notes that definitions of the status and roles of women in many traditional patriarchal families differ from those to which the dominant society subscribes. These conflicting definitions may precipitate an identity crisis in, for example, the working woman, who encounters both value systems on a daily basis. Another source of stress is the childlike image often associated with Asian-American women. Sexual stereotypes of Asian women (e.g., images such as "Suzie Wong" for Chinese women and the "geisha girl" for Japanese women) only serve to reinforce their oppression in U.S. society (Chow, 1987; Matthaei and Amott, 1990; True, 1990). And then there is the widespread tendency to view Asian-American women as employees of choice because of the popular impression that they are hard-working, uncomplaining or passive, and submissive—the very attributes that render them vulnerable to exploitation at work (Chow 1994b; Hossfeld, 1994; True, 1990). Socialized to aspire to be good wives and mothers, Asian-American women who have to work out of economic necessity and who work long hours mount a superhuman effort to be good mothers, wives, and workers. The stress and strain of shifting among multiple roles and the tension associated with role conflicts render these women vulnerable to mental health and physical complaints. Another source of stress for Asian-American women is involvement in interracial relationships. True (1990) maintains that many Asian-American families still discourage interracial relationships, yet the trend is increasing among younger Asian Americans.

Another mental health issue among Asian Americans is family violence and its impact on the individual, the family, and the community. The dynamics of violence render women and children especially vulnerable to abuse. Ho (1987) refers to reports of the use of physical violence on wives and children among a select sample of Vietnamese, Khmer, Laotian, and Southeast Asian Chinese women, and she discusses the cultural implications of this abuse for each subgroup. Young (1995) attributes the incidence of physical abuse among a sample of recent Korean immigrants to the strain of dealing with the stress of immigration and adapting to the demands of a new culture, especially one in which women's status is defined so differently. Incidents of abuse have also been documented among many of the estimated 200,000 Asian-American women married to U.S. military men. These women experience adjustment difficulties and psychosocial isolation, and many husbands, instead of helping their wives to adapt to the transition, became abusive. Matthaei and Amott (1990) report that many wives are unaware of their legal rights and have been divorced without their knowledge, losing financial support and custody of their children. Some have even faced deportation.

Sue (1994) notes that recent immigrants are at greater risk than others for mental health problems. They encounter numerous difficulties, including English language limitations, minority group status, cultural conflicts, and unemployment. Sue adds that Southeast Asian refugees are at particular risk for depression and post-traumatic stress disorder because of "premigration traumas and the postmigration stressors of adapting to and living in a new culture" that is very different from the one they left (p. 271). Trueba, Jacobs, and Kirton (1990) describe the difficult adjustment and acculturation experiences that different refugee groups have encountered. They also refer to the bride-price tradition practiced among Hmong families, which involves pay-ing a dowry to the bride's family, and the adverse effect it has had on young women in the community. Hmong women complain of feeling owned by their husbands and of having no control over their lives.

Gardner (1994) addresses health issues, drawing on data obtained by the National Center for Health Statistics in 1991. He notes that for all age groups in 1988, Asian Americans had the lowest death rates, compared to whites, African Americans, and Native Americans. He also refers to a 1987 U.S. Office of Disease Prevention and Health Promotion publication that reported "the health status of Asian Americans as a group is remarkably good" (p. 18–19). The leading causes of death among Asian-American women are cancer, heart disease, cerebrovascular disease, and accidents. Death rates for Asian-American males are higher than for females at almost every age except ages five to fourteen years. Gardner concludes that as Asian-American immigrants and their descendants adopt more and more of the majority culture's patterns in diet, exercise, smoking, and the like, it is reasonable to expect that their mortality levels and patterns will increasingly approximate those of whites. Any differences would come to be dominated by sociodemographic and economic factors and differences.

Empowerment and Transcendence

Despite the challenges of a racially and sexually segregated labor market, many Asian-American women have made the necessary economic adaptations in order to survive and thrive (Yamanaka and McClelland, 1994). However, the relative economic parity they have achieved tends to come at a price: indifference to family needs, less income than their educations might merit, or longer working hours. One adaptation that women have made is to work more hours per year and more consistently throughout their lives, regardless of family circumstances. Another strategy evidenced among well-educated recent immigrants, especially Filipino and Asian Indian women, is to secure professional employment commensurate with their qualifications, and the income advantage is even more evident when these women are able to become self-employed in professional situations. For Vietnamese women, the way to overcome a discriminatory job market appears to lie with English language proficiency and long hours of work. Native-born Japanese and Chinese Americans have been able to carve a niche for themselves in the public sector (with help from affirmative action provisions), both at the core of the sector, in government bureaucracies, and at the periphery, in schools and hospitals.

Chow (1994b) documents ways in which "Asian American women struggle at work to ensure family survival and to cope with racist oppression, patriarchal domination, and economic exploitation within the work bureaucracy" (p. 221). Contrary to the popular impression of Asian women as submissive and passive, the women in her study were assertive, challenging supervisors and coworkers who threatened their survival, willing to fight to protect work rights, and able to set boundaries to maintain self-respect and dignity. Only 6 percent of her sample of 161 women chose not to respond. Even in their silent protests, Chow claims that the women who participated demonstrated "the inner strength, resourcefulness, and perseverance of Asian American women" (p. 222).

Asian-American women draw strength from their families (Chow, 1994b; Matthaei and Amott, 1990; Yamanaka and McClelland, 1994). When organizational oppression and resistance seem to hamper their occupational outlook and weaken their work involvement, the family becomes an important resource to sustain them in the work world. This phenomenon only increases their dependence on the patriarchy, however, "thus creating a paradox for women in Asian American families" (Chow, 1994b, p. 223). The role of males in the life struggle of Asian-American women remains unresolved (Chow, 1994a). Women should be free to decide whether to work independently or with Asian-American men in partnership.

On a community-wide basis, Wei (1993) notes that one of the vehicles for nurturing Asian-American women's gender and ethnic identities has been the alternative press. He attributes to these publications an early and indispensable role in the development of the women's movement and a distinct pan-Asian identity, "legitimating [women's groups] even before they had gained popular acceptance" (p. 100). These publications presented the Asian-American community with a diversity of perspectives, stimulating them to ponder contemporary social issues and mobilizing them for specific social actions.

At the state level, the California Asian/Pacific Women's Network has played an especially important role in the lives of Asian-American women. Established in the mid-1980s, its priorities have been child care, meeting the needs of women refugees, and combating media stereotypes of Asian-American women. Its Los Angeles chapter has sponsored workshops on personal development, social issues, and professional growth. The chapter has also organized around the issue of mail-order brides, advocating for the cessation of the industry and its exploitation of women. Both the Los Angeles chapter and its sister organization, the Pacific and Asian American Women Bay Area Coalition, are well known for the scholarships they award to Asian-Pacific women seeking to pursue life changes and for their Women Warrior Awards, which "honor distinguished individuals in business, government, education, the arts, and the sciences who have contributed to the advancement of Asian Pacific women" (Wei, 1993, p. 100).

At the national level, activists from the Organization of Asian Women, the Organization of Chinese Americans, and the Japanese American Citizen's League were instrumental in the formation of the Coalition Against Anti-Asian Violence (CAAAV) in 1986. This effort began in response to the concern over rising anti-Asian sentiment, increasing racially motivated acts of violence against Asian businesses and individuals, and police brutality in the New York area. Mindful of the need for a united front, organizers "consciously invited diverse Asian American groups in order to have the broadest possible participation" (Wei, 1993, p. 194).

Educational activities sponsored by CAAAV have included a forum that focused on violence against Asians in America. Careful planning ensured that the session addressed root causes of anti-Asian violence and the importance of building partnerships and coalitions across diverse racial, economic, and political communities (Wei, 1993). The forum emphasized taking a proactive stance as opposed to a reactive approach to problem resolution. The coalition has drawn on advocacy, community mobilization, lobbying, coalition building, applying pressure on government agencies, and developing public and media relations as strategies to advance its cause and to accomplish desired ends. At the membership level, participating organizations have been careful to offer brochures and publications in several different Asian languages, and CAAAV has formed bilingual community outreach teams to reach members. Wei (1993) credits CAAAV's success as a credible community-based organization to its leadership, all of whom have been Asian-American women. Described as culturally sensitive and politically mature, these leaders have been farsighted enough to be inclusive and expansive in their vision and their work. They have also been "astute in avoiding some of the political problems that have adversely affected community-based organizations" (Wei, 1993, p. 196).

Conclusion

Unfortunately, racism, sexism, classism, and the "model minority" stereotype continue to be salient issues in the lives of all Asian-American women. Not only do women confront these pernicious forms of oppression in the dominant society; they also encounter oppression within their own homes and in the community. But women have shown that they are no longer willing to respond with either silence or inaction.

At the personal or individual level, the diversity of experiences and predicaments made complex by a host of multivariate factors (including ethnicity and gender) warrant unique and customized responses to plights and predicaments. In this regard, Cowger's (1994) prescription for a strengths perspective on assessment is particularly pertinent. It is summarized below:

Give preeminence to the client's understanding of the facts
Believe the client
Discover what the client wants
Move the assessment toward personal and environmental strengths
Adopt a multidimensional approach to assessment
Use language the client can understand
Make assessment a joint activity between worker and client
Reach a mutual agreement on the assessment
Avoid blame and blaming
Avoid cause-and-effect thinking
Assess; do not diagnose

Nationally, the challenge for Asian-American women leaders and activists is to be able to mobilize Asian-American women across national, ethnic, and class lines into collective action. The foundations have already been laid through the establishment of umbrella and local women's organizations. These are the representative segments of what Wei (1993) refers to as the Asian-American women's movement. This movement, which started in the 1960s, has been able to endure and expand because it has been responsive to the needs of the growing numbers of Asian women from various subgroups, adapting to changing issues of importance to these women. These issues range from concern with racial equality, social justice, equal opportunities, and political visibility to concrete day-to-day issues, such as the availability and access to supplemental income resources and first-class and affordable child care. Pan-Asian solidarity will be critical as women specifically, and the community in general, work towards these goals. In the meantime, political and socioeconomic empowerment remains a vital process facilitating the mobilization of Asian women into a powerful and cohesive unit of substance and change.

THIRTEEN

Empowering Lesbian and Bisexual Women of Color: Overcoming Three Forms of Oppression*

Larry Icard,† Teresa Jones, and Stephanie Wahab

Lesbian or bisexual women occupy a position in society that can be described as one of triple jeopardy. Three social forces—racism, sexism, and homophobia—result in their being devalued and stigmatized. Each of these forces functions separately as a determinant of oppression. As such, the psychological stress, dehumanizing experiences, and blocked opportunities that lesbian and bisexual women of color encounter are compounded by their exposure to all three.

Although the professional literature is giving increasing attention to lesbian and bisexual women, most has focused on white women. Likewise, most of the attention by scholars to women of color has focused on heterosexual minority women. The dearth of information on lesbian and bisexual women of color restricts efforts to address their empowerment appropriately. Toward filling the gap in the literature, this chapter provides an overview of issues on empowerment among lesbian and bisexual women of color. We explore the powerlessness and supports as described by lesbian and bisexual women of color who participated in focus groups conducted for gathering information for this chapter. We view the experiences of these women through their

* The authors extend their deepest appreciation to the women who contributed information for this chapter through their participation in their focus groups. Thanks to Deborah Ortega for her invaluable assistance and much needed suggestions. Special thanks to
Virginia Senechal for her priceless professional services. They also wish to thank Kathryn
Calderwood for her assistance in transcribing the audio recordings of the focus groups.

† Address replies to Larry D. Icard, School of Social Work, University of Washington, 4101
Fifteenth Avenue NE, Seattle, WA 98195.

involvements in the communities significantly affecting their lives. We then present two examples of empowerment from the field. The first concerns a group of African-American lesbian and bisexual women and their efforts to form a self-help organization. The second pertains to an African-American lesbian's experiences as she tries to effect change through her role as an elected public official. We conclude with a summary of strengths that are critical for lesbian and bisexual women of color in dealing with oppression from racism, sexism, and homophobia and suggestions to help lesbian and bisexual women of color working together and with empowerment practitioners to make changes for themselves and their communities.

In developing this chapter, we were mindful that our objective—to present information representative of the diverse racial and ethnic groups that make up lesbian and bisexual women of color as an oppressed population—was extremely ambitious. We have attempted to be as inclusive as possible. In addition to discussing the concerns of lesbian and bisexual women who are members of historical minority groups such as Native Americans and African Americans, we also consider those of nonhistorical minority groups such as Asians and Pacific Islanders. While emerging research suggests that bisexual and homosexual women share similar experiences, particularly with regard to "being out" with family and friends (Weinberg, Williams and Pryor, 1994), it also suggests that there are more differences than similarities. We have therefore limited our discussion of bisexual women of color and directed the focus of this chapter primarily to lesbian women of color.

Empowerment Issues Among Lesbian and Bisexual Women of Color

Several issues emerge that are central to responding to the personal and collective empowerment needs of lesbian and bisexual women of color. These issues center around racism, heterosexism, and sexism. Racism significantly impacts the lives of women of color who are lesbian or bisexual (Greene, 1994a, 1994b; Smith, 1983). In addition to their encounters with racism in the larger society, lesbian and bisexual women of color must also contend with prejudice and discrimination within the communities that should offer them solace: the broader gay and lesbian communities (Moraga and Anzaldúa, 1983; O'Leary, 1978; Swignoski, 1995a).

The issue of heterosexism takes on a particular dynamic in the lives of lesbian and bisexual women of color. Similar to lesbian and bisexual women and gay men who are white, lesbian and bisexual women of color are vulnerable to the physical, emotional, and economic suffering resulting from homophobia in the larger society (Swignoski, 1995a; Vazquez, 1992). This is intensified when coupled with the strong social hostilities that accompany racism. Historically, society has issued stiffer penalties for homosexuality to minorities than those issued to nonminority homosexuals (Katz, 1983). Given these inequities, another concern is the denigration and ostracism they experience in their ethnic community, a resource crucial in providing a foundation for their personal power (Swignoski, 1995b). Strong ethnic identification, particularly for lesbian or bisexual women of color who have recently immigrated to the United States, can make it extremely difficult for them to resist perceiving themselves as immoral and as social deviants (Chan, 1995).

People of color are disproportionately poor. For women of color who are lesbian or bisexual, the challenges that accompany poverty prevent many from affirming their sexual identities and having access to empowering opportunities available to nonminority lesbian and bisexual women. The obstacles to obtaining an adequate standard of living without a male companion prevent many women of color from affirming their sexual identities. Of equal concern is the classism and elitism that exist in the gay and lesbian communities. The potential for many of these communities to serve as a resource for lesbian or bisexual women of color is hampered because of their implicit and explicit emphasis on middle-class values. While lesbian and bisexual women of color collectively share common social stigmas, their experiences with discrimination and their empowerment needs vary. Of concern to bisexual women of color is that, in general, bisexual women are likely to feel denigrated in the lesbian community. Myths and misperceptions about bisexuality are not uncommon among lesbian women of color, as well as in the larger gay and lesbian community. Misunderstandings and prejudiced attitudes about bisexuality may become intertwined with racist attitudes in the larger gay and lesbian community, resulting in bisexual women of color being deprived both of the support offered through collectives of lesbian women of color and by the larger gay and lesbian community (George, 1993; Weise, 1992).

Methodology

Our effort to develop a fuller understanding of the empowerment issues of lesbian and bisexual women of color led us to conduct two focus groups, composed of a total of ten women: six African Americans, two Latinas, one Japanese American, and one Native American, all of whom live in Seattle, Washington. They ranged in age from thirty-five to fifty-four, and all were recruited by word of mouth and volunteered to participate in the focus groups. Some are in long-term relationships; some are parents as well as grandparents. While their incomes varied from low to middle level, most of the women were highly educated, with at least some college education. Their views are not presented as representative of all lesbian and bisexual women of color.

The groups were asked to address three issues central to this chapter: (1) what the concept of "gay community" meant to them; (2) what concerns and issues they would like to have addressed through the larger gay and lesbian community, through lesbian and bisexual support groups and organizations, or through other groups and organizations; and (3) what strengths would help offset their negative encounters with racism, sexism, and homophobia. Their responses to these questions are included in the following discussion on the ways in which particular communities affect the lives of lesbian or bisexual women of color.

Lesbian/Bisexual Women of Color and Their Communities

Communities offer useful boundaries for understanding from a cultural context the stigmas and the support lesbian and bisexual women of color encounter (Reynolds, 1934; Solomon, 1987). As noted by Lee (1994), "community" is both subjective and objective, place specific and place nonspecific. We consider five communities as having a significant effect on the personal and collective power of lesbian and bisexual minority women: the ethnic community, the gay community, the lesbian community, the ethnic gay and lesbian community, and the community of lesbian and bisexual women of color. The dynamic interplay among the social, cultural, and personal factors distinguishing a lesbian or bisexual woman of color as an individual determines her level of participation in and reference to each community. Each community functions as a resource as well as an obstacle in her life.

ETHNIC COMMUNITY

The affirmations and validations received from one's racial community help to offset negative societal valuations that can affect one's self-concept and personal power (Gary, 1978). For members who are lesbian, however, ethnic communities are often less than nurturing. These communities not only fail to buffer but often contribute to the homophobia and sexism experienced by their lesbian members.

There can also be incongruence between the expectations a lesbian or bisexual woman of color experiences from her ethnic community and the expectations she experiences from the gay community. For example, her racial or ethnic community expects women to marry, have children, and repress any same-sex desires. The gay community, on the other hand, encourages the open acknowledgement of homosexual conduct and identity. The following statement made by a women in our focus groups illustrates this point. "I feel myself . . . in the middle between the African-American community over here—the African-American straight community—and the gay/lesbian community over there. If I go to my ethnic community, I don't know if I'm okay over there, and if I go to the lesbian/gay community, I don't know if I'm okay over there either."

Feelings such as these can contribute to a sense of isolation, which can result in the loss of personal power. Personal powerlessness as described by Solomon (1976) involves the low self-esteem resulting from an individual's experiences with personal resources such as family, friends, and community. Encounters with homophobia in her ethnic community can cause a lesbian women of color to suppress a very important element of her self-concept: her sexual identity (Greene, 1990; Kitzinger, 1987). In her ethnic community, she may never be able to be completely herself. As one of the participants in our focus groups stated, "We socialize with straight African Americans, and we can't be ourselves, we're not comfortable, we have to just enjoy whatever we're doing, and if it's a play or if it's a meeting, whatever, we can't give our whole selves into the project, whatever, whatever that is."

The sexism coupled with the homophobia that lesbian and bisexual women of color experience in their ethnic communities cannot go unnoticed. In all cultures, gender inequities exist between the norms and role expectations of women and men. These double standards are often intertwined with religious values. For example, among Asian-American and Pacific Island populations, Buddhist and Confucian philosophies have a significant influence on the gender role expectations of women and cultural values on homosexuality (Chan, 1992; Sohng and Icard, 1996). Because of religious values, Chinese, Japanese, Taiwanese, Vietnamese, Korean, Laotian, and other Asian women are often relegated to roles subservient to men (Chow, 1989; Lee, 1991). In addition, many Asian cultures devalue homosexuality not for religious reasons but because it disrupts the kinship tradition (Hahm, 1986; Hinsch, 1990). Throughout the Mediterranean world, Arab and Islamic customs subordinate women to men, and homosexual conduct is ridiculed (El Bassel, personal communication; Hocquenqhem, 1994).

As Lorde (1984) comments, the racist believes that miscegenation can contaminate a whole lineage, while the homophobic minority considers lesbians so powerful as to threaten not just to contaminate a lineage but to obfuscate the sex of a racial lineage. Thus many lesbian and bisexual women of color receive no support for their sexual orientation from their ethnic communities (Chrystos, 1993). Many share this concern, made by a participant in our focus groups: "It is my hope in all this to be able to find, you know, a comfortable segment of the African-American community. It's hard, it's very hard, and I don't know if I've figured out what makes it so hard to find them. I don't know."

GAY COMMUNITY

In many parts of the country the gay community is one of the primary resources through which lesbian and bisexual women of color can meet and affiliate with other lesbian and bisexual women of color. We view the gay community as the civic groups, choruses, bars, restaurants, political organizations, media, and other institutions formed by and for lesbians and gays. Researchers and theorists point out the importance of close associations with other homosexuals for the mental health of homosexuals (Cass, 1979). For lesbian and bisexual women of color, however, the gay community does not afford the same benefits that it does their white lesbian and bisexual counterparts. Often the gay community is viewed by lesbian women of color as serving primarily the social, emotional, and political needs of white gay men, as reflected in the following comment: "You know, I guess my sense of the gay community . . . I just look at the white, gay community because there hasn't been a community for women of color. We haven't formed yet, I imagine, although there are some groups that are trying to do that now. But when I came out, there wasn't that sense of community; it was just the gay community, and that was a white, gay community."

Of major concern is the racism that exists in the gay community. Discrimination in bars and restaurants, indifference and segregatation in predominately white social gatherings, and racial slurs are among the forms of racism lesbian and bisexual women of color encounter through the gay community.

Many of the women in our focus groups stated that they felt as if they were caught in the middle of two major forces of racism: the discrimination that exists in the gay community and that in the larger society. As one women stated: "The gay and lesbian community as a whole imposes its racism on us, you know. So that separateness that we feel, or that we go through, I think comes from both directions. Nobody wants to be, nobody wants to participate with a group that is racist or espouses racist ideas. So it happens both ways."

Sadly, many white gays and lesbians fail to recognize how they contribute to the racism lesbian and bisexual women of color experience in the gay community. As one participant pointedly described: "A lot of times they don't know they're behaving in that way, or sometimes they do and sometimes they don't. But a lot of times they don't realize some of the comments they make are offensive or the things they say are offensive. . . . [This]) coworker, who's a lesbian, she says something one day that's very racist. And she says, 'I cannot be a racist. I'm a lesbian!' "

Another concern is the sexism that exists within the gay community. Many of the women in our focus groups felt that their concerns were pushed to the back while attention was directed first to the needs and issues of gay men and second to the concerns of white lesbian women. Daily encounters with the oppression of sexism may translate into less outward expression of wants and desires by lesbians, as compared to gays. These and other factors contribute to the empowerment issues of lesbian and bisexual women of color going largely unnoticed in the gay community. One woman recounted in our focus groups: "Another thing that comes to mind is . . . the fact that the gay community has been AIDS identified for such a long time, and I think, because it [AIDS] has been primarily striking men, that women's health issues are being neglected. So, another concern is trying to get the [gay] men to understand that, you know, it isn't about you [men] all the time. Sorry!"

As a result of their encounters with racism combined with sexism, many lesbian and bisexual women of color may avoid or severely limit their involvement in the gay community. One woman in our focus group reported: "We just separate ourselves. We just say, 'No, I'm not going be a part of this.' "

LESBIAN COMMUNITY

Historically, lesbian groups, social networks, and organizations have been composed largely of white women. As such, the lesbian community may serve as a refuge to buffer the subjugation lesbian women of color experience from homophobia and sexism, yet racial issues mitigate the support that it offers lesbian women of color. Race influences the relationship between lesbian women of color and the lesbian community. The racial oppression that lesbian women of color experience is not shared by their white lesbian cohorts (Cornwell, 1983). As one woman in our focus groups stated: "Yes, there are some common grounds: being lesbian and, uh, being . . . both of us being lesbian, a white person and myself are both lesbian, so we know that oppression, but the lesbian of the majority group does not know the oppression of racism. So, you know, in that way I feel separate from them." Another observed: "You know, they [white lesbians] can always hide that they are lesbians. In fact, well, I've heard people say things, 'Well, maybe I won't say this, 'cause they might think I'm a lesbian, and I really don't want that to happen,' but my being of color, it's not like you can hide that."

For many lesbian women of color, day-to-day survival issues, poverty, housing, and other problems related to racism are more of a priority than issues related to their sexual orientation. Consequently, lesbian women of color are less likely to turn to the lesbian community for political support. Organizations and efforts that focus on racism are more likely to receive their political involvement, as demonstrated in the following comment by one of the participants in our focus groups: "One of the groups that I'm involved with . . . is a group that is of gay and lesbian and bisexual Asian people and Asian-American people . . . working together to raise awareness about us. And to attempt some reconciliation [on gay and lesbian rights]. Some of us are immigrants, some of us have immigrant parents, and they have, uh, you know, just a whole real, different kind of idea a lot of times about what's appropriate in general and much less focus on things around, uh, being gay."

Moreover, as reflected in the next comment made by one of our focus group participants, experiences with racism in the lesbian community are causing many lesbian women of color to turn to racial and ethnic groups for their political involvement, regardless of the group's composition. "In terms of lesbian and gay community groups, I have to say that a lot of times I probably, unless it's like, targeted toward a particular issue that I'm interested in, I usually don't become involved. I'm not even a part of the kinds of organizations I was involved in a lot when I was in Phoenix. When I lived in Phoenix, I didn't know a lot of [gay and lesbian] people of color. I didn't know a lot of gay and lesbian people, period, in Phoenix. I think my tolerance level was a lot higher then than it is now, and I just think that I'm more likely to get involved in something with other people of color who are gay or straight than I am with a white lesbian organization."

Of additional concern is the racism that lesbian and bisexual women of color experience in the lesbian community. One form of racism—sexual racism—occurs when the racial physical attributes of a woman of color become the primary basis of sexual attraction for a white women. Thus the woman of color is viewed as an object rather than an individual. "I've come from a reservation that's really closed, especially to the gay community or the homosexual world at all. So when I came here I was so excited to be able to go into places and dance and, uh, and have other women around, and nobody was looking at you like you had twelve heads. You know. And it was like very comfortable. But then I saw that a lot of the women that were there in that setting were, uh, a lot of them were white, and they always had a person of color on their arm, and I watched as our women were being treated as if they were a flavor of the month, and it was like 'wait a minute!' You know. So I would just withdraw."

Perhaps more important for both lesbian and bisexual women of color, but for lesbian women of color in particular, is the pressure from the lesbian community for them to choose between men and heterosexual women of their own race and the lesbian community. As stated earlier, identification with one's ethnic community is a major source of emotional support. Many lesbian women of color therefore choose not to jeopardize their connection to their ethnic community in exchange for the support the lesbian community offers.

COMMUNITIES OF LESBIANS, BISEXUAL WOMEN, AND GAY MEN OF COLOR

Frustrated by traditional efforts' lack of success in reducing the disproportionate number of people of color, particularly African Americans, who are afflicted with AIDS; angered by the level of racism that exists in the gay and lesbian communities; disappointed over their own racial and ethnic communities' inability to respond effectively to AIDS; enraged by the homophobia they encounter in their own ethnic communities, lesbian and bisexual minority women of color and gay men of color are increasingly coming together to form self-help groups and organizations that are separate from the white gay and lesbian communities (Icard, 1996). This phenomenon, while relatively recent, is not new. (See, for example, Albertson's [1972] and Graber's [1989] discussions on homosexuality among African Americans in the 1920s.) Unlike earlier groups, today's lesbian and bisexual women and gay men of color are joining forces not just for socializing but for political, economic, health, social, and emotional needs as well. As more lesbian and bisexual women of color openly affirm their sexuality and form groups, the opportunities for sharing their experiences of oppression increase. The collective exploration of their encounters with racism, sexism, and homophobia facilitates their liberation, thus freeing them from what Shaull (1994) calls a culture of silence.

LESBIAN AND BISEXUAL WOMEN OF COLOR COMMUNITIES

Among the various communities discussed thus far, those formed by and for lesbian and bisexual women of color come closest to responding fully to their empowerment needs. Groups and organizations formed by lesbian and bisexual women of color offer support for ethnic identity and help counteract the negative valuations of racism. In addition, they serve as a resource for developing the personal and collective power to surmount stigmas and discrimination based on gender. As one participant in our groups stated: "I do not think the lesbian and gay community can address my needs as an African-American lesbian, because my needs are a sense of community among my own. [This is] one of the reasons why groups such Lesbian Women of Color have been established. . . . I think the primary thing for me, again, is that wholeness that I feel around being around my own."

Social groups and networks of lesbian and bisexual minority women are also important in helping to overcome the negative attitudes about homosexuality encountered in the ethnic community. These groups and networks play an important role in prevailing over the cultural barriers that keep lesbian and bisexual women from joining forces. For many lesbians of color, bisexuality continues to be misunderstood. These groups and networks also serve as a resource for bringing lesbian and bisexual women of color together.

Case Examples from the Field

We turn our attention next to presenting two examples of empowerment efforts by lesbian and bisexual women of color. The first example, Sistah-2-Sistah, summarizes the process by which a group of African-American lesbian and bisexual women of color formed an organization. The second discusses a different approach to empowerment, that of working inside a political system, as experienced by Sherry Harris, who at the time this information was collected was a member of the City Council of Seattle. The information in these examples was gathered through structured interviews.

SISTAH-2-SISTAH

Sistah-2-Sistah was founded in 1993 in Seattle, Washington, with the intention of creating a sense of community and empowerment for lesbian, bisexual, and transgender women of African descent. The organization evolved from conversations among six lesbian women of African descent who were associated with an agency specializing in the prevention of AIDS and offering social services to people of color affected by HIV and AIDS. These six founding women recognized the need of the lesbian and bisexual community of African-American women for support, cohesion, and education. The mission statement of Sistah-2-Sistah reads: "Our goals are to offer each woman spiritual, emotional, and educational resources, while providing the means that will enable each woman to help herself; and to become a positive and visible force in the African American community in order to reverse the inaccurate and negative portrayal of Lesbian, Bisexual, and Transgender women of African Descent."

Beginnings. Grassroots organizing calls for a lot of work and often presents many challenges. Sistah-2-Sistah was no exception. The obstacles, however, were mainly logistical; finding women to participate in the group was not a problem: there was a true thirst for such a group in the community. Susan (a fictitious name), one of the founders, states that "women were starved for such a group." Each of the six founding members agreed to invite ten women to the first meeting to develop the organization. Their first meeting attracted over forty women. In developing a list of projects, events, and goals to undertake, the group had to make decisions such as: Are we going to be a profit or nonprofit group? What will our structure look like? How do forty women come to consensus? Bringing forty African-American lesbian women together with different opinions, values, and beliefs was no easy task. But although it has been impossible to meet everyone's needs all of the time, Susan observes that the joy of empowerment comes from working collectively on one issue or goal "together."

Power through filling a need. Seattle has responded well to Sistah-2-Sistah. As stated by Susan, "They, too, have been waiting for this." Many agencies and individuals have turned to Sistah-2-Sistah for information, resources, and help. "The fact that there is a need for our organization gives us power." Sistah-2-Sistah does not speak for all lesbian women of African descent. "Instead, we try to create a path for change: change for us and change for the community," states Susan.

Currently, Sistah-2-Sistah is concentrating on furthering internal development and providing social support to members; however, the mere existence of the organization has had political ramifications. The organization has helped mobilize African-American lesbians and gays around civil rights issues and anti-gay initiatives, both locally and in the state of Washington. Sistah-2-Sistah has focused on raising the local African-American community's awareness of and sensitivity to gay and lesbian issues through offering educational programs and engaging in outreach activities such as speaking to church groups and holding community forums. As Susan states, "The members of Sistah-2-Sistah get involved with organizations and groups in the African-American community and demand change."

Struggles and gains. One of the greatest struggles for Sistah-2-Sistah has been, and continues to be, the acceptance (or nonacceptance) of bisexual African-American women by lesbians in the organization. For many of the reasons previously mentioned in this chapter, lesbian women are not always accepting of bisexual women. Susan states, "We are all sisters, no matter what. We need to understand each other, we need to learn to lift one another up, we need to be compassionate and nonjudgmental."

Susan feels that the most empowering moment for her through all the organizing of Sistah-2-Sistah was their first meeting. She says, "I didn't know there were so many sistahs!" Since that first meeting, three hundred women showed up at a "coming-out" event sponsored by Sistah-2-Sistah. Susan thinks that in order to survive as an organization the women need to work and play together. It is necessary that "we take care of ourselves and each other."

Sistah-2-Sistah has a current membership of one hundred fifty with approximately twenty to forty women regularly attending meetings. The organization is still in an infancy stage, with meetings held four times a month. Two of these are organizational administrative meetings, and two are social meetings. In addition to the coming-out event mentioned earlier, the organization has sponsored workshops on such topics as safer sex, bonding, communication, and spirituality. Susan describes Sistah-2-Sistah as dealing with a wide range of issues. "We have to deal with being people of color, being lesbian and bisexual, and the racism and the sexism in the gay community and the larger community."

WORKING FROM INSIDE POLITICAL SYSTEMS

In 1991 Sherry Harris was elected to the city council of Seattle, thus becoming the first publicly elected, openly lesbian African American in the United States (Thompson, 1994). In addition to her duties as a member of the Seattle City Council, Sherry is a member of the board of the National Black Gay and Lesbian Leadership Forum and an officer of the Gay and Lesbian Association of Elected Officials.

Her journey of personal empowerment. Sherry describes her childhood background as being ordinary. She recalls: "My family was like other families. When I was a youth I was told that I should be thinking about dating boys. However, I remember feeling different. I knew that I was attracted to girls instead of boys. Yet even as I got older I could not find a forum through which I could validate my feelings or develop a clear understanding of my sexuality. I only knew that I was different."

She views two things as important in helping her understand and acknowledge her lesbian sexuality. One was moving away from her family to attend college, which she believes allowed her to be free to explore her feelings. The second was joining a feminist consciousness-raising group. This, she recalls, was perhaps the most instrumental event in facilitating her development of a positive sexual identity as a lesbian. She reminisces how an openly identified lesbian in the group became her role model. Prior to meeting this woman, Sherry remembers only being exposed to lesbians who reflected stereotypes. Discomfort in perceiving herself as fitting the lesbian stereotype and feeling that there was no one with whom she could identify, she suppressed her sexuality. She recollects being impressed because the woman in the consciousness-raising group had a college education, appeared feminine, and was open and positive about being a lesbian. As she stated: "All of a sudden, click!" Through that experience, she feels, she began to get in touch with her sexual identity.

Becoming an advocate for lesbian women of color. Sherry reports: "When I ran for office, I had built up a very broad resume that included my involvement in working on children's issues, transportation issues, and land use, as well as gay rights issues. I felt that I should be up front and honest when questioned about my sexual orientation. However, I did not view my sexuality as an issue or as the basis for my political agenda." She explained how the label "lesbian" became firmly attached to her name through the local media during her campaign.

As she recalls: "Every article discussing my political campaign in one of the local papers would mention that I was gay. In fact, one would not have known that I was African American, because so much attention was placed on my being a lesbian. Every article would start, 'Sherry Harris, lesbian.' " The local media's sensationalizing of her sexuality has resulted in Sherry's being identified locally and nationally as a political advocate for gay and lesbian rights. Her election as the first publicly elected, openly lesbian African American was heralded in the gay press across the country.

Sherry has zealously accepted the role of advocate for lesbian and gay rights that has been thrust upon her. She comments, "I have always been politically active and fought for what I believed in, and I was not going to run away or hide from the challenge that was being presented to me."

Challenges. In the city of Seattle, elections are citywide, therefore Sherry's constituents are all citizens of Seattle. However, as an elected official who is a minority, Sherry feels obligated to represent the issues of minority groups. She also feels that as a minority she is held to higher standards by all the minority groups she represents.

One of the difficulties she continually encounters is trying to respond to all those who turn to her to represent their issues. She views her greatest challenge as trying to advocate and develop policies for minorities. The primary barrier to her effectiveness is the lack of a common agenda among minority groups. She notes, "As I go around the city, I ask various groups of people, 'What is the most important issue for you, and what can I do to help?' I get as many different answers as the number of people being represented in a particular group and the number of different groups I contact. It is difficult for me to be the representative they envision because I've got so many different things on my plate. I may pick one [issue], and the one that I pick may not be yours. So to you I'm not a leader, but to your friend or neighbor I am the greatest thing since sliced bread. Because there is no consensus on the problem, there is no agreement on strategies and solutions."

The upshot is that while she views this as a really exciting time to be a political advocate for racial and sexual minorities, for her it is also a challenging time. She notes, "Gay people and, to a large extent, Hispanics, are the only two groups against whom lawmakers are trying to craft laws to discriminate intentionally." Being an advocate for gay rights and lesbian women of color is even more difficult. She reiterates, "There isn't any clarity on issues, locally or nationally."

Summary and Conclusions

Throughout this chapter we have pointed out how the problems individual lesbian and bisexual women of color experience are influenced by societal forces resulting from racism, sexism, and homophobia. The theme of this chapter has been that once lesbian and bisexual women of color achieve an increased sense of personal power, they can they act collectively to overcome their encounters with racism, sexism, and homophobia.

A necessary condition for the empowerment of lesbian women of color is the rejection of the negative self-image imposed on them by their ethnic communities and by society. Meeting this condition requires consideration of the gender prescriptions, sexual attitudes, and religious values held by ethnic communities; socioeconomic status; and the temporal and social context of each ethnic group's assimilation into U.S. society. Each community to which a lesbian woman of color turns for emotional and social support serves a unique function as a resource. Conscious consideration is required both to coordinate the supports available through each community and to minimize each community's negative effects on the lesbian woman of color's life.

Overcoming oppression requires recognizing the strengths of lesbian and bisexual women of color as individuals and as a community. The women who participated in our focus groups are somewhat unique. Through the very act of volunteering to participate in this project they have distinguished themselves as individuals who are aware of and struggling to overcome their oppression. We therefore thought it appropriate to draw heavily from their experiences in identifying and discussing the strengths necessary to overcome the oppression of racism, sexism, and homophobia that afflicts the lives of lesbian and bisexual women of color. In reviewing their comments, four overlapping prerequisites to nurturing such strengths emerged: self-liberating dialogue, the ability to transform dehumanizing experiences into something empowering, solidarity with others, and love and mutual trust.

As Freire (1994) notes, one of the fundamental requirements for overcoming oppression is to enter a critical dialogue with oneself. This dialogue sets the stage for the struggle for liberation. Central to oppression is a group's acceptance and adoption of the negative attitudes held by its oppressors. Thus, for a lesbian woman of color, self-perceptions are apt to become impaired by her submersion in the way others define her reality. By having a critical self-dialogue, a lesbian or bisexual woman of color can challenge the perceptions about her sexual orientation, race, and gender that she has acquired through the socialization in her ethnic community and society. This process of critical self-discourse is reflected in the views of our focus group participants: "I think one of the interesting things about being a Latino lesbian is recognizing my own power. . . . The more I recognize that I am a Latino lesbian the more powerful I become." Similarly another participant stated: "One of my strengths is finding my pace, my path, and being able to walk that walk and truly believe that I'm okay." These statements reflect how both women have come to recognize their value and worth as individuals who are homosexual, minorities, and women.

Becoming aware of herself through critical self-dialogue only allows a lesbian or bisexual woman of color to achieve a partial understanding of the societal oppression she is experiencing. Her existence as a socially oppressed person is characterized by a dialectical relationship between her perceptions of herself and the experiences she encounters in her social environment. It is this dialectical relationship between a lesbian or bisexual woman of color and the communities that constitute her social world that determines the basis of her decisions about herself and how she views and responds to oppression from her environment. Freire (1994) refers to this process as a separation from and objectification of the world in order to transform it. This process of transforming one's world is reflected in the following comment made by one of our focus group participants: "I draw my strength from . . . the racism I feel from the larger society. . . . The homophobia that I feel from my church strengthens me, too."

Creating solidarity with others means working with members of other oppressed groups who are experiencing similar oppression. This allows two things to occur. First, it allows the lesbian or bisexual women of color to step outside her own experience and see the world from the viewpoint of another. Second, it allows her to gain a better understanding of the size and scope of the oppression she is encountering. One of the participants in our focus groups succinctly described this process: "I get a lot of my strength from working with diverse populations and having to deal with the racism in the society through my work, which is in an agency that serves people of color who are gay and straight."

Love in essence is an act of courage. No matter who is oppressed, the act of love offers a reason for liberation. This is particularly true for lesbian and bisexual women of color. Through loving others, they acknowledge their commitment to the cause of their own liberation. In addition, by allowing herself to be loved by another, the lesbian or bisexual woman of color acknowledges a challenge to which she must respond, and she concedes and accepts the difficulty of trusting in others to support her empowerment. The strength and power gained through love come in many forms. One woman in our focus groups described how coming out to a close friend gave her the personal support that she needed to proceed with her own empowerment. Another spoke of how the love and support she received from her teenaged son helped her overcome the pressures she experienced on daily basis. Others remarked on the support they received from their sexual partners.

For those considering forming an organization for lesbian and bisexual women of color, it is important to develop common agreement on the purpose and goals of the organization. Such an understanding constitutes a basic covenant among members and helps to socialize new members as they join the organization. A clear statement of purpose and goals can be modified to meet the changing needs of the members. The founding members of Sistah-2-Sistah spent a considerable amount of time and energy in the first few months in developing a mission statement. At times, many of members felt too much time was being devoted to this task, but the effort paid off in the long run.

Also important is recognizing that not all lesbian and bisexual women of color have the same interests or needs to organize. Some may want to be members but not take on an active role; others may want to be fully involved. Some may want to focus more on political action; others may want to focus more on socializing. Continual attention must be given to these diverse needs and interests by recognizing how each member makes a contribution to the organization and focusing on common issues.

Additionally, opportunities must be provided to allow all interested women to participate in the formation of the organization. One of the mistakes recognized by the founders of Sistah-2-Sistah was that much of the formative work (i.e., developing drafts of the mission statement and seeking tax-exempt status as a nonprofit organization) occurred outside the general membership meetings. Many members who were not part of these formative meetings felt that they were being left out of the important planning and decision making for the organization.

Learning from the experiences of similar organizations is also important. By drawing early on the experiences of one of the founders of Brother-to-

Brother, an organization for African-American gay men, the founding members of Sistah-2-Sistah were spared many of the hardships of starting an organization. Most importantly, knowledge is essential for empowerment. There are few role models to which lesbian and bisexual women of color can turn for guidance and direction. Likewise, there are few reports of personal and collective empowerment by lesbian women of color from which others may draw. Therefore the development of personal as well as collective knowledge is imperative for beginning the process of empowerment. In particular, knowledge and awareness of oneself is fundamental to allowing all the other conditions of empowerment to occur. The views of one of the women in our focus group best summarize the importance of knowledge: "You know, that 'you're a homosexual and you're not African' stuff, I'm not buying it, 'cause I've been doing some reading. You're not going to beat me down with that. You know, that 'you're a homosexual and you can't be Christian' stuff, I'm just not going to have it 'cause I've done a lot of reading on that. I guess strength is just knowledge for me, is just knowledge, knowledge, and more knowledge."

REFERENCES

◆

Ackelsberg, M., and Diamond, I. (1987). Gender and political life: New directions in political science. In B. Hess and M. Feree (Eds). *Analyzing gender: A handbook of social science.* Newbury Park, CA: Sage.

Acosta, F., and Yamamato, J. (1984). The group work practice with Hispanics. *Social Work with Groups,* 7(3): 63–73.

Acuña, R. (1988). *Occupied America: A history of Chicanos.* New York: Harper and Row.

Adair, M., and Howell, S. (1994). *Breaking old patterns, weaving new ties: Alliance building.* San Francisco: Tools for Change.

Adebimpe, V. R. (1982). Psychiatric symptoms in Black patients. In S. R. Turner and R. T. Jones (Eds). *Behavior modification and Black populations.* New York: Plenum, 57–72.

Adebimpe, V. R., Gigandet, J., and Harris, E. (1979, January). MMPI diagnosis of Black psychiatric patients. *American Journal of Psychiatry,* 136(1): 85–89.

Albee, G. (1986, August). *Powerless, politics, and prevention.* Paper presented at the meeting of the American Psychological Association, Washington, DC.

Albee, G. (1996). Toward a just society: Lessons from observations on the primary prevention of psychopathology. *American Psychologist,* 41(8): 891–898.

Albertson, C. (1972). *Bessie.* New York: Stein and Day.

Albrecht, L., and Brewer, R. (Eds.). (1990). *Bridges of power: Women's multicultural alliances.* Santa Cruz, CA: New Society Publishers.

Allen, W. (1978). Black family research in the United States: A review assessment and extension. *Journal of Comparative Family Studies,* 9 (Summer): 167–189.

Amaro, H. (1988). Women in the Mexican-American community: Religion, culture, and reproductive attitudes and experiences. *Journal of Community Psychology,* 16(1): 6–20.

American Psychiatric Association. (1994). *Diagnostic and statistical manual of mental disorders*. (4th Ed.). Washington, DC: APA.

Andersen, M. A., and Hill-Collins, P. (Eds.) (1995). *Race, class, and gender: An anthology*. (2d Ed.). Belmont, CA: Wadsworth.

Applewhite, S. R., and Daily, R. (1988). *Hispanic elderly in transition: Theory, research, policy, and practice*. New York: Greenwood.

Aragon de Valdez, T. (1980). Organizing as a political tool for the Chicana. *Frontiers*, 5: 7–13.

Arce, C. (1982). A reconsideration of Chicano culture and identity. *Daedalus*, 110: 177–191.

Arguelles, L., and Rivero, A. (1993). Gender/sexual orientation violence and transnational migration: Conversations with some Latinas we think we know. *Urban Anthropology and Studies of Cultural Systems and World Economic Development*, 22: 259–275.

Aries, E. (1977). Male-female interpersonal styles in all male, all female and mixed groups. In A. Sargent (Ed.). *Beyond sex roles*. (Pp. 292–298). St. Paul, MN: West.

Aswad, B. C. and Bilge, B. (1996). *Family and gender among American Muslims: Issues facing Middle Eastern immigrants and their descendants*. Philadelphia: Temple University Press.

Aswad, B. C., and Gray, N. (1996). Challenges to the Arab-American family and ACCESS (Arab Community Center for Economic and Social Services). In B. Aswad and B. Bilge (Eds). *Family and gender among American Muslims: Issues facing Middle Eastern immigrants and their descendants*. (Pp. 223–240). Philadelphia: Temple University Press.

Attneave, C. (1982). American Indians and Alaska Native families: Emigrants in their own homeland. In M. McGoldrick, J. Pearce, and J. Giordano (Eds.). *Ethnicity and family therapy*. (Pp. 55–83). New York: Guilford.

Baca Zinn, M. (1994). Feminist rethinking from racial-ethnic families. In M. Baca Zinn and B. T. Dill (Eds.). *Women of color in U.S. society*. (Pp. 303–314). Philadelphia: Temple University Press.

Baca Zinn, M. (1980). Gender and ethnic identity among Chicanos. *Frontiers*, 5: 18–24.

Baca-Zinn, M., and Dill, B. T. (1994a). Difference and domination. In M. Baca Zinn and B. T. Dill (Eds.). *Women of color in U.S. society*. (Pp. 3–12). Philadelphia: Temple University Press.

Baca-Zinn, M., and Dill, B. T. (Eds.). (1994b). *Women of color in U.S. society*. Philadelphia: Temple University Press.

Baines, D. (1997). Feminist social work in the inner city: The challenges of race, class and gender. *Affilia*, 12(3): 297–317.

Bambara, T. C. (1970). *The Black woman: An anthology*. New York: New American Library.

Bandura, A. (1982, September). The assessment and predictive generality of self-percepts of efficacy. *Journal of Behavior Therapy and Experimental Psychiatry*, 13(3): 195–199.

Bandura, A. (1984, June). Recycling misconceptions of perceived self-efficacy. *Cognitive Therapy and Research*, 8(3): 231–255.

Bandura, A. (1986). *Social foundations of thought and action*. Englewood Cliffs, NJ: Prentice-Hall.

Barrera, M. (1987). Chicano class structure. In R. Takaki (Ed.). *From different shores: Perspectives on race and ethnicity in America*. (Pp. 130–138). New York: Oxford University Press.

Bean, F. D., and Tienda, M. (1987). *The Hispanic population in the United States*. New York: Russell Sage Foundation.

Beckman, L. (1979). The relationship between sex roles, fertility, and family size preferences. *Psychology of Women Quarterly*, 4: 43–60.

Bell, D. (1992). *Faces at the bottom of the well: The permanence of racism*. New York: Basic.

Ben-Porath, Youssef S. (1987). *Issues in the psycho-social adjustment of refugees*. An unpublished report prepared for the National Institute of Mental Health's Refugee Assistance Program, Mental Health Technical Assistance Center, University of Minnesota (Contract No. 278-85-0024 CH).

Bergmann, S. J. and Surrey, J. L. (1997). The woman-man relationship: Impasses and possibilities. In J. Jordan (Ed.). *Women's growth in diversity*. (Pp. 260–287). New York: Guilford.

Bernal, G., and Flores-Ortiz, Y. (1982). Latino families in therapy. *Journal of Marital and Family Therapy*, 8(3): 357–365.

Biegel, D. E., and Naparstek, A. (1982). *Neighborhood networks for humane mental health care*. New York: Plenum.

Billingsley, A. (1968). *Black families in White America*. Englewood Cliffs, NJ: Prentice-Hall.

Bock, S. (1980). Conscientization: Paolo Freire and class-based practice. *Catalyst*, 2: 5–25.

Boes, M., and van Wormer, K. (1997). Social work with homeless women in emergency rooms: A strengths-feminist perspective. *Affilia*, 12(4): 427–451.

Boss, P., Doherty, W., La Rossa, R., Schumm, W., and Steinmetz, S. (1993). *Sourcebook of family theories and methods: A contextual approach*. New York: Plenum.

Boyd-Franklin, N. (1989). *Black families in therapy: A multisystems approach*. New York: Guilford.

Boyd-Franklin, N. (1987, July). Group therapy for Black women: A therapeutic support model. *American Journal of Orthopsychiatry*, 57(3): 394–401.

Bradshaw, C., Soifer, S., and Gutiérrez, L. (1993). Toward a hybrid model for effective organizing in communities of color. *Journal of Community Practice*, 1: 25–42.

Brandon, W. (1974). *The last Americans: The Indian in American culture*. New York: McGraw-Hill.

Bredeson, P. V. (1989, October–November). Redefining leadership and the roles of school principals: Responses to changes in the professional worklife of teachers. *High School Journal,* 73(1): 9–20.

Bricker-Jenkins, M., Hooyman, N., and Gottlieb, N. (Eds). (1991). *Feminist social work practice.* Newbury Park, CA: Sage.

Bricker-Jenkins, M., and Hooyman, N. (1986). *Not for women only: Social work practice for a feminist future.* Silver Springs, MD: NASW.

Brown, P. (1994). Participatory research: A new paradigm for social work. In L. Gutiérrez and P. Nurius (Eds.). *Education and research for empowerment practice.* (Pp. 291–302). Seattle: Center for Policy and Practice Research, University of Washington.

Brower, A. M., Garvin, C. D., Hobson, J., Reed, B. G., and Reed, H. Exploring the effects of leader, gender, and race on group behavior. (1987). In J. Lassner, K. Powell, and E. Finnigan (Eds.). *Social group work: Competence and values in practice.* (Pp. 129–148). New York: Haworth.

Brownell, P. (1997). Multicultural practice and domestic violence. Chapter 13 in E. P. Congress (Ed.). *Multicultural perspectives in working with families.* (Pp. 217–235). New York: Springer.

Burghardt, S. (1982). *Organizing for community action.* Beverly Hills: Sage.

Burr, W. R. (1979). *Contemporary theories about the family.* New York: Free Press.

Burwell, N. Y. (1995). Shifting the historical lens: Early economic empowerment among African Americans. *Journal of Baccalaureate Social Work,* 1(1): 25–37.

Carpenter, E. (1980). Social services, policies, and issues. *Social Casework,* 61: 455–461.

Cass, V. C. (1979). Homosexual identity formation: A theoretical model. *Journal of Homosexuality,* 4: 219–235.

Castex, G. M. (1993). Frames of reference: The effects of ethnocentric map projections on professional practice. *Social Work,* 38(6): 713–726.

Ceballo, R. E. (1995). *Living in dangerous neighborhoods: The effects on poor, African-American single mothers and their children.* Doctoral dissertation, University of Michigan, Ann Arbor.

Chan, C. S. (1992). Cultural considerations in counseling Asian American lesbian and gay men. In S. Dworkin, and F. Guitierres (Eds.). *Counseling gay men and lesbians: Journey to the end of the rainbow.* (Pp. 115–124). Alexandria, VA: American Association for Counseling and Development.

Chan, C. S. (1995). Issues of sexual identity in an ethnic minority: The case of Chinese American lesbians, gay men, and bisexual people. In A. R. D'Augelli and C. J. Patterson (Eds.). *Lesbian, gay and bisexual identities over the lifespan.* (Pp. 87–101). New York: Oxford University Press.

Chau, K. L. (1990). Social work practice: Towards a cross-cultural practice model. *Journal of Applied Social Sciences,* 14(2): 249–275.

Checkoway, B. (1997). Core concepts of community change. *Journal of Community Practice,* 4(1): 11–29.

Checkoway, B., and Norsman, A. (1986). Empowering citizens with disabilities. *Community Development Journal,* 21: 270–277.

Cheetham, J. (1982). *Social work and ethnicity.* Boston: Allen and Unwin.

Chernesky, R. (1997). Managing agencies for multicultural services. Chapter 2 in E. P. Congress (Ed.). *Multicultural perspectives in working with families.* (Pp. 17–33). New York: Springer.

Chesler, M., and Chesney, B. (1988). Self-help groups: Empowerment attitudes and behaviors of disabled or chronically ill persons. In H. Yucker (Ed.). *Attitudes toward persons with disabilities.* (Pp. 230–247). New York: Springer.

Chesler, M., and Chesney, B. (1991). *Self-help groups for parents of children with cancer.* Madison, WI: University of Wisconsin Press.

Chow, E. N. (1985). Acculturation experience of Asian American women. In A. Sargent (Ed.). *Beyond sex roles.* (Pp. 238–251). St Paul, MN: West.

Chow, E. N. (1987). The development of feminist consciousness among Asian American women. *Gender and Society,* 1(3): 284–299.

Chow, E. N. (1989). The feminist movement: Where are all the Asian American women? In Asian Women United of California (Ed.). *Making waves: An anthology of writings by and about Asian American Women.* (Pp. 362–376). Boston: Beacon.

Chow, E. N. (1994a). The feminist movement: Where are all the Asian American women? In Ronald Takaki (Ed.). *From different shores: Perspectives on race and ethnicity in America.* (Pp. 184–208). New York: Oxford University Press.

Chow, E. N. (1994b). Asian American women at work. In M. Baca Zinn and B. T. Dill (Eds.). *Women of color in U.S. society.* (Pp. 247–264). Philadelphia: Temple University Press.

Chrystos. (1993). Ya don't wanna eat pussy. In J. Penelope and S. J. Wolfe (Eds.). *Lesbian culture: An anthology.* (P. 207). Freedom, CA: Crossing.

Chu, J., and Sue, S. (1984, Fall). Asian/Pacific-Americans and group practice. *Social Work with Groups,* 7(3): 23–36.

Churchill, W., and LaDuke, W. (1992). Native North America: The political economy of radioactive colonialism. In M. A. Jaimes (Ed.). *The state of Native America: Genocide, colonization, and resistance.* (Pp. 241–266). Boston: South End.

Clayton, S., and Crosby, F. (1987). The search for connections. *Journal of Social Issues,* 42. 1–10.

Cohen, H. (1997). The impact of culture in social work practice with groups: The grandmothers as mothers again case study. Chapter 18 in E. P. Congress (Ed.). *Multicultural perspectives in working with families.* (Pp. 311–331). New York: Springer.

Cohen, H. (1990). My client, myself. *Family Therapy Networker, 14 (3).* 19–23.

Cole, E. (1993). *Women of the protest generation at midlife: Personality development, political consciousness, and activism.* Doctoral dissertation, University of Michigan, Ann Arbor.

Coll, C., Cook-Nobles, R., and Surrey, J. (1997). Building connection through diversity. In J. Jordan (Ed.). *Women's growth in diversity.* (Pp. 176–198). New York: Guilford.

Comas-Diaz, L. (1981, October). Effects of cognitive and behavioral group treatment on the depressive symptomatology of Puerto Rican women. *Journal of Consulting and Clinical Psychology,* 49(5): 627–632.

Comas-Diaz, L., and Greene, B. (1994). *Women of color: Integrating ethnic and gender identities in psychotherapy.* (Pp. 389–427.) New York: Guilford.

Comas-Diaz, L., and Griffith, E. (1988). *Clinical guidelines in cross-cultural mental health.* New York: Wiley.

Congress, E. (1997). *Multicultural perspectives in working with families.* New York: Springer.

Congress, E., and Lynn, M. (1997). Family and group approaches with culturally diverse families: A dialogue to increase collaboration. In E. Congress (Ed.). *Multicultural perspectives in working with families.* (Pp. 275–287). New York: Springer.

Coppola, M., and Rivas, R. (1985). The task-action group technique: A case study of empowering the elderly. In M. Parenes (Ed.). *Innovations in social group work: Feedback from practice to theory.* (Pp. 133–147). New York: Haworth.

Cordova, F. (1983). *Filipinos: Forgotten Asian Americans.* Dubuque, IA: Kendall/Hunt.

Cormier, L. S., and Cormier, W. (1998). *Interviewing strategies for helpers: Fundamental skills and cognitive behavioral interventions.* (4th Ed.). Pacific Grove, CA: Brooks/Cole.

Cornwell, A. (1983). *Black lesbian in White America.* Tallahassee: NAIAD.

Cowger, C. D. (1994). Assessing client strengths: Clinical assessment for client empowerment. *Social Work,* 39(3): 262–267.

Cox, E. (1992). The critical role of social action in empowerment oriented groups. *Social Work with Groups,* 14(3/4): 77–90.

Cox, T. (1993). *Cultural diversity in organizations: Theory, research, and practice.* San Francisco, CA: Berrett-Koehler.

Cromwell, V., and Cromwell, R. (1978). Perceived dominance in decision-making and conflict resolution among Anglo, Black, and Chicano couples, *Journal of Marriage and the Family,* 40: 749–759.

Crosbie-Burnett, M., and Lewis, E. (1993a). A social-cognitive model of couples and families: An integration of contributions from psychological theories. In P. Boss, W. Doherty, R. La Rossa, W. Schumm, and S. Steinmetz (Eds.). *Sourcebook of family theories and methods: A contextual approach.* (Pp. 531–557). New York: Plenum.

Crosbie-Burnett, M., and Lewis, E. (1993b). Use of African-American family structures and functioning to address the challenges of European-American post-divorce families. *Family Relations, 42(July):* 243–248.

Crosby, F., and Hereck, G. (1987). Male sympathy and the situation of women: Does personal experience make a difference? *Journal of Social Issues,* 42: 55–66.

Cross, T. (1986). Drawing on cultural tradition in Indian child welfare practice. *Social Casework,* 67: 283–289.

Crow Dog, M., and Erdoes, R. (1990). *Lakota woman.* New York: Harper Perennial.

Crowfoot, J. E. (1972). *Planning and social systems: Organizations as a special case.* Ann Arbor: Center for Research on Utilization of Scientific Knowledge, Institute for Social Research, University of Michigan, Ann Arbor.

Danziger, S. K. (1995). Family life and teenage pregnancy in the inner-city: Experiences of African-American youth. *Children and Youth Services Review,* 17(1–2): 183–202.

Darabi, K., Dryfoos, J., and Schwartz, D. (1986). Hispanic adolescent fertility. *Hispanic Journal of the Behavioral Sciences,* 8: 157–171.

Davis, A. (1983). *Women, race, and class.* New York: Vintage.

Davis, L. E. (1984). Essential components of group work with Black Americans. *Social Work with Groups,* 7(3): 97–109.

Davis, L. E., Cheng, L., and Strube, M. (1996). Differential effects of racial compositions on male and female groups: Implications for group work practice. *Social Work Research,* 20(3): 157–167.

Davis, L. E., Galinsky, M. J., and Schopler, J. H. (1995). RAP: A framework for leadership of multicultural groups. *Social Work,* 40(2): 156–165.

Davis, L. E., and Proctor, E. K. (1989). *Race, gender and class: Guidelines for practice with individuals, families, and groups.* Englewood Cliffs, NJ: Prentice-Hall.

Davis, S., and Harris, M. (1982). Sexual knowledge, sexual interests, and sources of sexual information of rural and urban adolescents from three cultures. *Adolescence,* 17: 471–492.

Delgado, M. (1983). Hispanics and psychotherapeutic groups. *International Journal of Group Psychotherapy,* 33(4): 507–520.

Delgado, M., and Hum-Delgado, D. (1982). Natural support systems: Source of strength in Hispanic communities. *Social Work,* 27: 83–89.

DeLois, K. (1998). Empowerment practice with lesbians and gay men. In L. Gutiérrez, R. Parsons, and E. Cox (Eds). *Empowerment in social work: A sourcebook.* (Pp: 40–51). Pacific Grove, CA: Brooks/Cole.

Devore, W., and Schlesinger, E. (1996). *Ethnic-sensitive social work practice.* (4th Ed.). Boston: Allyn and Bacon.

Devore, W., and Schlesinger, E. (1987). *Ethnic-sensitive social work practice.* Columbus: Merrill.

Dill, B. T. (1994). Fictive kin, paper sons, and compadrazgo: Women of color and the struggle for family survival. In M. Baca Zinn and B. T. Dill (Eds.). *Women of color in U.S. society.* (Pp. 149–170). Philadelphia: Temple University Press.

Dodd, P. (1994). *On being a bright and ambitious woman: Four voices from upper management.* Doctoral dissertation, University of Michigan, Ann Arbor.

Ellis, A. (1962). *Reason and emotion in psychotherapy.* New York: Lyle Stuart.

Erlich, J. (1992). *Community organizing in a diverse society.* Boston: Allyn and Bacon.

Estrada, L., Garcia, C., Macias, R., and Maldonado, L. (1982). Chicanos in the United States: A history of exploitation and resistance. *Daedalus,* 110: 103–131.

Evans, S. (1980). *Personal politics.* New York: Vintage.

Ewalt, P. (1994). On not knowing. *Social Work,* 39(3): 245–246.

Fagan, H. (1979). *Empowerment: Skills for parish social action.* New York: Paulist.

Falicov, C. J. (1982). Mexican families. In M. McGoldrick, J. K. Pearce, and J. Giordano (Eds.). *Ethnicity and family therapy.* (Pp. 134–163). New York: Guilford.

Fay, B. (1987). *Critical social science: Liberation and its limits.* Ithaca, NY: Cornell University Press.

Feldman-Summers, S., and Ashworth, C. (1981). Factors related to intentions to report a rape. *Journal of Social Issues,* 37: 53–70.

Fighting Back: Frances Sandoval and her mother's crusade take aim at gangs. (1988, October 16). *Sunday Chicago Tribune Magazine,* pp: 10–24.

Figueira-McDonough, J., Netting, F. E., and Nichols-Casebolt, A. (1998). *The role of gender in practice knowledge: Claiming half the human experience.* New York: Garland.

Fischer, G. (1987). Hispanic and majority student attitudes toward forcible date rape as a function of differences in attitudes toward women. *Sex Roles,* 17: 93–101.

Fitzpatrick, J., and Gomez, T. (1997). Still caught in a trap: The continued povertization of women. *Affilia,* 12(3): 318–341.

Flynn, J. (1994). Social justice in social agencies. In R. Edwards (Ed.). *Encyclopedia of social work.* (19th Ed.). (Pp. 2173–2179). Washington, DC: NASW.

Fong, R. (1992). A history of Asian Americans. In S. M. Furuto, R. Biswas, D. K. Chung, K. Murase, and F. Ross-Sheriff (Eds.). *Social work with Asian Americans.* Newbury Park, CA: Sage.

Frankenberg, R. (1993). *The social construction of Whiteness: White women, race matters.* Minneapolis: University of Minnesota Press.

Freire, P. (1970). Cultural action for freedom. *Harvard Educational Review,* 40: 205–225, 452–477.

Freire, P. (1973). *Education for critical consciousness.* New York: Seabury.

Freire, P. (1994). *Pedagogy of the oppressed.* New York: Continuum.

Fuchs, V. (1983). *Who shall live? Health, economics, and social choice.* New York: Basic.

Gallegos, J. (1982). The ethnic competence model for social work education. In B. White (Ed.). *Color in a White society.* (Pp. 1–9). Silver Springs, MD: NASW.

Garcia, J., and Montgomery, P. (1991). *The Hispanic population in the United States: March 1990.* Washington, DC: U.S. Department of Commerce.

Gardner, R. (1994). Mortality. In N. W. S. Zane, D. T. Takeuchi, and K. N. J. Young (Eds.). *Confronting critical health issues of Asian and Pacific Islander Americans.* (Pp: 53–104). Thousand Oaks, CA: Sage.

Garvin, C. (1985). Work with disadvantaged and oppressed groups. In M. Sundel, P. Glasser, R. Sarri, and R. Vinter (Eds.). *Individual change through small groups.* (2d Ed.). (Pp. 461–472). New York: Free Press.

Garvin, C., and Reed, B. (1995). Sources and visions for feminist group work: Reflective processes, social justice, diversity, and connection. In N. Van Den Bergh (Ed.). *Feminist practice in the twenty-first century.* (Pp. 41–69.) Washington, DC: NASW.

Garvin, C. D., and Seabury, B. A. (1997). *Interpersonal practice in social work: Promoting competence and social justice.* (2d Ed.) Boston: Allyn and Bacon.

Gary, L. E. (1978). Mental health: A conceptual overview. In L. E. Gary (Ed.). *Mental health: A challenge to the Black community.* Philadelphia: Dorrance.

Gaventa, J. (1980). *Power and powerlessness: Quiescence and rebellion in an Appalachian valley.* Urbana: University of Illinois Press.

George, S. (1993). *Women and bisexuality.* London: Scarlet.

Germain, C. (1979). *Social work practice: People and environments.* New York: Columbia University Press.

Germain, C. B. (1973). An ecological perspective in casework practice. *Social Casework,* 54(7): 323–330.

Germain, C. B., and Gitterman, A. (1980). *The life model of social work practice.* New York: Columbia University Press.

Germain, C., and Gitterman, A. (1996). *The life model of social work practice: Advances in theory and practice.* (2d Ed.). New York: Columbia University Press.

Gerschick, T., Israel, B., and Checkoway, B. (1990). *Means of empowerment in individuals, organizations, and communities.* Ann Arbor: University of Michigan Center for Research on Social Organizations.

Gibson, G. (1983). *Our kingdom stands on brittle glass.* Silver Springs, MD: NASW.

Giddings, P. (1984). *When and where I enter: The impact of Black women on race and sex in America.* New York: Morrow.

Gilder, G. (1981). *Wealth and poverty.* New York: Basic.

Gilkes, C. (1983). Going up for the oppressed: The career mobility of Black women community workers. *Journal of Social Issues,* 39(3): 115–139.

Gilkes, C. (1981). Holding back the ocean with a broom: Black women and community work. In L. F. Rodgers-Rose (Ed.). *The Black woman.* (Pp. 217–233). Beverly Hills: Sage.

Giovanni, N. (1996). Nikki Rosa. In *Selected poems of Nikki Giovanni.* (P. 43). New York: Morrow.

Giovanni, N. (1994). *Racism 101.* New York: Morrow.

Gitterman, A., and Schulman, L. (1994). *Mutual aid groups, vulnerable populations, and the life cycle.* New York: Columbia University Press.

GlenMaye, L. (1998). Women as an oppressed group. In L. Gutiérrez, R. Parsons, and E. Cox (Eds.). *Empowerment in social work: A sourcebook.* (Pp: 30–39). Pacific Grove, CA: Brooks/Cole.

Glenn, E. N. (1984). The dialectics of wage work: Japanese American women and domestic service, 1905–40. In L. Cheng and E. Bonacich (Eds.). *Labor immigration under capitalism: Asian workers in the United States before World War II.* Berkeley: University of California Press.

Glenn, E. N. (1986). *Issei, Nisei, war bride: Three generations of Japanese women in domestic service.* Philadelphia: Temple University Press.

Glenn, E. N. (1983). Split household, small producer, and dual wage earner: An analysis of Chinese-American family strategies, *Journal of Marriage and the Family*, 45(1): 35–46.

Goldberg, S., and Deutsch, F. (1977). Theories and methodologies: The study of individuals and families. In S. Goldberg and F. Deutsch (Eds.). *Life-span individual and family development*. (Pp: 51–58). Monterey, CA: Brooks/Cole.

Gordon, L. W. (1987). Southest Asian refugee migration to the United States. In J. T. Fawcett and B. V. Carino (Eds.). *Pacific bridges: The new immigration from Asia and the Pacific Islands*. (Pp. 153–174). New York: Center for Migration Studies.

Gould, K. (1987). Feminist principals and minority concerns: Contributions, problems, and solutions. *Affilia*, 3(1): 6–19.

Graber, E. (1989). A spectacle in color: The lesbian and gay subculture of jazz age Harlem. In M. Duberman, M. Vicinus, and G. Chauncey, Jr. (Eds.). *Hidden from history: Reclaiming the gay and lesbian past*. (Pp. 318–331). New York: Meridian.

Greene, B. (1994a). Ethnic-minority lesbians and gay men: Mental health and treatment issues. Special issue: Mental health of lesbians and gay men. *Journal of Consulting and Clinical Psychology*, 62(2): 243–251.

Greene, B. (1994b). Lesbian women of color: Triple jeopardy. In L. Comas-Diaz and B. Greene (Eds.). *Women of color: Integrating ethnic and gender identities in psychotherapy*. New York: Guilford.

Greene, B. (1994c). *Women of color: Integrating ethnic and gender identities in psychotherapy*. New York: Guilford.

Greene, B. (1993). Psychotherapy with African-American women: Integrating feminist and psychodynamic models. Special issue: Psychotherapy with women from a feminist perspective. *Journal of Training and Practice in Professional Psychology*, 7(1): 49–66.

Greene, B. (1990). African American lesbian: The role of family, culture and racism. *BF Magazine*, pp. 6, 26.

Gunn Allen, P. (1986). *The sacred hoop: Recovering the feminine in American Indian traditions*. Boston: Beacon.

Gurin, P. (1975). *Black consciousness, identity and achievement: A study of students in historically Black colleges*. New York: Wiley.

Gurin, P. (1985). Women's gender consciousness. *Public Opinion Quarterly*, 49(2): 143–163.

Gurin, P., Miller, A. H., and Gurin, G. (1980). Stratum identification and consciousness. *Social Psychology Quarterly*, 43(1): 30–47.

Gutiérrez, L. (1994). Beyond coping: An empowerment perspective on stressful life events. *Journal of Sociology and Social Welfare*, 21(3): 201–220.

Gutiérrez, L. (1992). Empowering clients in the twenty-first century: The role of human service organizations. In Y. Hasenfeld (Ed.). *Human service organizations as complex organizations*. (Pp. 320–338). Newbury Park, CA: Sage.

Gutiérrez, L. M. (1991). Empowering women of color: A feminist approach. In Hooyman, N., and Bricker-Jenkins, M. *Feminist social work practice in clinical settings.* (Pp. 199–214). Beverly Hills: Sage.

Gutiérrez, L. M. (1990). Working with women of color: An empowerment perspective. *Social Work*, 35(2): 149–153.

Gutiérrez, L., DeLois, K., and GlenMaye, L. (1995). Understanding empowerment practice: Building on practitioner based knowledge. *Families in Society*, 76(9): 534–542.

Gutiérrez, L., GlenMaye, L., and DeLois, K. (1995). The organizational context of empowerment practice: Implications for social work administration. *Social Work*, 40(2): 249–258.

Gutiérrez, L., and Lewis, E. (1994). Community organizing with women of color: A feminist perspective. *Journal of Community Practice*, 1(2): 23–44.

Gutiérrez, L., and Lewis, E. (1992). A feminist perspective on organizing with women of color. In J. Erlich and F. Rivera (Eds.). *Community organizing in a diverse society.* (Pp. 113–132). Boston: Allyn and Bacon.

Gutiérrez, L., Lewis, E., and Nagda, B. A. (1995, June). *Creative multicultural work within organizations.* Workshop presented at Bertha Capen Reynolds Society Annual Meeting, Philadelphia, PA.

Gutiérrez, L., and Nagda, B. (1996). The multicultural imperative in human services organizations: Issues for the 21st century. In P. Raffoul and A. McNeece (Eds.). *Future issues for social work practice.* Boston: Allyn and Bacon.

Gutiérrez, L., Oh, H., and Gillmore, M. R. (1997, August). *Understanding perceptions of risk and (em)power(ment) for STD prevention.* Paper presented at the American Psychological Association Conference. Chicago, IL.

Gutiérrez, L., and Ortega, R. (1991). Developing methods to empower Latinos: The importance of groups. *Social Work with Groups*, 14(2): 23–43.

Gutiérrez, L., Ortega, R., and Suarez, Z. (1990). Self help and the Latino community. In T. Powell (Ed.). *Working with self-help.* Silver Springs, MD: NASW.

Gutiérrez, L., Parsons, R., and Cox, E. (Eds.). (1998). *Empowerment in social work practice: A sourcebook.* Pacific Grove, CA: Brooks/Cole.

Gutiérrez, L., Reed, B. G., Ortega, R., and Lewis, E. (1998). Teaching about groups in a gendered world: Toward curricular transformation in group work education. In J. Figueira-McDonough, F. E. Netting, and A. Nichols-Casebolt (Eds). *The role of gender in practice knowledge: Claiming half the human experience.* (Pp. 170–204). New York: Garland.

Hahm, P. C. (1986). *Korean jurisprudence, politics and culture.* Seoul: Yonsei University Press.

Hanke, L. (1959). *Aristotle and the American Indians: A study in race prejudice in the modern world.* Chicago: Henry Regnery.

Hansen, J. *Cultural perspectives in family therapy.* Aspen, CO: Aspen Systems Corp.

Hardy-Fanta, C. (1986). Social action in Hispanic groups. *Social Work*, 31(2): 119–123.

Hartman, A., and Laird, J. (1978). Diagrammatic assessment of family relationships. *Social Casework*, 59: 465–476.

Haslett, D. C. (1997). Hull House and the birth control movement: The untold story. *Affilia*, 12(3): 261–277.

Hayes-Bautista, D., and Chapa, J. (1987). Latino terminology: Conceptual bases for standardized terminology. *American Journal of Public Health*, 77: 61–68.

Henderson, D. (1994). Feminist participatory nursing research with women in drug treatment. Doctoral dissertation, School of Nursing, University of Michigan, Ann Arbor.

Henly, J. (1994). *Surviving without welfare: The informal support networks of former general assistance recipients.* Doctoral dissertation, University of Michigan, Ann Arbor.

Hernández, S., Jorgensen, J., and Parsons, R. (1988). Integrated practice: A framework for problem solving. *Social Work*, 33: 417–421.

Hill-Collins, P. (1997, November). *Women in families: Race, gender and class.* Keynote speech presented at the annual meeting of the National Council on Family Relations, Chicago, IL.

Hill-Collins, P. (1990). *Black feminist thought.* New York: Routledge.

Hinsch, B. (1990). *Passions of the cut sleeve: The male homosexual tradition in China.* Berkeley: University of California Press.

Hirayama, H., and Hirayama, K. (1985). Empowerment through group participation: Process and goal. In M. Parnes (Ed.). *Innovations in social group work: Feedback from practice to theory.* (Pp. 119–131). New York: Haworth.

Hirsch, K. (1991). Clementine Barfield takes on the mean streets of Detroit. *Ms.: The World of Women*, 1(4): 54–58.

Ho, C. K. (1990). An analysis of domestic violence in Asian American communities: A multicultural approach to counseling. *Women and Therapy, 9(1/2)*: 129–150.

Ho, M. K. (1987). *Family therapy with ethnic minorities.* Newbury Park, CA: Sage.

Hocquenghem, G. (1994). Towards an irrecuperable pederasty. In J. Goldberg (Ed.). *Reclaiming Sodom.* (Pp. 233–246). New York: Routledge.

Hodges, V., Burwell, Y., and Ortega, D. (1998). Empowering families. In L. Gutiérrez, R. Parsons, and E. Cox (Eds.). *Empowerment in social work: A sourcebook.* Pacific Grove, CA: Brooks/Cole.

Holman, A. M. (1983). *Family assessment: Tools for understanding and for intervention.* Beverly Hills: Sage.

hooks, b. (1981). *Ain't I a woman: Black women and feminism.* Boston: South End.

hooks, b. (1995). *Killing rage: Ending racism.* New York: Henry Holt.

hooks, b. (1994). *Outlaw culture: Resisting representatives.* New York: Routledge.

hooks, b. (1993). *Sisters of the yam: Black women and self-recovery.* Boston: South End.

hooks, bell (1990a). Choosing the margins as a space of radical openness. Ch. 15 in *Yearning: Race, gender, and cultural politics.* (Pp. 145–153). Boston: South End.

hooks, b. (1990b). *Yearning: Race, gender, and cultural politics.* Boston: South End.

Horseman, R. (1981). *Race and manifest destiny.* Cambridge: Harvard University Press.

Hossfeld, K. J. (1994). Hiring immigrant women: Silicon Valley's "simple formula." In M. Baca Zinn and B. T. Dill (Eds.), *Women of color in U.S. society.* (Pp: 65–93). Philadelphia: Temple University Press.

Hunter, A. (1997). Counting on grandmothers: Black mothers' and fathers' reliance on grandmothers for parenting support. *Journal of Family Issues,* 18: 251–269.

Hunter, A. (1993). Making a way: Strategies of southern urban African-American families, 1900 and 1936. *Journal of Family History,* 18: 231–248.

Hunter, A., and Ensminger, M. (1992a). Diversity and fluidity in children's living arrangements. In E. Congress (Ed.). *Multicultural perspectives in working with families.* New York: Springer.

Hunter, A., and Ensminger, M. (1992b). Family transitions in an urban Afro-American community. *Journal of Marriage and the Family,* 54: 418–426.

Hurtado, A. (1996). *The color of privilege: Three blasphemies on race and feminism.* Ann Arbor: University of Michigan Press.

Hurtado, A. (1982). *Domination and intergroup relations: The impact on Chicano linguistic attitudes.* Unpublished doctoral dissertation, University of Michigan, Ann Arbor.

Hurtado, A. (1997). Understanding multiple group identities. *Journal of Social Issues,* 53(2): 299–329.

Hyde, C. (1996). A feminist response to Rothman's "The interweaving of community intervention approaches." *Journal of Community Practice, 3(3/4):* 127–45.

Hyde, J. (1986). *The psychology of gender: Advances through meta-analysis.* Baltimore: Johns Hopkins University Press.

Icard, L. (1996). Assessing the strengths and needs of African American gays: A multidimensional perspective. *Journal of Gay and Lesbian Social Services.* 25–50.

Ichioka, Y. (1988). *The Issei: The world of the first-generation Japanese immigrants, 1885–1924.* New York: Free Press.

Iglehart, A. P., and Becerra, R. M. (1995). *Social services and the ethnic community.* Needham Heights, MA: Allyn and Bacon.

Israel, B., Checkoway, B., Schulz, A., and Zimmerman, M. (1994). Health education and community empowerment: Conceptualizing and measuring perceptions of individual, organizational, and community control. Special issue: Community empowerment, participatory education, and health: I. *Health Education Quarterly,* 21(2): 149–170.

Jackson, B., and Holvino, E. (1988). *Multicultural organizational development.* Ann Arbor: Program on Conflict Management Alternatives.

Jackson, J., Neighbors, H., and Gurin, G. (1986). Findings from a national survey of Black mental health: Implications for practice and training. In M. Miranda and H. Kitano (Eds.). *Mental health research and practice in minority communities: Development of culturally sensitive training programs.* (Pp: 91–116). Rockville, MD: NIMH.

Jackson, J. S., Tucker, M. B., and Bowman, P. J. (1982). Conceptual and methodological problems in survey research on Black Americans. In W. T. Lui (Ed.). *Methodological problems in minority research.* (Pp: 11–39). Chicago: Pacific/Asian American Mental Health Research Center.

Jaimes, M. A. (1992). American Indian women: At the center of indigenous resistance in contemporary North America. In M. A. Jaimes (Ed.). *The state of Native America: Genocide, colonization, and resistance.* (Pp. 311–344). Boston: South End.

Jansson, B. S. (1994). *The reluctant welfare state.* (2d Ed.). Pacific Grove, CA: Brooks/Cole.

Jansson, B. S. (1997). The reluctant welfare state. *American social welfare policies: Past present and future* (3d ed.). Pacific Grove, CA: Brooks/Cole.

Johnson, H. (1990). Empowerment in practice: An interview with Dr. Maria Chavez. *Networking Bulletin: Empowerment and Family Support,* 1(2): 1–2, 16–20.

Jordan, J. (1997). *Women's growth in diversity: More writings from the Stone School Center.* New York: Guilford.

Jorgenson, S., and Adams, R. (1987). Family planning needs and behavior of Mexican American women: A study of health care professionals and their clientele. *Hispanic Journal of the Behavioral Sciences,* 9: 265–286.

Kahn, A., and Bender, E. (1985). Self help groups as a crucible for people empowerment in the context of social development. *Social Development Issues,* 9(2): 4–13.

Kalbacken, J. (1994). *The Menominee.* Chicago: Children's.

Katz, J. N. (1983). *Gay/lesbian almanac.* New York: Carroll and Graf.

Kazdin, A. (1982). *International handbook of behavior modification and therapy.* New York: Plenum.

Keefe, T. (1980). Empathy skill and critical consciousness. *Social Casework,* 61: 387–393.

Kelley, P., and Kelley, V. R. (June, 1985). Supporting natural helpers: A cross-cultural study. *Social Casework,* 66(6): 358–366.

Kelly, G. P. (1978). Schooling, gender and the reshaping of occupational and social expectation: The case of Vietnamese immigrants into the United States. *International Journal of Women's Studies,* 1: 323–335.

Kessel, J. L. (1987). *Kiva, cross, and crown.* Albuquerque: University of New Mexico Press.

Kettner, P. M. (1987). *Purchase of service contracting.* Newbury Park, CA: Sage.

Kettner, P. M., Daley, J., and Nichols, A. (1985). *Initiating change in organizations and communities: A macro practice model.* Monterey, CA: Brooks/Cole.

Khoury, R. (1995). *Mental health practice with Arab-Americans.* Videotaped presentation, Department of Community Health, Lansing, MI.

Kibria, N. (1994). Migration and Vietnamese American women: Remaking ethnicity. In M. B. Zinn and B. T. Dill (Eds.). *Women of color in U.S. society.* (Pp. 247–264). Philadelphia: Temple University Press.

Kieffer, C. H. (1984). Citizen empowerment: A developmental perspective. *Prevention in Human Services,* 3(2–3). 9–36.

Kirk, G., and Okazawa-Rey, M. (1998). *Women's lives: Multicultural perspectives.* Mountain View, CA: Mayfield.

Kirk, S., and Kutchins, H. (1992). *The selling of DSM.* New York: Aldine De Gruyter.

Kitzinger, C. (1987). *The social construction of lesbianism.* Beverly Hills: Sage.

Kleugel, J., and Smith, E. (1981). Beliefs about stratification. *Annual Review of Sociology,* 7: 29–56.

Knoll, T. (1982). *Becoming Americans: Asian sojourners, immigrants, and refugees in the western United States.* Portland, OR: Coast to Coast.

Kopasci, R., and Faulkner, A. (1988). The powers that might be: The unity of White and Black feminists. *Affilia,* 3(2): 33–50.

Kranau, E. J., Green, V., and Valencia-Weber, G. (1982). Acculturation and the Hispanic woman: Attitudes toward women, sex-role attribution, sex-role behavior and demographics. *Hispanic Journal of Behavioral Studies,* 4(1): 21–40.

LaBonte, R. (1997). Community, community development, and the forming of authentic partnerships. Chapter 6 in M. Minkler (Ed.). *Community organizing and community building for health.* (Pp: 88–102). New Brunswick, NJ: Rutgers.

Lacayo, R. (1989). On the front lines. *Time.* September 11, 1989, p. 8.

Lai, T. A. (1986). Asian women: Resisting the violence. In Marviolet C. Burns (Ed.). *The speaking profits us: Violence in the lives of women of color.* (Pp. 8–11). Seattle: Center for the Prevention of Sexual and Domestic Violence.

Lamphere, L. (1992). *Structuring diversity: Ethnographic perspectives on the new immigration.* Chicago: University of Chicago Press.

Land, P. (1988). *In our experience: Workshops at the Women's Therapy Center.* London: Women's.

Latting, J. K. (1994). Diffusion of computer-mediated communication in a graduate social work class: Lessons from the class from hell. *Computers in Human Services,* 10(3): 21–45.

Latting, J. K. (1993). Soliciting individual change in an interpersonal setting: The case of racially or sexually offensive language. *Journal of Applied Behavioral Science,* 29(4): 464–484.

Latting, J. K., and Blanchard, A, (1994). Empowering staff in a "poverty agency": An organization development intervention. *Journal-of-Community-Practice,* 4(3): 59–75.

Laval, R. A., Gomez, E. A., and Ruiz, P. (1983, Spring). A language minority: Hispanic/Americans and mental health care. *American Journal of Social Psychiatry,* 3(2): 42–49.

Lazarus, A. A. (1968). Aversion therapy and sensory modalities: Clinical impressions. *Perceptual and Motor Skills,* 27(1): 178.

Lee, C. A. (1991). An Asian lesbian's struggle. In M. Silvera (Ed.). *Piece of my heart: A lesbian of color anthology.* (Pp. 115–118). Toronto, Ontario: Sister Vision.

Lee, J. (1986). Asian-American elderly: A neglected minority group. *Journal of Gerontological Social Work,* 9 (4): 103–116.

Lee, J. A. (1994). *The empowerment approach to social work practice.* New York: Columbia University Press.

Leigh, J. (1985). Primary prevention approaches. In S. Grey, A. Hartman, and E. Saalberg. (Eds.). *Empowering the Black family: A round table discussion.* Ann Arbor: National Child Welfare Training Center.

Lewis, E. A. (1993a). African-American populations. In G. Walker-Burt and J. Herrick (Eds.). *Cultural diversity in Michigan: Culturally competent mental health services.* Module 1. Lansing, MI: Michigan Department of Mental Health.

Lewis, E. A. (1993b). Continuing the legacy: On the importance of praxis in the education of social work student and teachers. In D. Schoem, L. Frankel, X. Zuniga, and E. Lewis (Eds.). *Multicultural Teaching in the University.* (Pp: 26–36). New York: Praeger.

Lewis, E. (1989). Role strain in African-American women: The efficacy of support networks. *Journal of Black Studies,* 20(2): 155–169.

Lewis, E. A. (1988). Role strengths and strains of African-American women: Social support as a prevention strategy. *Journal of Primary Prevention,* 9(1&2): 77–91.

Lewis, E. A., and Ford, B. (1990). The network utilization project: Incorporating traditional strengths of African-American families into group work practice. *Social Work with Groups,* 13(3): 7–22.

Lewis, E. A., and Kissman, K. (1989). Factors in ethnic-sensitive feminist social work practice. *Arete,* 14(2): 23–31.

Lewis, E. A., and Suarez, Z. (1995). Natural helping networks. In NASW. *Encyclopedia of Social Work.* (19th Ed.). (Pp. 1765–1772). Silver Springs, MD: NASW.

Lewis, R. (1993). American-Indian populations. G. Walker-Burt and J. Herrick (Eds.). *Cultural diversity in Michigan: Culturally competent mental health services.* Module 3. Lansing, MI: Michigan Department of Mental Health.

Lipchik, E. (1991). Spouse abuse: Challenging the party line. *Family Therapy Networker,* 15(3): 59–63.

Longres, J. (1990). *Human behavior in the social environment.* Itasca, IL: F. E. Peacock.

Longres, J., and McLeod, E. (1980). Consciousness raising and social work practice. *Social Casework,* 61: 267–277.

Lorde, A. (1983). *Movement in Black: The collected poetry of Pat Parker.* Trumansburg, NY: Crossing.

Lorde, A. (1984). *Sister outsider: Essays and speeches.* Trumansburg, NY: Crossing.

Loring, M., and Powell, B. (1988). Gender, race and DSM-III: A study of the objectivity of psychiatric diagnostic behavior. *Journal of Health and Social Behavior,* 29. 1–22.

Lum, D. (1992). *Social work practice and people of color: A process-stage approach.* Pacific Grove, CA: Brooks/Cole.

Lum, D. (1996). *Social work practice and people of color: A process-stage approach.* (3d Ed.). Pacific Grove, CA: Brooks/Cole.

Lum, D. (1982). Toward a framework for social work practice with minorities. *Social Work,* 27: 244–249.

Lyman, S. (1977). *The Asians in North America.* Santa Barbara: Clio.

Macht, M., and Quam, J. (1986). *Social work: An introduction.* Columbus, OH: Merrill.

Macht, M., Wirth, Q., and Jean, H. (1986). *Social work: An introduction.* Columbus, OH: Merrill.

Mail, P. D. (1990). *Indian health conditions.* U.S. Department of Health and Human Services, Public Health Service, Indian Health Service monograph. Washington, DC: U.S. Government Printing Office.

Manning, S. (1998). Empowerment in mental health programs: Listening to the voices. In L. Gutiérrez, R. Parsons, and E. Cox (Eds.). *Empowerment in social work practice: A sourcebook.* (Pp: 89–109). Pacific Grove, CA: Brooks/Cole.

Marin, G., and Van Oss Marin, B. (1991). *Research with Hispanic Populations.* Newbury Park, CA: Sage.

Mason, P. (1998). Race, cognitive ability, and wage inequality. *Challenge,* 3(41): 63–75.

Mathis, T., and Richan, D. (March 1986). *Empowerment: Practice in search of a theory.* Paper presented at the Annual Program Meeting of the Council on Social Work Education, Miami, FL.

Matsumoto, V. (1984). Japanese-American women during World War II. *Frontiers,* 8(1): 6–14.

Matthaei, J., and Amott, T. (1990). Race, gender, work: The history of Asian and Asian-American women. *Race and Class,* 31(3): 61–80.

Mattis, J. S. (1995). *Workings of the spirit: Spirituality, meaning construction and coping in the lives of Black women.* Doctoral dissertation. University of Michigan, Ann Arbor.

Maultsby, M. C. (1979). A historical view of Blacks' distrust of psychiatry. In S. Turner and R. Jones. (Eds.). *Behavior modification in Black populations.* (Pp: 39–56). New York: Plenum.

Maultsby, M. C., and Brandsma, J. M. (1990). *Outpatient treatment of alcoholism: A review and comparative study.* Baltimore: University Park.

Mays, V., and Cochran, S. D. (1988). Issues in the perception of AIDS risk and risk reduction activities by Black and Hispanic/Latino women. *American Psychologist,* 43(11): 949–957.

McAdoo, H. (1982). Demographic trends for people of color. *Social Work,* 27: 15–23.

McGoldrick, M., and Gerson, R. (1982). *Ethnicity and family therapy.* New York: Guilford.

McGoldrick, M., and Gerson, R. (1985). *Genograms in family assessment.* New York: Norton.

McGoldrick, M., Pearce, J., and Giordano, J. (Eds.). (1982). *Ethnicity and family therapy.* New York: Guilford.

McGoldrick, M., Pearce, J., and Giordano, J. (Eds.). (1994). *Ethnicity and family therapy.* (2d Ed.). New York: Guilford.

McInnis, K., Petracchi, H. E., and Morganbesser, M. (1990). *The Hmong in America:*

Providing ethnic sensitive health, education, and human services. Dubuque, IA: Kendall/Hunt.

McIntosh, P. (1995). A personal account of coming to see correspondence through work in women's studies. In M. L. Andersen and P. Hill-Collins (Eds.). *Race, class, and gender: An anthology.* (2d Ed.). (Pp. 7–82). Belmont, CA.: Wadsworth.

McMahon, M. O. (1990). *The general method of social work practice: A problem-solving approach.* Englewood Cliffs, NJ: Prentice-Hall.

McNickle, D. (1973). *Native American tribalism: Indian survivals and renewals.* London: Oxford University Press.

McWhirter, E. H. (1994). *Counseling for empowerment.* Alexandria, VA: American Counseling Association.

Melville, M. (1988). Hispanics: Race, class or ethnicity? *The Journal of Ethnic Studies,* 16: 67–83.

Miley, K., O'Melia, M., and DuBois, B. (1998). *Generalist social work practice: An empowering approach.* Boston: Allyn and Bacon.

Miller, J., Jordan, J., Kaplan, A., Stiver, I., and Surrey, J. (1997). Some misconceptions and reconceptions of a relational approach. In J. Jordan (Ed.). *Women's growth in diversity: More writings from the Stone School Center.* (Pp: 25–49). New York: Guilford.

Minkler, M. (1997). *Community organizing and community building for health.* New Brunswick, NJ: Rutgers University Press.

Mizio, E. (1981). *Training for service delivery to minority clients.* New York: Family Service Association of America.

Mondros, J., and Wilson, S. (1994). *Organizing for power and empowerment.* New York: Columbia University Press.

Moore, J. W., and Pachon, H. (1985). *Hispanics in the United States.* Englewood Cliffs, NJ: Prentice-Hall.

Moraga, C., and Anzaldúa, G. (Eds.). (1983). *This bridge called my back: Writings by radical women of color.* Brooklyn: Kitchen Table.

Morales, A. (1981). Social work with third world people. *Social Work,* 26: 48–51.

Morell, C. (1987). Cause is function: Toward a feminist model of integration for social work. *Social Science Review,* 61: 144–155.

Moriyama, A. (1984). The causes of emigration: The background of Japanese emigration to Hawaii, 1885–94. In L. Cheng and E. Bonacich (Eds.). *Labor immigration under capitalism: Asian workers in the United States before World War II.* Berkeley: University of California Press.

Morrell, J. A. (1984). *Prevention planning in mental health.* Beverly Hills: Sage.

Morrow, D. F. (1996). Coming out issues for adult lesbians: A group intervention. *Social Work,* 41(6): 647–656.

Mukherjee, S. (1983). Misdiagnosis of schizophrenia in bipolar patients: A multiethnic comparison. *American Journal of Psychiatry,* 140(12): 1571–1574.

Muñoz, C. (1989). *Youth, identity and power: The Chicano movement.* London: Verso.

Nagel, J. (1994). Constructing ethnicity: Creating and re-creating ethnic identity and culture. *Social Problems*, 41 (1): 152–176.

Nee, V., and Wong, H. Y. (1985). Asian American socioeconomic achievement: The strength of the family bond. *Sociological Perspectives*, 28(3): 281–305.

Neighbors, H. W., and Jackson, J. (Eds.). (1996). *Mental health in Black America*. New York: Sage.

Neighbors, H, and Taylor, R. (1985). The use of social service agencies by Black Americans. *Social Service Review*, 59: 258–268.

Nelson, C., and Tienda, M. (1985). The structuring of Hispanic ethnicity: Historical and contemporary perspectives. *Ethnic and Racial Studies*, 8: 49–73.

Netting, E. (1993). *Social work macro practice*. New York: Longman.

Netting, E., Kettner, P., and McMurty, S. (1995). Selecting appropriate tactics. In J. Tropman, J. Erlich, and J. Rothman (Eds.). *Tactics and techniques of community intervention*. Itasca, IL: Peacock.

Ogbu, J. V. (1981). Black education: A cultural-ecological perspective. In H. McAdoo (Ed.). *Black families*. (Pp. 139–154). Beverly Hills: Sage.

O'Hanlon, William Hudson (1990). Debriefing myself: When a brief therapist does long-term work. *Family Therapy Networker*, 14(2): 48–49, 68–69.

Okazawa-Rey, M. (1998). Empowering poor communities of color: A self-help model. In L. Gutiérrez, R. Parsons, and E. Cox (Eds.). *Empowerment in social work practice: A sourcebook*. (Pp: 52–64). Pacific Grove, CA: Brooks/Cole.

O'Leary, J. (1978). Legal problems and remedies. In G. Vida (Ed.). *Our right to love: A lesbian resource book*. (Pp. 196–203). Englewood Cliffs, NJ: Prentice Hall.

Ortiz, S., and Casas, J. (1990). Birth control and low-income Mexican-American women: The impact of three values. *Hispanic Journal of the Behavioral Sciences*, 12: 83–92.

Ortiz, V. (1994). Women of color: A demographic overview. In M. Baca Zinn and B. T. Dill (Eds.). *Women of color in U.S. society*. (Pp: 13–40). Philadelphia: Temple University Press,.

Padilla, F. M. (1985). *Latino ethnic consciousness: The case of Mexican-American and Puerto Ricans in Chicago*. Notre Dame, IN: University of Notre Dame Press.

Padilla, Y. (1990). Social science theory on the Mexican-American experience. *Social Service Review*, 64: 261–275.

Parsons, R. (1991). Empowerment: Purpose and practice in social work. *Social Work with Groups*, 14(2): 7–22.

Parsons, R., Jorgensen, J. D., and Hernández, S. H. (1994). *The integration of social work practice*. Pacific Grove, CA.: Brooks/Cole.

Paulino, A., and Burgos-Servido, J. (1997). Working with immigrant families in transition. In E. Congress. (Ed.). *Multicultural perspectives in working with families*. (Pp: 13–40, 125–141). New York: Springer.

Peluso, E., and Peluso, L. S. (1988). *Women and drugs: Getting hooked, getting clean*. Minneapolis: CompCare Publishers.

Pernell, R. (1985). Empowerment and social group work. In M. Parenes (Ed.). *Inno-*

vations in social group work: Feedback from practice to theory. (Pp. 107–117). New York: Hawthorn.

Pinderhughes, E. (1989). *Understanding race, ethnicity, and power: The key to efficacy in clinical practice.* New York: Free Press.

Pinderhughes, E. (1983). Empowerment for our clients and for ourselves. *Social Casework,* 64(6): 331–338.

Portes, A. (1984). The rise of ethnicity: Determinants of ethnic perceptions among Cuban exiles in Miami. *American Sociological Review,* 49(3): 383–397.

Portes, A., Parker, R., and Cobas, J. (1980). Assimilation or consciousness: Perceptions of U.S. society among recent Latin American immigrants to the United States. *Social Forces,* 59: 200–224.

Portes, A., and Truelove, C. (1987). Making sense of diversity: Recent research on Hispanic minorities in the United States, *Annual Review of Sociology,13*: 359–385.

Posadas, B. (1981). Crossed boundaries in interracial Chicago: Filipino American families since 1925. *Amerasia Journal,* 8: 31–52.

Powers, M. N. (1986). *Oglala women: Myth, ritual, and reality.* Chicago: University of Chicago Press.

Pretsby, J., Wandersman, A., Florin, P., Rich, R., and Chavis, D. (1990). Benefits, costs, incentive management and participation in voluntary organizations: A means to understanding and promoting empowerment. *American Journal of Community Psychology,* 18: 117–149.

Purnell, R. (1996). *Child sexual abuse, alcohol and drug (mis)use, and human immunodeficiency virus (*HIV*).* Doctoral dissertation, School of Social Work, University of Michigan, Ann Arbor.

Pyant, C. T., and Yanico, B. J. (1991, July). Relationship of racial identity and gender-role attitudes to Black women's psychological well-being. *Journal of Counseling Psychology,* 38(3): 315–322.

Queralt, M. (1984). Understanding Cuban immigrants: A cultural perspective. *Social Work,* 29(2): 115–121.

Rabaya, V. (1971). Filipino immigration: The creation of a new social problem. In A. Tachiki, E. Wong, and F. Odo (Eds.). *Roots: An Asian American reader.* Los Angeles: UCLA Asian American Studies Center.

Randle, M. (1994). *Civil resistance.* London: Fontana.

Rappaport, J. (1981). In praise of paradox: A social policy of empowerment over prevention. *American Journal of Community Psychology,* 9(1): 1–25.

Reagon, B. J. (1983). Coalition politics. In B. Smith (Ed.). *Home girls: A Black feminist anthology.* (Pp. 356–369). New York: Kitchen Table.

Reed, B., Newman, P. A., Suarez, Z., and Lewis, E. (1997). Interpersonal practice beyond diversity and towards social justice: The importance of critical consciousness. In C. Garvin and B. Seabury (Eds.). *Interpersonal Practice in Social Work.* (Pp: 44–77). New York: Garland.

Reimers, D. M. (1985). *Still the golden door: The third world comes to America.* New York: Columbia University Press.

Reischl, T., Zimmerman, M., and Rappaport, J. (1986, August). *Mutual help mechanisms in the empowerment of former mental patients.* Paper presented at the annual meeting of the American Psychological Association, Washington, DC.

Renz-Beaulaurier, R. (1998). Empowering people with disabilities: The role of choice. In L. Gutiérrez, R. Parsons, and E. Cox (Eds.). *Empowerment in Social Work Practice: A Sourcebook.* (Pp: 73–81). Pacific Grove, CA: Brooks/Cole.

Reynolds, B. C. (1934). *Between client and community: A study of responsibility in social casework.* New York: Oriole.

Rhoades, E. R., Hammond, J., Welty, T. K., Handler, A. O., and Amler, R. W. (1980). The Indian burden of illness and future health interventions. *Public Health Report,* 102(4): 361–368.

Ristock, J. (1990). Canadian feminist social service collectives: Caring and contradictions. In L. Albrecht and R. Brewer. (Eds.). *Bridges of power: Women's multicultural alliances.* Philadelphia: New Society.

Rivera, F., and Erlich, J. (1995). *Community organizing in a diverse society.* (2d Ed.). Needham Heights, MA: Allyn and Bacon.

Robnett, B. (1997). *How long? How long? African-American women in the struggle for civil rights.* New York: Oxford University Press.

Rogler, L., Cooney, R., Constantino, G., Earley, B., Grossman, B., Gurak, D., Malgady, R., Rodriguez, R. (1983). *A conceptual framework for mental health research on Hispanic populations.* New York: Hispanic Research Center.

Rooney, R. (1992). *Practice strategies for work with involuntary clients.* (Pp. 201–230). New York: Columbia University Press.

Rose, S. (1989). *Working with adults in groups: Integrating cognitive behavioral and small group strategies.* San Francisco: Jossey Bass.

Rose, S., and Black, B. (1985) *Advocacy and empowerment: Mental health care in the community.* Boston: Routledge and Kegan Paul.

Rose, W. (1992). The great pretenders: Further reflections on White shamanism. In M. A. Jaimes (Ed.). *The state of Native America: Genocide, colonization, and resistance.* (Pp. 403–422). Boston: South End.

Rosenberg, M. (1981). The self concept: Social product and social force. In M. Rosenberg and R. Turner. (Eds.). *Social Psychology.* New York: Basic.

Rothman, S. (1994). *Giving for social change: Foundations, public policy, and the American political agenda.* Westport, CT: Praeger.

Ruiz, A. (1990). Ethnic identity: Crisis and resolution. *Journal of Multicultural Counseling and Development,* 18: 29–40.

Rumbaut, R. G. (1995). Vietnamese, Laotian, and Cambodian Americans. In Pyong Gap Min (Ed.). *Asian Americans: Contemporary trends and issues.* (Pp. 232–270). Thousand Oaks, CA: Sage.

Sanchez, G. (1993). *Becoming Mexican American: Ethnicity, culture, and identity in Chicano Los Angeles, 1900–1945.* New York: Oxford University Press.

Sanderlin, G. (1971). *Bartolome De Las Casas: A selection of his writings.* New York: Knopf.

Santopietro, M. C. S., and Lynch, B. A. (1980). Indochina moves to main street: What's behind the "inscrutable mask"? *RN*, 43: 921–922.

Scanzoni, J., and Fox, G. L. (1980). Sex roles, family, and society: The seventies and beyond. *Journal of Marriage and the family*, 42: 43–58.

Schacter, D. (1996). The puzzle of the past. *Family Therapy Networker*, 20(6): 30–35.

Scharff, D. E., and Scharff, J. (1991). Joining the family: Countertransference can be the therapist's compass. *Family Therapy Networker*, 15(5): 73–81.

Schechter, S. (1982). *Women and male violence: The visions and struggles of the battered women's movement.* Boston: South End.

Schechter, S., Szymanski, S., and Cahill, M. (1985). *Violence against women: A curriculum for empowerment.* (Facilitator's Manual). New York: Women's Education Institute.

Schulz, A., Israel, B., Zimmerman, M., and Checkoway, B. (1993). *Empowerment as a multi-level construct: Perceived control at the individual, organization and community levels.* Program for Conflict Management Alternatives Working Paper #40. Ann Arbor: University of Michigan Center for Research on Social Organizations.

Scott, J., and Delgado, M. (1979). Planning mental health programs for Hispanic communities. *Social Casework*, 60: 451–456.

Scrimshaw, S., and Pasquariella, B. (1971). Variables associated with the demand for female sterilization in Spanish Harlem. *Advances in Planned Parenthood*, 6: 133–141.

Sermabeikian, P. (1994). Our clients, ourselves: The spiritual perspective and social work practice. *Social Work*, 39(2): 178–183.

Shapiro, J. (1984). Commitment to disenfranchised clients. In A. Rosenblatt and D. Waldfogel (Eds.). *Handbook of clinical social work.* San Francisco: Jossey-Bass.

Shaull, R. (1994). Foreword. In P. Freire, *Pedagogy of the oppressed.* New York: Continuum.

Sherman, W., and Wenocur, S. (1983). Empowering public welfare workers through mutual support. *Social Work, 28(5)*: 375–379.

Shimkin, D. B., Shimkin, E. M., and Frote, D. A. (Eds). (1979). *The extended family in Black societies.* Paris: Mouton.

Shon, S. P., and Ja, D. Y. (1982). Asian families. In M. McGoldrick, J. Pearce, and J. Giordano (Eds.). *Ethnicity and family therapy.* New York: Guilford.

Silva, J. (1983). Cross-cultural and cross-ethnic assessment. In G. Gibson (Ed.). *Our kingdom stands on brittle glass.* (Pp: 59–66). Silver Springs, MD: NASW.

Simmons, C., and Parsons, R. (1983a). Developing internality and perceived competence: The empowerment of adolescent girls. *Adolescence, 18(72)*: 917–922.

Simmons, C. H., and Parsons, R. J. (1983b, Spring). Empowerment for role alternatives in adolescence. *Adolescence*, 18(6a): 193–200.

Simon, B. L. (1994). *The empowerment tradition in American social work: A history.* New York: Columbia University Press.

Simon, B. L. (1990). Rethinking empowerment. *Journal of Progressive Human Services,* 1(1): 27–40.

Smeeding, T., Danziger, S., and Rainwater, L. (1996). Child well-being in the west. Toward a new model of antipoverty policy. In G. Cornia, S. Danziger (Eds). *Child poverty and deprivation in the industrialized countries.* (pp. 368–389). New York: Clarendon Press.

Smith, E. D. (1995). Addressing the psychospiritual distress of death as reality: A transpersonal approach. *Social Work,* 40(3): 402–412.

Smith, B. (1983). *Home girls: A Black feminist anthology.* New York: Women of Color, Kitchen Table.

Social Work with Groups, 13(4): 1990. Special Issue: Ethnicity and biculturalism: Emerging perspectives of social group work.

Social Work with Groups 7(3): 1984. Special Issue: Ethnicity in social group work.

Soderfeldt, M., Soderfeldt, B., and Warg, L. (1995). Burnout in social work. *Social Work,* 40(5): 638–647.

Sohng, S., and Icard, L. (1996). Cultural imperatives for practice with Korean gay men. *Journal of Gay and Lesbian Social Services*: 115–138.

Solomon, B. (1976). *Black empowerment.* New York: Columbia University Press.

Solomon, B. (1987). Empowerment: Social work in oppressed communities. *Journal of Social Work Practice,* 2(4): 79–91.

Solomon, B. (1982). Empowering women: A matter of values. In A. Weick S. Vandiver. (Eds.). *Women, power and change.* (Pp. 206–214). Silver Springs, MD: NASW.

Soto, E. (1983, October). Sex-role traditionalism and assertiveness in Puerto Rican women living in the United States. *Journal of Community Psychology,* 11(4): 346–354.

Soto, E., and Shaver, P. (1982). Sex-role traditionalism, assertiveness, and symptoms of Puerto Rican women living in the United States. *Hispanic Journal of the Behavioral Sciences,* 4: 1–19.

Specht, H., and Courtney, M. E. (1994). *Unfaithful angels: How social work has abandoned its mission.* New York: Free Press.

Spencer, M. (1983, December). Children's cultural values and parental child rearing strategies. *Developmental Review,* 3(4): 351–370.

Spiegel, J. (1982). An ecological model of ethnic families. In M. McGoldrick, J. Pearce, and J. Giordano (Eds.). *Ethnicity and family therapy.* (Pp: 31–51). New York: Guilford.

Starhawk (1992). *Truth or dare.* New York: Harper and Row.

Starret, R. H., Mindell, C. H., and Wright, R. (1983, Winter). Influence of support systems on the use of social services of the Hispanic elderly. *Social Work Research and Abstracts,* 19(4): 35–40.

Stehno, S. (1982). Differential treatment of minority children in service systems. *Social Work,* 27: 39–45.

Stensrud, R., and Stensrud, K. (1981, January). Counseling may be hazardous to your health: How we teach people to feel powerless. *Personnel and Guidance Journal,* 59(5): 300–304.

Strand, V. (1997). The impact of ethnicity and race on the treatment of mothers in incest families. In E. Congress (Ed.). *Multicultural perspectives in working with families.* (Pp. 201–216). New York: Springer.

Strand, P. J., and Jones, W., Jr. (1985). *Indochinese refugees in America: Problems of adaptation and resettlement.* Durham, NC: Duke University Press.

Suarez, Z., Lewis, E., and Clark, J. (1995). Preparing for the 21st century: Women of color and feminist social work practice. In N. Van Den Bergh (Ed.). *Feminist practice in the twenty-first century.* (Pp. 195–210). Silver Springs, MD.: NASW.

Sue, S. (1994). Mental health. In N. W. S. Zane, D. T. Takeuchi, and K. N. J. Young (Eds.). *Confronting critical health issues of Asian and Pacific Islander Americans.* (Pp. 266–288). Thousand Oaks, CA: Sage.

Sue, D., and Sue, D. (1990). *Counseling the culturally different.* New York: Wiley.

Sundhagul, M. (1981). Situation and role of refugee women: Experiences and perspectives from Thailand. *International Migration,* 19: 102–107.

Suzuki, B. (1980). Education and socialization of Asian Americans in the model minority thesis. In R. Endo, S. Sue, and N. Wagner (Eds.). *Asian Americans: Social and psychological perspectives.* Vol. 2. (Pp. 155–175). Ben Lomond, CA: Science and Behavior.

Swift, C., and Levin, G. (1987, Fall–Winter). Empowerment: An emerging mental health technology. *Journal of Primary Prevention, 8(1–2)*: 71–94.

Swignoski, M. E. (1995a). For the White social worker who wants to know how to work with lesbians of color. *Journal of Gay and Lesbian Social Services,* 3(2): 7–21.

Swignoski, M. E. (1995b). The social service needs of lesbians of color. *Journal of Gay and Lesbian Social Services,* 3(2): 67–83.

Szapocznik, J., Kurtines, W., and Fernandez, T. (1980). Bicultural involvement and adjustment in Hispanic American youths. *International Journal of Intercultural Relations, (4)*: 353–365.

Takaki, R. (1993). *A different mirror: A history of multicultural America.* Boston: Little, Brown.

Takaki, R. (1989). *Strangers from a distant shore: A history of Asian Americans.* Boston: Little, Brown.

Tatum, B. (1997). *"Why are all the Black kids sitting together in the cafeteria?" and other conversations about race.* New York: Basic.

Taylor, D., and Dubé, L. (1986). Two faces of identity: The "I" and the "we." *Journal of Social Issues,* 42: 81–98.

Taylor, R., Chatters, L., Tucker, M., and Lewis, E. (1990). Developments in research on Black families. *Journal of Marriage and the Family: A Decade Review,* 52: 24–36.

Thompson, C. E., and Jenal, S. T. (1994, October). Interracial and intraracial quasi-counseling interactions when counselors avoid discussing race. *Journal of Counseling Psychology*, 41(4): 484–491.

Thompson, M. (1994). *Long road to freedom: The advocate history of the gay and lesbian movement.* New York: St. Martin's.

Thornton, A., and Camburn, A. (1983) Causes and consequences of sex-role attitudes and attitude change. *American Sociological Review*, 48: 211–227.

Thurow, L. (1993). Affirmative action as a zero-sum game. In R. Takaki, (Ed.). *From different shores.* London: Oxford University Press.

Tienda, M., and Ortiz, V. (1986). Hispanicity and the 1980 census. *Social Science Quarterly*, 67: 3–20.

Toffler, A. (1990). *Powershift: Knowledge, wealth, and violence at the edge of the 21st century.* New York: Bantam.

Triandis, H. C. (1983, October). Some dimensions of intercultural variation and their implication for community psychology. *Journal of Community Psychology*, 11(4): 285–302.

Troll, L. E., Bengston, V. L., and McFarland, D. (1979). Generations in the family. In W. R. Burr, R. Hill, F. I. Nye, and I. L. Reiss (Eds.). *Contemporary Theories about the Family.* Vol. 1. (Pp. 127–161). New York: Free Press.

True, R. H. (1990). Psychotherapeutic issues with Asian American women. *Sex Roles*, 22(7/8): 477–485.

Trueba, H., Jacobs, L., and Kirton, E. (1990). *Cultural conflict and adaptation.* New York: Farmer.

Turner, C. W. (1997). Clinical applications of the Stone Center theoretical approach to minority women. In J. Jordan (Ed.) *Women's growth and diversity.* (Pp: 74–90). New York: Guilford.

U.S. Bureau of the Census. (1992). *1990 census of the population.* Vol. 1, *Characteristics of the population.* Washington, DC: U.S. Department of Commerce.

Van Den Bergh, N. (1995). *Feminist practice in the twenty-first century.* Silver Springs, MD.: NASW.

Van Den Bergh, N., and Cooper, L. (Eds.) (1986). *Feminist visions for social work.* Silver Springs, MD: NASW.

Van Soest, D. (1994). Peace and social justice. In *The encyclopedia of social work.* Washington, DC: NASW.

Vasquez-Nuttall, E., Romero-Garcia, I., and De Leon, B. (1987). Sex roles and perceptions of femininity and masculinity of Hispanic women: A review of the literature. *Psychology of Women Quarterly*, 11: 409–425.

Vazquez, C. (1992). Appearances. In W. J. Blumenfeld (Ed.). *Homophobia: How we all pay the price.* (Pp. 157–166). Boston: Beacon.

Wakatsuki, Y. (1979). Japanese immigration to the United States, 1866–1924. *Perspectives in American History*, 12: 387–516.

Wallack, L. (1997). Media advocacy: A strategy for empowering people. In M. Minkler (Ed.). *Community organizing and community building for health.* (Pp. 339–352). New Brunswick, NJ: Rutgers.

Wallerstein, N. (1992). Empowerment and popular education applied to youth. *New designs for youth development,* 10(1): 17–22.

Wallerstein, N., Sanchez, M., and Dow, L. (1997). Freirian praxis in health education and community organizing: A case study. In M. Minkler (Ed.). *Community building for health.* (Pp. 195–211). New Brunswick, NJ: Rutgers,.

Washington, R. (1982). Social development: A focus for practice and education. *Social Work,* 27: 104–109.

Watts-Jones, D. (1990) Towards a stress scale for African-American women. *Psychology of Women Quarterly,* 14: 271–275.

Wei, W. (1993). *The Asian American movement.* Philadelphia: Temple University Press.

Weick, A. (1982). Issues of power in social work practice. In A. Weick and S. Vandiver. (Eds.). *Women, power, and change.* Silver Springs, MD: NASW.

Weick, A., and Vandiver, S. (1982). *Women, power, and change.* Washington, DC: NASW.

Weil, M. (1986). Women, community and organizing. In N. Van Den Bergh and L. Cooper (Eds.). *Feminist visions for social work.* (Pp. 187–210). Silver Springs, MD: NASW.

Weinberg, M. S., Williams, C. J., and Pryor, D. W. (1994). *Dual attraction: Understanding bisexuality.* New York: Oxford University Press.

Weingarten, H., and Leas, S. (1989) Levels of marital conflict model: A guide to assessment and intervention in troubled marriages. *American Journal of Orthopsychiatry,* 57(3): 407–417.

Weise, E. R. (1992). *Closer to home: Bisexuality and feminism.* Seattle: Seal.

West, C. (1998). *On Martin Luther King.* Keynote address for the Rev. Dr. Martin Luther King Jr. Day Symposium, University of Michigan, Ann Arbor.

West, G. (1990). Cooperation and conflict among women in the welfare rights movement. In L. Albrecht and R. Brewer (Eds.). *Bridges of power: Women's multicultural alliances.* (Pp. 149–171). Philadelphia: New Society.

Westermeyer, J. (1977). The drunken Indian: Myths and realities. In S. Unger (Ed.). *Destruction of American Indian families.* New York: Association on American Indian Affairs.

Williams, L (1990) The challenge of education to social work: The case of minority children. *Social Work,* 35: 236–242.

Withorn, A. (1984). *Serving the people: Social services and social change.* New York: Columbia University Press.

Wolpe, J. (1969). Basic principles and practices of behavior therapy of neuroses. *American Journal of Psychiatry,* 125(9): 1242–1247.

Womack, A. (1994). The lowdown on lupus. *Health Quest: The Publication for Black Women,* 4 (spring): 12–15.

Wong, H. Z. (1985). Training for mental health providers to Southeast Asian refugees: Models, strategies, and curricula. In T. C. Owan (Ed.). *Southeast Asian mental health treatment, prevention, services, training, and research*. (Pp. 345–390). Washington, DC: National Institute of Mental Health.

Wong, M. G., and Hirschman, C. (1983). Labor force participation and socioeconomic attainment of Asian-American women. *Sociological Perspectives*, 26(4): 423–426.

Woo, D. (1985). The socio-economic status of Asian American women in the labor force: An alternative view. *Sociological Perspectives*, 28(2): 307–338.

Yamada, M. (1983). Asian Pacific American women and feminism. In C. Moraga and G. Anzaldúa (Eds.). *This bridge called my back: Writings by radical women of color.* (Pp: 71–75). Brooklyn: Kitchen Table.

Yamanaka, K., and McClelland, K. (1994). Earning the model-minority image: Diverse strategies of economic adaptation by Asian-American women. *Ethnic and Racial Studies*, 17(1): 79–114.

Ybarra, L. (1982). When wives work: The impact on the Chicano family. *Journal of Marriage and the Family*, 44(1): 169–178.

Yeich, S., and Levine, R. (1992). Participatory research's contribution to a conceptualization of empowerment. *Journal of Applied Social Psychology*, 22–24. 1894–1908.

Yoshioka, R. B., Tashima, N., Chew, M., and Murase, K. (1981). *Mental health services for Pacific/Asian Americans.* San Francisco: Pacific American Mental Health Project.

Young, I. (1995). Social movements and the politics of difference. In J. Arthur, J. Shapiro, and A. Shapiro (Eds.). *Campus wars: Multiculturalism and the politics of difference.* Boulder: Westview.

Zander, A. (1979). The psychology of group processes. *Annual Review of Psychology*, 30: 417–431.

Zavella, P. (1986). The politics of race and gender: Organizing Chicana cannery workers in Northern California. In A. Bookman and S. Morgan (Eds.). *Women and the politics of empowerment.* Philadelphia: Temple University Press.

Zimmerman, M. (In press). Empowerment: Forging new perspectives in mental health. In J. Rappaport and E. Seidman (Eds.). *Handbook of community psychology.* New York: Plenum.

Zimmerman, M. (1995). Psychological empowerment: Issues and illustrations. Special issue: Empowerment theory, research, and application. *American Journal of Community Psychology* 23(5): 581–599.

skill building: advocacy and, 184; in
assessment, 36, 37; community
empowerment and, 101; confidence
and, 162–64, 182; connection and,
10; education methods for, 18, 19, 20;
empowerment and, 11, 12, 22; in
engagement, 28, 47; evaluation and,
127; family practice and, 53, 63;
group practice and, 79, 183; in Native
American parenting group, 144;
organization empowerment and, 82,
84, 95, 96, 98–99; termination and,
120, 121; women of the African diaspora and, 166t
slavery, 138, 153, 157
social action: Asian-American women
and, 201–2, 205–6; community
empowerment and, 102, 104, 105, 112;
critical consciousness and, 7–8, 19,
116; decision making and, 55;
empowerment and, xii, 10, 223; family pracitice and, 65; individual practice and, 14, 43; Native American
empowerment and, 141; political
empowerment and, 11–12
social class. *See* status
social environment: of African-American women, xvi–xvii; assessment
and, 26, 30–36, 37, 177–78; community empowerment and, 101, 102–3,
107, 111, 112, 115; confidence and, 182;
connection and, 165–66; cultural
variance perspective and, 60; eclectic
systems framework and, 57; engagement and, 30, 36; evaluation and,
122; family practice and, 53, 56, 61,
63, 65; group practice and, 69, 72,
77; homosexuality and, 210–12; individuals and, xii, xiii, 4, 6, 8, 9, 40,
44–45, 50, 51; Latinos and, 173,
177–79; lesbian and bisexual women
of color and, 211, 212, 213, 217,

222–25; Native American women
and, 140; organization empowerment
and, 95–96; poverty and, 16; power
analysis of, 19; Stone School model
and, 63; women of the African diaspora and, 157, 159, 160
social environment perspective, xii, xiv,
16
social justice, 4, 10, 101, 165, 201–2, 207
social services organizations: client
empowerment in, 81–82; ethnic-sensitive approach and, 16, 17; ethnocentrism practices of, 14–15; immin-
grants' rights and, 43; organization
empowerment and, 85–87, 95–96,
99; use of by Latinas, 173
social status. *See* status
social support networks: for Asian-
American women, 200; assessment
and, 32; connection and, 10; lesbian
and bisexual women of color and,
218–19; political empowerment and,
12; power analysis of, 19
social welfare systems, xi–xiii, xvii, 15,
16, 43, 175, 189
social work practice: bias in, 158; development of techniques for, 51;
empowerment perspective in,
xiii–xv, 4, 11–23, 36; ethnocentrism
in, 14–15; goal of, 129; role of, xi–xii
social work practitioners: burn out in,
82, 88; connection and, 165–66; critical consciousness of, 60–62, 73; as
enabler, 179, 184; relationship with
consumer, 44–47, 64; role of, 20, 23,
166t, 177, 179; self-analysis of, 164;
spirituality of, 13, 162
Soifer, S., 104
Solomon, B., 212
SOSAD (Save Our Sons and Daughters), 113
South Africa, 6